TALES FROM
SPANISH PICARESQUE NOVELS
A Motif-Index

J. Wesley Childers

STATE UNIVERSITY OF NEW YORK PRESS
ALBANY, 1977

First published in 1977 by
State University of New York Press
Albany, New York 12246

©1977 State University of New York
All rights reserved

Made and printed in the United States of America

Library of Congress Cataloging in Publication Data

Childers, James Wesley, 1906-
Tales from Spanish picaresque novels.

Bibliography: p.
1. Spanish fiction—Classical period, 1500-1700—
Themes, motives—Indexes. 2. Picaresque literature—
Themes, motives—Indexes. I. Title.
PQ6147.P5C55   863'.3'0924   77-8780
ISBN 0-87395-188-3

To Margaret Alcorn Childers

PREFACE

Many years ago Dr. Ralph Boggs suggested to this writer through Professor Stith Thompson that the Spanish picaresque novel was an important source of folktales worthy of a motif index. After years of off-and-on work, the present index is a result of that suggestion. It includes tales from thirty Spanish picaresque novels: The twenty-two included in Ángel Valbuena y Prat's anthology, La novela picaresca española (Madrid: Aguilar, 1946), and eight additional ones. The Casamiento engañoso, listed in the Bibliography, is the prologue to Cervantes' Coloquio de los perros and is not a separate novel. All of the major Spanish picaresque novels are indexed herein.

In the Introduction which follows, this writer gives a definition of the picaresque genre, some general comments on the influence of this realistic type of fiction on Spanish and other literatures, and some of the problems encountered in indexing stories from the novels. These comments are not intended to be a definitive study of the vast scholarship relating to the picaresque genre, but rather they are comments which pertain especially to aspects of compiling a motif-index from the thirty novels chosen.

This Motif-Index is based on the plan of classification in the revised edition of Professor Stith Thompson's Motif-Index of Folk Literature, 6 volumes (Bloomington, Indiana: Indiana University Press, 1955-1958). The numerous new entries not found in the Thompson work are given as close a classification as possible to other similar motifs already listed by Thompson, and are marked with an asterisk (*).

-v-

INTRODUCTION

The picaresque novel was one of Spain's great literary developments during her Golden Age. It was a new genre of realistic fiction in which the rogue was the central character. It was usually a comic autobiography of an anti-hero who was a peripatetic character, moving about from job to job and from city to city. As the _pícaro_ (rogue) went from master to master, he satirized their personal faults and their trades and professions. The rogue and his tricks and the manners he satirized were the two principal identification marks of the genre. Although the rogue and his tricks constitute the main interest in the novels, the satirical comments on various trades and professions give a wealth of information on the social, political, and religious background of the sixteenth and seventeenth centuries in Spain. The rogue came from the low life of Spanish society and was the antithesis of the social, moral, and human order. He was the exact opposite of the high-born nobles and wealthy gentry. He was not a villain resorting to murder, but rather a vagabond who survived through trickery and theft. The very fact that he could survive by tricking his more fortunate fellow creatures made him a popular hero.

Although the rogue is usually a male, there are several outstanding female tricksters. Among these are Lozana (_La Lozana Andaluza_), Justina (_La pícara Justina_), Elena (_La hija de Celestina_), Flora (_La sabia Flora malsabidilla_), Teresa (_La niña de los embustes, Teresa de Manzanares_), Rufina (_La garduña de Sevilla y anzuelo de las bolsas_), and Feliciana and Luisa (_Las harpías en Madrid_).

Animals, instead of humans, are the protagonists in
Cervantes' <u>El coloquio de los perros</u>, where two dogs, Ber-
ganza and Cipión, have been given human speech for one night
and relate their adventures with various masters. Their
speech is overheard by a sick soldier behind whose hospital
bed they are talking. Likewise, in Salas Barbadillo's <u>La</u>
<u>peregrinación sabia</u> the adventures of two foxes constitute
the chief interest.

Authors of the picaresque novel used this realistic type
of fiction in a subtle manner to satirize the absurd idealistic
chivalric and pastoral novels in vogue at the time. In addition, the rogue novel was used to protest against the social,
religious, and political corruption in Spain at a time when
the nation appeared to be at the zenith of her power and pros-
perity. Under Charles I and Philip II numerous wars and high
taxes had depleted the nation's and its citizens' financial
resources, and poverty was wide-spread. In an effort to
impose the Spanish way of life on the rest of Europe and on
the New World colonies, Spanish monarchs had brought the
nation to the verge of bankruptcy. Bands of beggars roamed
the streets of the large cities soliciting alms, stealing,
and tricking the more affluent in order to survive.

Almost all of the novels portray the poverty of the
lower classes and protest against it. In <u>Lazarillo de Tormes</u>,
however, there is an interesting twist: The novel also
exposes the hollow aspects of Spanish society by satirizing
the impoverished squire who is too proud to work, but who is
willing to eat food which his young servant, Lázaro, has
acquired through begging. Quevedo in <u>La vida del Buscón</u>

describes with exaggerated details the poverty which existed in stingy schoolmaster Cabra's house. Because of their poverty, the rogues do not receive equal justice with the rich before the law, and numerous stories are told (especially in Guzmán de Alfarache) of how policemen, judges, and jailers dispense justice according to the size of the bribes given.

Some of the most powerful protest stories are against certain practices of the church and its representatives in Spain. In Rinconete y Cortadillo Cervantes satirizes the phony religious practices of the pimps, prostitutes, and thieves in gangster Monipodio's house in Sevilla. Some of these low-life characters go into a chapel and light candles, others toss coins in a basket for special masses, and still others carry rosaries with jangling beads. Lazarillo de Tormes protests against the deceitful priests who sell indulgences, as well as the lechery of certain priests. The pícaro relates how he married an archpriest's mistress and followed the priest's advice concerning people's gossip: "Therefore, pay no attention to what they may say; but consider only what concerns you - your own advantage." In several of the novels there is protest against the Inquisition. Authors take recourse to relating a pícaro's dreams, as in Lazarillo de Manzanares, or they tell fables and interpolate stories into the novel to call attention to the awesome power of the Inquisition. Some typical examples are the following: (1) A priest threatens to report Justina to the Inquisition for criticizing a church (Q221.3.1.*); (2) a frightened woman gives a trickster student her hens when he threatens to expose her "heresy" (K335.0.9.1.*); (3) a terrified peasant digs up his

pear tree and sends the tree with its fruit to the Grand
Inquisitor when the latter asked for pears (J829.4.*); and
(4) the fable of the lion's bad breath (J811.2.2.*) is a
subtle protest against the way courts of the Inquisition
dealt with non-Christian Jews and Arabs.

A composite picture of Spanish society emerges from the
picaresque novels as the peripatetic rogue satirizes the
social classes and their professions and trades. Nobles,
priests, soldiers, doctors, merchants, peasants, thieves, and
prostitutes pass in review. The rogue affirms that robbing
has shifted from the nobles down to the lower classes and
has become legalized in certain professions and trades with
doctors, merchants, and law-enforcement officers being the
chief offenders. According to the pícaro, officers and judges
bear great hatred toward thieves because the officers want
to be the only thieves.

Numerous writers in other countries imitated the style
and framework of the Spanish picaresque novel. F. W. Chandler
in his two-volume work, The Literature of Roguery (New York:
Macmillan, 1907), gives a comprehensive study of picaresque
literature outside of Spain. Further proof of the European
vogue of the Spanish rogue novel were the numerous translations
from the Spanish into English, French, German, Italian, and
other languages.

Foreign authors made references in their works to episodes
in the Spanish picaresque novels and, in some instances, borrowed whole episodes from these novels. Shakespeare, for
example, in Much Ado About Nothing, Act II, Sc. 1, refers to
two episodes in Lazarillo de Tormes in which Lázaro tricked his

blind master by eating a sausage and then later tricked him into jumping into a stone pillar (see motifs J1144.1.1.*) and (K1043.4.*): "Ho now you strike like the blind man: 'twas the boy that stole your meat, and you'll beat the post." Scholars also think that Shakespeare drew on the Lazarillo in King Lear, Act IV, Sc. 6, when Edgar with a compassionate motive rather than a malevolent one tricks the blind Earl of Gloucester into "falling" over an imaginary cliff. In French literature Moliere in his play, Le Tartuffe, borrowed his great "unmasking scene" of the hypocritical Tartuffe (Act III, Sc. 6), from Salas Barbadillo's La hija de Celestina (K1961.1.5.2.*). Earlier, Scarron had used this scene in his novel, Les Hypocrites. Lesage's Gil Blas was so Spanish in flavor that scholarly readers thought that he had taken it from the Spaniard Padre Isla, instead of the latter having translated it into Spanish from the French. Lesage, however, borrowed from Vicente Espinel's Marcos de Obregon the episode in which a trickster flatters Gil Blas as a great Latin scholar in order to get a free meal (J2337.1.*). Furthermore, Lesage's Le diable boiteux (The Limping Devil) has the style and framework of Vélez de Guevara's El diablo cojuelo which appeared 66 years earlier.

Most of the Spanish picaresque novels appeared in the sixteenth and seventeenth centuries; however, Vida de Torres Villarroel came out about the middle of the eighteenth century. Many sequels and translations were made of the principal novels, especially of Lazarillo de Tormes and Guzmán de Alfarache. Interpolated folktales, fables, and riddles occurred in nearly all of the novels. Alonso, mozo de muchos

amos has the richest collection of folktales, and La pícara
Justina, the largest number of puns and riddles.

Most of the narratives in the picaresque novels center
around the pícaro and his tricks; therefore, the majority of
the story motifs in this index are found under two classifi-
cations: J, The Wise and the Foolish; and K, Deceptions.
Several stories have more than one appropriate motif or salient
characteristic. For example, the motif of a story might be
clever repartee, but at the same time the rogue's clever
remarks served to deceive someone. Such a story would be listed
in both the J and K categories with cross-references. In most
cases, the page reference under a story motif from a novel
indicates the beginning of the main story in question.

Difficulties encountered in indexing story motifs often
centered around the meaning of vocabulary items used by the
low-class pícaro. In La Lozana Andaluza, for example, there
were many unfamiliar terms which referred to the prostitutes
and their type of life. In La pícara Justina it was difficult
to be sure of the meaning of many puns and riddles. Quevedo's
exaggerated style in La vida del Buscón was difficult to
interpret. Also, there was the problem of how to handle the
rogue's autobiography. Most of it was narrative fact and had
no folktale motif. For example, Lázaro states that he was born
in a mill in the River Tormes; therefore, he "was born in the
river." This statement does not fall under the classification
of verbal cleverness, in the opinion of this writer; it is part
of the autobiographical framework of the novel. On the other
hand, Guzmán's account of his illegitimate conception is a
folklore motif of deception (K1514.11.1.*), because his mother

tricked her husband by feigning illness in order to meet her lover who engendered Guzmán.

There was the question of whether to include the three additional stories in James Mabbe's 1622 translation of the Guzmán (The Rogue: or The Life of Guzmán de Alfarache, New York: Alfred A. Knopf, Vol. 4, 1924). These three stories come from Part II, Book III, chapters II and III, and are listed in this index under J1442.3.1.*, Q272.1.2.*, and Z134.3.*. Although these tales do not appear in the present Spanish versions, they were in Barezzo Barezzi's 1615 Italian translation of Part II of the Guzmán, and Mabbe translated into English the Italian version which may have been available to him before Part II of the Spanish; and this may presuppose an earlier Spanish edition in Italy.

Despite the fact that the picaresque novel was often a crude, unpolished, and disjointed work of fiction, it had a four-fold effect on the literature of Spain and other countries. (1) It caused a decline in the popularity of the chivalric and pastoral novels, two idealistic types of fiction which flourished from the fifteenth into the seventeenth century. By giving his lengthy genealogy, the pícaro burlesqued the way chivalric and pastoral novels began with a detailed account of the hero's lofty, noble heritage. The rogue was a realistic anti-hero who could survive by his wits, and he became more interesting to readers than the make-believe knight or the moping pastoral lover. (2) The picaresque genre suggested new literary fields for authors in later generations. Writers discovered that many low-life people were not criminals, and they began to write about the realistic life of peasants and middle-class people. Out of the emphasis on the lower and middle classes was born the novel of manners. (3) The framework and technique of the picaresque novel shaped the style of many authors. Dickens, Thackeray, and Fielding are good examples in English literature; and Baroja and Cela, in modern Spanish literature. (4) The picaresque novel democratized world fiction, stimulating later writers to choose their fictional characters from real life and from all classes of society and from any trade or profession.

----- J. Wesley Childers

State University of New York at Albany
January, 1977

ABBREVIATED TITLES

(Full titles for the abbreviated ones used in the text follow, together with the name of the author. Consult Bibliography A or B as indicated.)

Alonso.	El donado hablador, Alonso mozo de muchos amos (Alcalá Yáñez- A).
Buscón.	La vida del Buscón (Quevedo- A).
Casamiento.	El casamiento engañoso (Cervantes- A).
Castigo.	El castigo de la miseria (Zayas- A).
Codicia.	La desordenada codicia de los bienes ajenos (García- A).
Coloquio.	Coloquio de los perros (Cervantes- A).
Diablo.	El diablo cojuelo (Vélez de Guevara- A).
Estebanillo.	Vida y hechos de Estebanillo González (González- A).
Flora.	La sabia Flora malsabidilla (Salas Barbadillo- B)
Fregona.	La ilustre fregona (Cervantes- A).
Garduña.	La garduña de Sevilla y anzuelo de las bolsas (Castillo- A).
Guadaña.	Vida de don Gregorio Guadaña (Enríquez Gómez- A)
Guzmán.	Guzmán de Alfarache (Alemán- A).
Guzmán (Luján).	Segunda parte de la vida del pícaro Guzmán de Alfarache (Luján- A).
Harpías.	Las harpías en Madrid y coche de las estafas (Castillo- B).
Hija.	La hija de Celestina (Salas Barbadillo- A).
Justina.	La pícara Justina (López de Úbeda- A).
Lazarillo.	La vida de Lazarillo de Tormes (Anonymous- A).
Lazarillo (Luna).	Segunda parte de Lazarillo de Tormes (Luna- A).
Lozana.	La lozana andaluza (Delicado- B).

Manzanares.   Lazarillo de Manzanares (Cortés de Tolosa- B).

Marcos.   La vida de Marcos de Obregón (Espinel- A).

Necio.   El necio bien afortunado (Salas Barbadillo- B).

Peregrinación.   La peregrinación sabia (Salas Barbadillo- B).

Periquillo.   Periquillo el de las gallineras (Santos- A).

Píndaro.   Varia fortuna del soldado Píndaro
                 (Céspedes y Meneses- B).

Rinconete.   Rinconete y Cortadillo (Cervantes- A).

Rogue.   The Rogue: or The Life of Guzmán de Alfarache
                 (Mabbe- B).

Teresa.   La niña de los embustes, Teresa de Manzanares
                 (Castillo- A).

Torres.   Vida de Torres Villarroel (Torres Villarroel- A).

Trapaza.   Aventuras del Bachiller Trapaza (Castillo- A).

Urdemalas.   El subtil cordovés, Pedro de Urdemalas
                 (Salas Barbadillo- B).

BIBLIOGRAPHY

A

The twenty-two picaresque novels listed below are contained in the following comprehensive anthology: Valbuena y Prat, Angel. La novela picaresca española. Madrid: Aguilar, 1946.

Alcalá Yáñez y Ribera, Jerónimo de. El donado hablador, Alonso mozo de muchos amos, pp. 1197-1339.

Alemán, Mateo. Guzmán de Alfarache, pp. 233-577.

Castillo y Solórzano, Alonso de. Aventuras del Bachiller Trapaza, pp. 1427-1527.

_____ La garduña de Sevilla y anzuelo de las bolsas, pp. 1528-1620.

_____ La niña de los embustes, Teresa de Manzanares, pp. 1342-1426.

Cervantes, Miguel de. El casamiento engañoso, pp. 196-202.

_____ Coloquio de los perros, pp. 203-232.

_____ La ilustre fregona, pp. 150-176.

_____ Rinconete y Cortadillo, pp. 177-195.

Enríquez Gómez, Antonio. Vida de don Gregorio Guadaña, pp. 1681-1719.

Espinel, Vicente. La vida de Marcos de Obregón, pp. 921-1087.

García, Carlos. La desordenada codicia de los bienes ajenos, pp. 1155-1195.

González, Estebanillo. Vida y hechos de Estebanillo González, pp. 1722-1850.

(Anonymous). Lazarillo de Tormes, pp. 83-111.

López de Úbeda, Francisco. La pícara Justina, pp. 703-885.

Luján de Sayavedra, Mateo. Segunda parte de la vida del pícaro Guzmán de Alfarache, pp. 579-702.

Luna, Juan de. Segunda parte de Lazarillo de Tormes,
    pp. 114-146.

Quevedo y Villegas, Francisco Gómez de. La vida del Buscón,
    pp. 1089-1153.

Salas Barbadillo, Alonso Jerónimo de. La hija de Celestina,
    pp. 887-919.

Santos, Francisco. Periquillo el de las gallineras, pp. 1854-1918.

Torres Villarroel, Diego de. Vida de Torres Villarroel,
    pp. 1921-2023.

Vélez de Guevara y Dueñas, Luis. El diablo cojuelo,
    pp. 1640-1677.

Zayas y Sotomayor, María de. El castigo de la miseria,
    pp. 1621-1637.

B

Castillo y Solórzano, Alonso de. Las harpías en Madrid y
    coche de las estafas. In Colección selecta de antiguas
    novelas españolas. Vol. VII. Madrid: Librería de los
    Bibliófilos Españoles, 1907.

Céspedes y Meneses, Gonzalo de. Varia fortuna del soldado
    Píndaro. In Biblioteca de autores españoles. Vol. XVIII.
    Madrid: Ediciones Atlas, 1946, pp. 273-375.

Cortés de Tolosa, Juan. Lazarillo de Manzanares. Barcelona:
    Selecciones Bibliófilas. Segunda Serie. Vol. I, 1960.

Delicado, Francisco. La lozana andaluza. Buenos Aires:
    Ediciones Nuevo Romance, 1942.

Mabbe, James (trans.). The Rogue: or The Life of Guzmán de
    Alfarache. New York: Alfred A. Knopf, Vol. IV, 1924.

Salas Barbadillo, Alonso Jerónimo de. El necio bien afortunado.

In La Sociedad de Bibliófilos Españoles. Vol. XXI.

Madrid: Imprenta de la Viuda e Hijos de M. Tello, 1894.

_____ La peregrinación sabia. Clásicos castellanos.

Madrid: Espasa-Calpe, 1958.

_____ La sabia Flora malsabidilla. Madrid: Revista

de Archivos. Vol. I, 1907, pp. 285-502.

_____ El subtil cordovés, Pedro de Urdemalas.

Madrid: Juan de la Cuesta, 1620.

GENERAL SYNOPSIS OF THE INDEX

A. MYTHOLOGICAL MOTIFS

A100 - A499. <u>Gods</u>

    A100 - A199. The gods in general

    A400 - A499. Gods of the earth

A600 - A899. <u>Cosmogony and cosmology</u>

    A700 - A799. The heavens

A1200 - A1699. <u>Creation and ordering of human life</u>

    A1300 - A1399. Ordering of human life

    A1500 - A1599. Origin of customs

A2200 - A2599. <u>Animal characteristics</u>

    A2200 - A2299. Various causes of animal characteristics

    A2400 - A2499. Causes of animal characteristics: appearance and habits

B. ANIMALS

B0 - B99. Mythical animals

B100 - B199. Magic animals

B200 - B299. Animals with human traits

B300 - B599. <u>Friendly animals</u>

    B300 - B349. Helpful animals - general

    B350 - B399. Grateful animals

    B400 - B499. Kinds of helpful animals

    B500 - B599. Services of helpful animals

B700 - B799. Fanciful traits of animals

B800 - B899. Miscellaneous animal motifs

C. TABU

C0 - C99. Tabu connected with supernatural beings

C200 - C299. Eating and drinking tabu

C300 - C399. Looking tabu

C600 - C699. Unique prohibitions and compulsions

D. MAGIC

D0 - D699. <u>Transformation</u>

    D10 - D99. Transformation: man to different man

    D100 - D199. Transformation: man to animal

    D200 - D299. Transformation: man to object

    D300 - D399. Transformation: animal to person

    D400 - D499. Other forms of transformation

    D500 - D599. Means of transformation

D700 - D799. Disenchantment

D800 - D1699. <u>Magic objects</u>

    D900 - D1299. Kinds of magic objects

    D1300 - D1599. Function of magic objects

    D1600 - D1699. Characteristics of magic objects

D1700 - D2199. <u>Magic powers and manifestations</u>

    D1710 - D1799. Possession and means of employment of
                   magic powers

    D1800 - D2199. Manifestations of magic power

E. THE DEAD

E0 - E199. Resuscitation

E200 - E599. <u>Ghosts and other revenants</u>

    E200 - E299. Malevolent return from the dead

    E300 - E399. Friendly return from the dead

    E400 - E599. Ghosts and revenants - miscellaneous

F. MARVELS

G. OGRES

H. TESTS

J. THE WISE AND THE FOOLISH

K. DECEPTIONS

K0 - K99. Contests won by deception

K100 - K299. Deceptive bargains

K300 - K499. Thefts and cheats

K500 - K699. Escape by deception

K700 - K799. Capture by deception

K800 - K999. Fatal deception

K1000 - K1199. Deception into self-injury

K1200 - K1299. Deception into humiliating position

K1300 - K1399. Seduction or deceptive marriage

K1400 - K1499. Dupe's property destroyed

K1500 - K1599. Deceptions connected with adultery

K1600 - K1699. Deceiver falls into own trap

K1700 - K2099. <u>Deception through shams</u>

    K1700 - K1799. Deception through bluffing

    K1800 - K1899. Deception by disguise or illusion

    K1900 - K1999. Imposters

    K2000 - K2099. Hypocrites

K2100 - K2199. False accusations

K2200 - K2299. Villains and traitors

K2300 - K2399. Other deceptions

L. REVERSAL OF FORTUNE

L100 - L199. Unpromising hero (heroine)

L400 - L499. Pride brought low

M. ORDAINING THE FUTURE

M0 - M99. Judgments and decrees

M100 - M199. Vows and oaths

M200 - M299. Bargains and promises

M300 - M399. Prophecies
M400 - M499. Curses

N. CHANCE AND FATE

N0 - N99. Wagers and gambling

N100 - N299. The ways of luck and fate

N300 - N399. Unlucky accidents

N400 - N699. <u>Lucky accidents</u>

    N440 - N499. Valuable secrets learned

    N500 - N599. Treasure trove

    N600 - N699. Other lucky accidents

N700 - N799. Accidental encounters

N800 - N899. Helpers

P. SOCIETY

P0 - P99. Royalty and nobility

P100 - P199. Other social orders

P200 - P299. The family

P300 - P399. Other social relationships

P400 - P499. Trades and professions

P500 - P599. Government

P600 - P699. Customs

P700 - P799. Society - miscellaneous motifs

Q. REWARDS AND PUNISHMENTS

Q10 - Q99. Deeds rewarded

Q100 - Q199. Nature of rewards

Q200 - Q399. Deeds punished

Q400 - Q599. Kinds of punishment

R. CAPTIVES AND FUGITIVES

R0 - R99. Captivity

R100 - R199. Rescues

R200 - R299. Escapes and pursuits

R300 - R399. Refuges and recapture

S. UNNATURAL CRUELTY

S0 - S99. Cruel relatives

S100 - S199. Revolting murders or mutilations

S300 - S399. Abandoned or murdered children

T. SEX

T0 - T99. Love

T100 - T199. Marriage

T200 - T299. Married life

T300 - T399. Chastity and celibacy

T400 - T499. Illicit sexual relations

T500 - T599. Conception and birth

T600 - T699. Care of children

U. THE NATURE OF LIFE

U0 - U99. Life's inequalities

U100 - U299. The nature of life - miscellaneous motifs

V. RELIGION

V0 - V99. Religious services

V100 - V199. Religious edifices and objects

V200 - V299. Sacred persons

V300 - V399. Religious beliefs

V400 - V449. Religious virtues

V450 - V499. Religious orders

V500 - V599. Religious motifs - miscellaneous

W. TRAITS OF CHARACTER

W0 - W99. Favorable traits of character

W100 - W199. Unfavorable traits of character

X. HUMOR

Z. MISCELLANEOUS GROUPS OF MOTIFS

A. MYTHOLOGICAL MOTIFS

A100 - A499. GODS

A100 - A199. THE GODS IN GENERAL

A100. Deity

A106.2.1. Revolting devil banished to hell. Is captured by
another devil and taken back to hell. Diablo: Tranco X
1677b.

A106.2.2. Satan's fall from heaven.

G303.4.5.2. Devil has a broken foot. He limps.

A106.2.2.1.* Didn't have time to observe stars. Devil's fall
from heaven was too fast for him to observe stars, he
tells a student questioner. Diablo: Tranco VI 1661a.

A120. Nature and appearance of the gods.

A132.6.2.1.* Goddess in form of cloud. Ixion unites with cloud
in form of goddess Juno. Guzmán (Luján): Pt. II, Bk. III,
Ch. V 668a.

Q501.5. Punishment of Ixion.

A180. Gods in relation to mortals.

A182.3.2.1.* God rebukes Elijah for flogging himself in the
desert. He should be in the crowds of men where his
words and life could save many souls. Periquillo:
Discurso XIV 1909A.

A400 - A499. GODS OF THE EARTH.

A450. God of trades and professions.

A454. God of healing. Alonso: Pt. I, Ch. VI 1244b.

D1711.6.2.1.* Aesculapius as god of healing.

Z100. Symbolism

A600 - A899. COSMOGONY AND COSMOLOGY

A700 - A799. THE HEAVENS

A720. Nature and condition of the sun.

A737.5.1.* Moon's eclipse caused by goddess' periods of weeping. Moon goddess decrees times of weeping for herself because she previously rejected Apollo's advances when she failed to recognize him. Justina: Bk. IV, Ch. I 869b.

A1200 - A1699. CREATION AND ORDERING OF HUMAN LIFE

A1300 - A1399. ORDERING OF HUMAN LIFE

A1310. Arrangement of man's bodily attributes.

A1313. Origin of sex-organs.

A1352.4.* Why men hurry in sexual intercourse.

A1320. Determination of span of life.

A1321. Men and animals readjust span of life. At first, thirty years are given to all animals and to man. For the animals it is too long, for man too short. Man is given a portion of animals' lives. Years 1-30 vigorous (man's own); 30-50 burdens and blows (ass's); 50-70 snarling and growling at others (dog's); 70-90 foolish (monkey's). Guzmán: Pt. II, Bk. I, Ch. III 403b.

B592. Animals bequeath characteristics to man.

A1330. Beginnings of trouble for man.

L482. Men too prosperous (happy): things are made more difficult.

A1331.3.* Paradise lost because men worship God of Contentment. Jupiter substitutes God of Discontentment who looks like his brother Contentment. Guzmán: Pt. I, Bk. I, Ch. VII 269b.

A1337.0.5. Disease as punishment. "French disease" (syphilis) is spread by an angel to the French soldiers in Italy as punishment for their killing the poor and sacking the city of Rapallo. Lozana: Mamotreto LIV 179.

A1337.8.1.* Plagues in Naples started from infected wine and water. Blood from dogs and lepers had been poured into wells. Lozana: Mamotreto LIV 179.

A1346.2.3. Men are too happy: pain and sickness created. Necio: Ch. III 250.

L482. Men too prosperous (happy): things are made more difficult.

A1350. Origin of sex functions.

A1352.4.* Why men hurry in sexual intercourse. At first, all men were eunuchs until the Lord made testicles for them. Men hurry in sexual intercourse for fear their testicles may be taken away from them. Lozana: LXIII 205.

A1313. Origin of sex-organs.

A1500 - A1599. ORIGIN OF CUSTOMS

A1580. Origin of laws.

A1581.2.1.* Origin of penalty for theft. First thief was an angel in heaven, the morning star. He tried to rob glory from God by wanting to outshine the sun. He was condemned to perpetual imprisonment. Codicia: Ch. V 1172a.

A1581.2.2.* Adam punished for theft. Tried to rob knowledge and wisdom from God. Banished from Garden of Eden. Codicia: Ch. V 1172b.

A2200 - A2599. ANIMAL CHARACTERISTICS

A2200 - A2299. VARIOUS CAUSES OF ANIMAL CHARACTERISTICS.

A2230. Animal characteristics as punishment.

A2232.3.1.* Beetle makes request for more noble appearance. Louse supports the request and he and beetle are crushed under a man's foot. Periquillo: Discurso IX 1884a.

Q338.4.* Request for higher condition punished.

A2270. <u>Animal characteristics from miscellaneous causes</u>.

A2281,3.1.* Why cat and mouse are enemies. Mouse ate up cat's possessions while she was away. <u>Justina</u>: Bk. II, Pt. III, Ch. II 834b.

    A2494.1.1. Enmity between cat and mouse.

   A2400 - A2499. CAUSES OF ANIMAL CHARACTERISTICS: APPEARANCE AND HABITS.

A2410. <u>Animal characteristics: color and smell</u>.

A2412.5.2.2.* Why frog has no hair. Unhappy because she could not sing like the swan nor sleep all winter like the fly, the frog asked Jupiter to change her. To accomplish the change it was necessary to pluck all of the frog's hair to make a pillow on which she could sleep all winter, and a tongue of nap which she could use in singing all summer. <u>Justina</u>: Introduction 713a.

A2430. <u>Animal characteristics: dwelling and food</u>.

A2433.3.1.2.* Fox puts curse of coldness on unborn kittens. This is why kittens are cold-natured and seek a fire. <u>Justina</u>: Bk. I, Ch. I 725b.

    J758.3. Fish refuse fox's invitation to live on dry land. M470. Curses on objects or animals. Q340. Meddling punished.

A2470. <u>Animal's habitual bodily movements</u>.

A2471.3.1.* Why dove is always looking into water. She is seeking picture of frog to whom she lent her chastity. <u>Justina</u>: Bk. III, Ch. VI 866b.

    D419.1.3.* Transformation: frog to dove.

A2490. <u>Other habits of animals</u>.

A2494.1.1. Enmity between cat and mouse. <u>Justina</u>: Bk. II,
Pt. III, Ch. II 834b.

A2281.3.1.* Why cat and mouse are enemies.

A2494.9.3.* Enmity between fox and wolf. Fox teaches wolf's
son to hunt chickens. Son is killed by cattle when his
parents send him to get a calf. <u>Marcos</u>: Bk. I,
Descanso VII 946a.

B. ANIMALS

B0 - B99. MYTHICAL ANIMALS

B10. <u>Mythical beasts and hybrids</u>.

B11.2.1.11. Dragon as modified eagle. Eagle lends wings to
dragon and agrees to fight him on the ground. <u>Justina</u>:
Bk. IV, Ch. IV 880b.

B15. Animals with unusual limbs or members.

B15.1.2.1.1.1.* Two-headed serpent. One is a frog's head
sticking out of the serpent's mouth. <u>Marcos</u>: Bk. III,
Descanso XIV 1064a.

    J1839.* Man thinks snake has two heads.

B16.1.2.2.* Knight-errant dog defeats two fighting bulls and
the herdsmen who come to their defense. <u>Peregrinación</u>:
p. 32.

B90. <u>Other mythical animals</u>.

B99.1. Mythical salamander.

    B768.2.1.* Salamander found attached to oven's
mortar where flames are located.

B.100 - B199. MAGIC ANIMALS

B120-B169. ANIMALS WITH MAGIC WISDOM

B120. <u>Wise animals</u>

    B152.1. Dog indicates adulteress.

    B211.1.7. Speaking dog.

B121.0.1.* Wise dog does not leap upon master. He recalls
the fable of the ass and lapdog, and he does not want
to displease his master. <u>Coloquio</u>: p. 209a.

B150. <u>Oracular animals</u>.

B152.1. Dog indicates adulteress. He attacks her at night when
she meets paramour. She tries to feed him a sponge fried
in lard, but the dog recognizes the danger and does not
eat it. <u>Coloquio</u>: p. 212b.

B120. Wise animals

B153.2.* Dog indicates where water is located. When untied,
dog finds water source, thus reviving shepherd and flock.
Marcos: Bk. I, Descanso XIV 971b.

B421. Helpful dog.

B170-B189. OTHER MAGIC ANIMALS

B180. Magic quadruped.

B184.1.10. Magic horse makes prodigious jump. Reverses its
direction in mid-air and returns to starting place.
Flora: p. 330.

B599.4.* High-jumping horse helps master.

B200 - B299. ANIMALS WITH HUMAN TRAITS

B210. Speaking animals.

J2415.1.3.* The two presents to the emperor: two
speaking birds.

B211.1.3.2. Speaking mule. Trickster tells crowd that a mule
speaks Greek. Dupe speaks to it in Italian and is kicked.
"No more dealing with Greek mules: They speak from
behind." Guadaña: Ch. III 1690a.

J2349.1.1.* Dupe is made to believe that mule
speaks Greek.

B211.1.7. Speaking dog. Coloquio: p. 205a.

K302.2.* Woman steals meat from basket carried by dog.

B211.3. Speaking bird.

J1118.2.* Speaking thrush helps king regain stolen
treasure. J2415.1.3.* The two presents to the
emperor: two speaking birds.

B220. Animal kingdom (or community).

B221.1.1.* Monkeys suspend play momentarily when one drowns.
Frolic resumes until another accident occurs. Alonso:
Pt. II, Ch. IV 1290b.

B230. <u>Parliament of animals</u>.

B234.1.* Animals gather in an academy. Four quadripeds and four birds meet in a literary society with the horse as president. <u>Peregrinación</u>: p. 44.

B260. <u>Animal warfare</u>.

B263.9.* War between knight-errant dog and villagers. The dog, a descendant of Alexander the Great's dog Mataleones, wins fight with armed peasants. <u>Peregrinación</u>: p. 31.

B264.4.1.* Fight between cat and snake. Cat kills snake after long fight. <u>Marcos</u>: Bk. II, Descanso IV 1007a.

B290. <u>Other animals with human traits</u>.

B291.2.2.1.* Dogs as messengers. Relay of dogs take messages to giants' king. Messages are placed inside a hollow cane. <u>Marcos</u>: Bk. III, Descanso XXII 1080a.

B300 - B599. FRIENDLY ANIMALS

B300 - B349. HELPFUL ANIMALS - GENERAL

B330. <u>Death of helpful animal</u>.

B335.6.1.* Fettered lamb warns lion of trap set by man. After lion falls into pit, the lamb tells him how to escape. The freed lion is too proud to rescue the lamb, and the man kills the lamb. <u>Periquillo</u>: Discurso III 1864a.

    W154.3.1.1.* Lion rescued from pit by following fettered lamb's advice, but is too proud to rescue lamb.

B350 - B399. GRATEFUL ANIMALS

B360. <u>Animals grateful for rescue from peril of death</u>.

B361. Animals grateful for rescue from pit. They warn rescuer that a man imprisoned with them is a monster. Latter kills rescuer for money. <u>Periquillo</u>: Discurso III 1863b.

    W154.2. Monster ungrateful for rescue. W154.8. Grateful animals; ungrateful man.

B400 - B499. KINDS OF HELPFUL ANIMALS

B400-B449. HELPFUL BEASTS

B400. **Helpful domestic beasts.**

B411.2. Helpful ox. Knocks down a ceremonious nobleman who
is blocking entrance to building, thus freeing the doorway.
<u>Píndaro</u>: Bk. II, Ch. XII 343b.

> P56.* Ceremonious noblemen block door while deter-
> mining who will enter first.

B421. Helpful dog.

> B153.2.* Dog indicates where water is located.
> B521.1.3.* Dog warns man against prostitutes.
> B579.7.1.* Dog earns money for master.

B421.1.* Obedient dog pursues fleeing man and attacks him.
The latter was his master. <u>Coloquio</u>: p. 218a.

B421.2.* Dog drags witch into yard. Witch goes into trance
and dog drags her out into yard. <u>Coloquio</u>: p. 223b.

B443.1.1.* Doe brings udder full of milk for thirsty traveler.
<u>Alonso</u>: Pt. I, Ch. VII 1251a.

> F900. Extraordinary occurrences.

B450. **Helpful birds.**

B450.0.1.* Helpful songbirds. Wild animals stop and listen
to bird songs, and hunters can shoot the wild beasts.
<u>Periquillo</u>: Discurso XIII 1904b.

> K756.4.* Hunters use songbirds in order to kill
> wild animals.

B451.5.1.* Raven brings bread to saint. <u>Alonso</u>: Pt. I, Ch. VII
1251a.

> F900. Extraordinary occurrences.

B469.9.2.* Helpful parrot humbles arrogant statesman. The
bird's repeated call of "Waterseller" reminds proud

statesman of his ancestor's humble business beginning.
Necio: Ch. IV 271.

L400. Pride brought low.

B500 - B599. SERVICES OF HELPFUL ANIMALS

B520. Animals save person's life.

B521.1.3.* Dog warns man against prostitutes. Dog tries to
tell mayor that diseased prostitutes are infecting city.
He can only bark, and is beaten for his noise.
Coloquio: p. 232a.

B421. Helpful dog.

B527.4.* Horse saves man from drowning. Man holds to horse's
tail and is pulled ashore. Marcos: Bk. III, Descanso III
1038b.

B530. Animals nourish men.

B535.0.3. Goat as nurse for child. On growing up he becomes
a swift runner. Alonso: Pt. II, Ch. II 1277b.

B535.0.15.* She-bear nurses Orson. Latter grows up to be
valiant French king of incredible strength. Alonso:
Pt. II, Ch. II 1277b.

B535.0.16.* Sow nurses child. On growing up, the youth undresses
daily and enters a quagmire. Alonso: Pt. II, Ch. II 1277b

B570. Animals serve men.

B579.7.1.* Dog earns money for master. His tricks include
running like a horse and jumping through a hoop.
Coloquio: p. 219a.

B421. Helpful dog.

B590. Miscellaneous services of helpful animals.

B592. Animals bequeath characteristics to man. Guzmán: Pt. II,
Bk. I, Ch. III 403b.

A1321. Men and animals readjust span of life.

B599.4.* High-jumping horse helps master read a paper which a
woman is reading on her balcony. <u>Flora</u>: p. 330.

B184.1.10. Magic horse makes prodigious jump.

B700 - B799. FANCIFUL TRAITS OF ANIMALS

B730. <u>Fanciful color, smell, etc. of animals</u>.

B731.12.1.* Murex fish has vivid blood color inside and outside. It disappears forever when Christ is crucified.
<u>Periquillo</u>: Discurso XIV 1909b.

B750. <u>Fanciful habits of animals</u>.

B752.1. Swan song. Swan sings as she dies. <u>Periquillo</u>:
Discurso VII 1880a.

J1309.4.* Does a dying swan sing?

B768.2.1.* Salamander found attached to oven's mortar where
flames are located. <u>Marcos</u>: Bk. III, Descanso XIV 1064b.

B99.1. Mythical salamander.

B800 - B899. MISCELLANEOUS ANIMAL MOTIFS

B870. <u>Giant animals</u>.

B875.1.1.* Large snake turns from chasing mule to pursuing
muleteer. The latter finally kills it. <u>Marcos</u>: Bk. I,
Descanso XV 975a.

C. TABU

C0 - C99. TABU CONNECTED WITH SUPERNATURAL BEINGS

C50. Tabu: offending the gods.

C51.1.1.1.* Tabu: birds not to perch on holy temple. Sharp
spikes on temple roof used to prevent birds from perching.
Alonso: P. I, Ch. III 1212a.

C200 - C299. EATING AND DRINKING TABU

C250 - C279. DRINKING TABUS

C270. Tabu: drinking certain things.

C273.3.* Tabu: drinking water from wells in Rome. Water
turned bad after Romans refused to give it to pilgrims.
Poor people prayed for water to turn bad so that pilgrims
would buy water from the Tiber from them. Lozana: LIV 176.

C300 - C399. LOOKING TABU

C320. Tabu: looking into certain receptacle.

C321.3.* Tabu: opening cave in which are locked all evils.
Curious woman wheedles key from man, unlocks cave, and
lets out evils. Periquillo: Discurso XVII 1917a.

C600 - C699. UNIQUE PROHIBITIONS AND COMPULSIONS

C600 -C649. THE ONE FORBIDDEN THING

C630. Tabu: the one forbidden time.

C631.1. Tabu: journeying on Sabbath. Man's mule slips and
falls down mountain on a Sunday-night trip. Marcos:
Bk. I, Descanso XVI 979b.

Q223.6. Failure to observe holiness of Sabbath
punished.

D. MAGIC

D0 - D699. TRANSFORMATION

D10 - D99. TRANSFORMATION: MAN TO DIFFERENT MAN

D20. <u>Transformation to person of different social class.</u>

D22.3.* Transformation: fool into a wise man. Company of
friends initiate foolish man into the society of the
wise. <u>Necio</u>: Ch. VII 320ff.

D100 - D199. TRANSFORMATION: MAN TO ANIMAL

D100. <u>Transformation: man to animal</u>

D128.* Transformation: Man to fish. D370.2.* "Fish"
with human characteristics.

D110 - D149. TRANSFORMATION: MAN TO MAMMAL

D110. <u>Transformation: man to wild beast (mammal).</u>

D110.1.* Goddess transforms men to wild animals. She lets
them keep their human understanding. <u>Guzmán</u>: Pt. II,
Bk. III, Ch. V 542a.

D118.2. Transformation: man to monkey. Trickster is converted
into a monkey. Boys play tricks on him, thus repaying
him for his former tricks. <u>Justina</u>: Bk. II, Pt. III,
Ch. II 838b.

D128.* Transformation: Man to fish. Shipwrecked man caught
in fishermen's nets. He is exhibited as a fish with
human characteristics. <u>Lazarillo</u> (Luna): Pt. II,
Ch. IV 120a.

D100. Transformation: man to animal. D370. Transformation: fish to man.

D130. <u>Transformation: man to domestic beast (mammal).</u>

D132.1.1.* Transformation: man to ass. Son is transformed to
ass and beaten because of father's sins. The father

does not change his ways on seeing the son's humiliation. <u>Periquillo</u>: Discurso XVII 1915b.

D150. <u>Transformation: man to bird</u>.

D161.1.* Woman transformed to parrot. She talked as parrot by day and as woman by night. Jupiter granted her request to revert to the status of woman. <u>Justina</u>: Bk. II, Pt. II, Ch. I 779a.

  D200 - D299. TRANSFORMATION: MAN TO OBJECT

D250. <u>Transformation: man to manufactured object</u>.

D263.1.1.* Devil locked up in a ring. It had formerly belonged to a doctor whose patients had died. <u>Diablo</u>: Tranco IV 1650b.

  D300 - D399. TRANSFORMATION: ANIMAL TO PERSON
  D310 - D349. TRANSFORMATION: MAMMAL TO PERSON

D330. <u>Transformation: domestic beast (mammal) to person</u>.

D332.1. Transformation of ass (donkey) to person. <u>Justina</u>: Bk. II, Pt. III, Ch. I 830b.

  J1908.4.* Ass transformed to man dances and turns his head around whenever he hears an ass bray.

D342. Transformation: cat to person. <u>Alonso</u>: Pt. II, Ch. VI 1302a.

  J1908.2. Cat transformed to maiden runs after mouse.

D370. <u>Transformation: fish to man</u>.

  D128.* Transformation: man to fish.

D370.2.* "Fish" with human characteristics. Shipwrecked man caught in fishermen's nets is exhibited as a fish with human characteristics. <u>Lazarillo</u> (Luna): Pt. II, Ch. IV 120a.

  D100. Transformation: man to animal.

D400 - D499. OTHER FORMS OF TRANSFORMATION

D410. <u>Transformation: one animal to another.</u>

D419.1.3.* Transformation: frog to dove. Frog asks Venus to
transform him to dove. Venus grants the request, but
hides a picture of the frog in the river so that he
would be humble whenever he saw his former self. <u>Justina</u>:
Bk. III, Ch. VI 866b.

> A2471.3.1.* Why dove is always looking into water.
> D521. Transformation through wish.

D500 - D599. MEANS OF TRANSFORMATION

D520. <u>Transformation through power of the word.</u>

D521. Transformation through wish.

> D419.1.3.* Transformation: frog to dove.

D560. <u>Transformation by various means.</u>

D579.1.* Thin man is transformed into a plump man by "magic"
mirror. Mirror is a gift from a man seeking favors.
<u>Necio</u>: Ch. IV 270.

> D1163. Magic mirror.

D700 - D799. DISENCHANTMENT

D760. <u>Disenchantment by miscellaneous means.</u>

D786.2.* King's ardor for war kindled then cooled by music.
<u>Guzmán</u> (Luján): Pt. II, Bk. II, Ch. VII 632b.

> D1275.1. Magic music. J1675.5.1.* King influenced
> by music.

D800 - D1699. MAGIC OBJECTS

D900 - D1299. KINDS OF MAGIC OBJECTS

D950. <u>Magic tree.</u>

D953.3.* Magic twig with bitter bark good for sheep.
Shepherd cuts branches and throws them into pool from
which sheep drink, thereby producing fine wool.
<u>Periquillo</u>: Discurso XIV 1908a.

D978. Magic herbs.

> D1323.13.1.* Magic powder made from herbs ensures
> good memory if snuffed into nostrils. K112.4.* Sale
> of pseudo-magic powdered herbs.

D1130. <u>Magic buildings and parts</u>.

D1132.2.* Magic palace of Prince World transforms animals
when they enter. Asses become men, and other animals
are transformed into different species. <u>Periquillo</u>:
Discurso VII 1878a.

D1150. <u>Magic furniture</u>.

D1163. Magic mirror.

> D579.1.* Thin man is transformed into a plump man
> by magic mirror. D1323.1. Magic clairvoyant mirror.

D1250. <u>Miscellaneous magic objects</u>.

D1273. Magic formula (charm).

> D1355.18.1.1.* Love charm (words) spoken into
> love-sick girl's ear cures her sickness. . . .

D1275.0.1.* Man's foolish songs and repetition of silly
words cure woman of melancholia. <u>Marcos</u>: Bk. II,
Descanso X 1020a.

D1275.1. Magic music.

> D786.2.* King's ardor for war kindled then cooled
> by music. J1675.5.1.* King influenced by music.

D1275.1.1.* Magical effect of music on army. Spartans carried
musicians to their battles. Their stirring music made
the soldiers fight better. <u>Necio</u>: Ch. I 170.

D1275.2.1.* Alexander the Great is excited by songs of Trojan
war. On hearing the songs, he grabs his sword and starts
slashing with it. <u>Marcos</u>: Bk. III, Descanso V 1042b.

> D1275.1. Magic music.

D1275.2.2.* Realistic song overcomes serenader. When he
sings, "Break the veins of my heart," he asks woman to
stab him. Marcos: Bk. III, Descanso V 1043a.

D1275.1. Magic music. J2450. Literal fool.

D1300 - D1599. FUNCTION OF MAGIC OBJECTS

D1310. Magic object gives supernatural information.

D1316.4.2.1.* Magic spectacles allow wearer to see through
wall. Necio: Ch. IV 269.

D1323.1. Magic clairvoyant mirror. Devil borrows woman's
mirror and shows her and a student what is happening
in a distant city. Diablo: Tranco VIII 1665b.

D1163. Magic mirror.

D1323.3.1.* Magic clairvoyant peep-hole. Trickster induces
dupe to look through magic hole in wall in order to see
far-away persons. He sees woman and man in next room.
Necio: Ch, I 193.

D1323.13.1.* Magic powder made from herbs ensures good memory
if snuffed into nostrils. Estebanillo: Bk. I, Ch. I 1728a.

D1350. Magic object changes person's disposition.

D1355.18.1.1.* Love charm (words) spoken into love-sick girl's
ear cures her sickness. Marcos: Bk. II, Descanso X 1019b.

D1273. Magic formula (charm).

D1360. Magic object effects temporary change in person.

D1368.2.1.* Magic ring causes illusions. Owner shows visitors
demons, dark cloud, smoke; and they hear Cupid's voice.
Necio: Ch. I 176ff.

D1421.1.6.1.* Magic ring summons demons.

D1400 - D1439. MAGIC OBJECT GIVES POWER OVER OTHER PERSONS

D1420. Magic object draws person (thing) to it.

D1421.1.6.1.* Magic ring summons demons. Man tells his
friends that his magic ring will summon demons when turned.
Necio: Ch. I 176.

D1500. Magic object controls disease.

D1500.1.18. Magic healing water. Doctors of Rome filled up
three ditches of water which had curative powers for
bathers, making one ditch on top. This ditch had curative
powers. Lozana: Mamotreto LIX 193.

D1500.1.18.1.3.* Man's bath water as remédy. Feverish man
drinks his filthy bath water, vomits, and is cured.
Marcos: Bk. I, Descanso XI 963a.

    N646.1.* Feverish man drinks filthy bath water.

    D1600 - D1699. CHARACTERISTICS OF MAGIC OBJECTS

D1620. Magic automata.

D1622.1. Crucifix bows as sign of favor. Man who has forgiven
his enemy prays before crucifix, asking that his sins be
forgiven. Crucifix nods head affirmatively, and man
retires to monastery. Guzmán: Pt. II, Bk. II, Ch. VIII
483b.

    D1700 - D2199. MAGIC POWERS AND MANIFESTATIONS

    D1710 - D1799. POSSESSION AND MEANS OF EMPLOYMENT
                OF MAGIC POWERS

D1710. Possession of magic powers.

D1711.6.2.1.* Aesculapius as god of healing. Picture
details his attributes. Alonso: Pt. I, Ch. VI 1244b.

    Z100. Symbolism.

D1720. Acquisition of magic powers.

D1731.2. Marvels seen in dreams.

    V513.1.1.* Monk sees vision of lawer's soul carried
away by demons.

D1760. Means of producing magic power.

D1766.1.4. Pain stopped by prayer.

    D2161. Magic healing power. D2161.3.12.* Toothache
    magically cured. J701.3.* "Prayer no good."

D1766.1.9.* Water turns bad by prayer. Poor Romans prayed
that water in Roman wells would turn bad so that pilgrims
would buy Tiber's water from them. Lozana: Mamotreto
LIV 176.

    C273.3.* Tabu: drinking water from wells in Rome.

    V52.16.* Prayers of poor cause water in Roman
    wells to turn bad.

      D1800 - D2199. MANIFESTATIONS OF MAGIC POWER

        D1800 - D1949. LASTING MAGIC QUALITIES

D1830. Magic strength.

D1831. Magic strength resides in hair. Periquillo: Discurso
XVI 1912b.

    K2213.4.3.* Samson's secret betrayed by his wife.

      D2050 - D2099. DESTRUCTIVE MAGIC POWERS

D2060. Death or bodily injury by magic.

D2063.1.1.1.* Witch torments girl's absent lover by sympathetic
magic. She sticks pins in a wax image and binds it with
steel wires in order to secure man for the girl.
Pindaro: Bk. I, Ch. XVI 308b.

    G259.2. Witch recognized by odor.

    D2100 - D2199. OTHER MANIFESTATIONS OF MAGIC POWER

D2100. Magic wealth.

D2106.1.5.1.* Christ multiplies five loaves and two fish.
Feeds a multitude of people. Alonso: Pt. I, Ch. VII 1251a.

    F900. Extraordinary occurrences.

D2120. Magic transportation.

D2121.5. Magic journey: man carried by spirit or devil. Student frees devil from bottle. Grateful devil takes him on a magic journey over a city at night. <u>Diablo</u>: Tranco Primero 1642a.

       G303.6.2.10. Devil appears to scholar.

D2150. <u>Miscellaneous magic manifestations</u>.

D2161. Magic healing power.

       D1766.1.4. Pain stopped by prayer. J701.3.* "Prayer no good."

D2161.3.12.* Toothache magically cured. Youth tells maid that he will write out a prayer to cure her toothache. He sends love letter instead, which girl tears up. <u>Fregona</u>: p. 166a.

       D1766.1.4. Pain stopped by prayer. J701.3.* "Prayer no good."

D2161.5.8.* Cure by French king. Latter cures patients suffering from "king's disease." "The king blesses and touches you; may God heal you." <u>Alonso</u>: Pt. I, Ch. VI 1242b.

E. THE DEAD

E0 - E199. RESUSCITATION

E50. <u>Resuscitation by magic.</u>

E58.1.* Soldier's weeping causes dead friend to return. Latter undresses and gets into bed with his friend, but he quickly leaves when friend is inhospitable. <u>Alonso</u>: Pt. II, Ch. IV 1290b.

> E361. Return from the dead to stop weeping.

E200 - E599. GHOSTS AND OTHER REVENANTS

E200 - E299. MALEVOLENT RETURN FROM THE DEAD

E230. <u>Return from dead to inflict punishment.</u>

> Q223.4.2.* Revenant punishes dueler for letting him die without confessing.

E236.4.3.* Ghost appears to remind murderer to set up dowry for dead man's daughter. <u>Marcos</u>: Bk. II, Introduction 1001a.

> E459.3. Ghost "laid" when its wishes are acceded to.

E300 - E399. FRIENDLY RETURN FROM THE DEAD

E360. <u>Other reasons for friendly return from the dead.</u>

E361. Return from the dead to stop weeping.

> E58.1.* Soldier's weeping causes dead friend to return.

E400 - E599. GHOSTS AND REVENANTS - MISCELLANEOUS

E440. <u>Walking ghost "laid."</u>

> E236.4.3.* Ghost appears to remind murderer to set up dowry for dead man's daughter.

E459.3. Ghost "laid" when its wishes are acceded to. Murderer agrees to set up dowry for dead man's daughter as specified in will. <u>Marcos</u>: Bk. II, Introduction 1001a.

> E440. Walking ghost "laid."

F. MARVELS

F500 - F599. REMARKABLE PERSONS

F530. Exceptionally large or small men.

F531.3.2.1.1.* Giants throw large rocks toward departing ships.
Marcos: Bk. III, Descanso XXIII 1081a.

F540. Remarkable physical organs.

F547.2.2.* Hermaphrodite with extraordinary sex organs. Penis
like that of a mule, and vagina like a cow's. Lozana:
Mamotreto XXXIX 137.

F547.2.3.* Hermaphrodite. A human hermaphrodite monster was
born with special physical characteristics and special
markings. These are explained symbolically. Guzmán:
Pt. I, Bk. I, Ch. I 246a.

F560. Unusual manner of life.

F562.6.* Man and wife live in carriage. They catch cold if
they stick heads or hands outside. Diablo: Tranco II 1645b.

F600 - F699. PERSONS WITH EXTRAORDINARY POWERS

F640. Extraordinary powers of perception.

F647.1.2.* Extraordinary olfactory sense. Woman detects that
partridges have been basted with bacon. She throws them
away. Marcos: Bk. I, Descanso XXII 994b.

F680. Other marvelous powers.

F692. Person(s) with remarkable memory. Numerous examples
given. Marcos: Bk. III, Descanso XIV 1063b.

F696.1.* Aged Christian swimmer confiscates a boat from five
Moors. Marcos: Bk. III, Descanso X 1056a.

F696.2.* Shipwrecked man swims all night. Refuses rescue
because others need help worse than he. Marcos: Bk. III,
Descanso X 1056a.

F700 - F899. EXTRAORDINARY PLACES AND THINGS

F700. <u>Extraordinary places</u>.

F709.3.1.* Town of thieves. Thieving soldiers, formerly
quartered in town, give it a reputation for harboring
thieves. <u>Guzmán</u>: Pt. I, Bk. II, Ch. IX 331b.

> J1399.2.* Mayor's house harbors two thieves:
> father and son.

> F900 - F1099. EXTRAORDINARY OCCURRENCES

F900. <u>Extraordinary occurrences</u>.

> B443.1.1.* Doe brings udder full of milk for
> thirsty traveler. B451.5.1.* Raven brings bread
> to saint. D2106.1.5.1.* Christ multiplies five
> loaves and two fish.

F930. <u>Extraordinary occurrences concerning seas or waters</u>.

F930.2.1.* Waters of Tiber rise to drown impertinent workmen.
They had requested emperor's son as hostage for work
payment. <u>Lozana</u>: Mamotreto LIII 173.

> Q338. Immoderate request punished. Q338.3.* Workmen
> punished for requesting emperor's son as hostage.
> Q552.19.5. Miraculous drowning as punishment for
> haughtiness.

F950. <u>Marvelous cures</u>.

F950.1.1.* House of miserly schoolmaster cures diseases.
It is so miserly that nothing thrives in it, and sick
people are cured by merely entering it. <u>Buscón</u>:
Bk. I, Ch. III 1099 a.

> W152.18.* Stingy schoolmaster.

F953.2.* Broken arm marvelously cured in two weeks. Soldier
attributes the cure to the great amount of wine which

he drank. <u>Estebanillo</u>: Bk. II, Ch. VI, 1842a.

 J1319.3.* "What kills some, cures others."

F959.6.2. Immunity to poison by eating poisons (Mithridates).
<u>Guzmán</u> (Luján): Pt. II, Bk. II, Ch. VI 628b.

F970. <u>Extraordinary behavior of trees and plants</u>.

F979.5.1. Unconsumed burning bush. Moses sees the burning
bush and is told to remove his shoes because he is on
hold ground. <u>Alonso</u>: Pt. I, Ch. III, 1212b.

F1010. <u>Other extraordinary events</u>.

F1021.2.1. Icarus's wings melt. Flight so high that sun
melts glue of artificial wings. <u>Guzmán</u> (Luján):
Pt. II, Bk. III, Ch. IV 664b.

 Q325.1.* Icarus disobeys father and flies too high

F1036. Hand from **heaven** writes on wall. Belshazzar punished
for desecrating the temple. <u>Alonso</u>: Pt. II, Bk. IV 1291a.

F1041.3. Person goes blind from overweeping. <u>Alonso</u>: Pt. I,
Ch. V 1229b.

F1068.2.3.* Woman dreams that a snake bites her while she is
picking an apple. An old man spits on the snake's head,
killing it and freeing the woman. She interprets the
dream to mean that her old servant's advice is saving
her from sin. <u>Marcos</u>: Bk. I, Descanso IV 936b.

 J157.1.1.* Woman dreams that an old man rescues her
from snake (temptation).

G. OGRES

G10 - G399. KINDS OF OGRES
G100 - G199. GIANT OGRES

G120. Physical characteristics of giant ogres.

G121.1.2.* Giants seize men. Giants have one eye, one arm, one nostril, and one ear. Marcos: Bk. III, Descanso XX 1076a.

> R11.3. Abduction by giant. R43. Captivity on island.

G200 - G299. WITCHES

G250. Recognition of witches.

G259.2. Witch recognized by odor. Strong odor of sulphur remains when witch disappears. Pindaro: Bk. I, Ch. XVI 307b.

> D2063.1.1.1.* Witch torments girl's absent lover by sympathetic magic.

G265.6.3. Witch causes horse (mule) to behave unnaturally. Rider cannot control the animal which takes him to house of witch. Pindaro: Bk. I, Ch. XVI 309a.

G300 - G399. OTHER OGRES

G300. Other ogres.

G303.4.5.2. Devil has a broken foot. He limps. He was first one thrown out of heaven and all other devils thrown out fell on him. Diablo: Tranco I 1643a.

> A106.2.2. Satan's fall from heaven.

G303.6.2.1.1.* Devil appears invisible among actors. He disappears when police come to arrest him. Diablo: Tranco V 1657b.

> P471.3.* Actress starts a fight when she does not get leading rôle.

G303.6.2.1.2.* Devil appears invisible among beggars. One
beggar is called "The Limping Devil" and an envoy from
hell tries to carry him away. He escapes because of
his invisibility. <u>Diablo</u>: Tranco IX 1672a.

G303.6.2.10. Devil appears to scholar. Student frees devil
from bottle, and grateful devil takes him on a magic
journey at night over the roof tops of Madrid..<u>Diablo</u>:
Tranco I, 1642a.

D2121.5. Magic journey: man carried by spirit
or devil.

G303.9.4.0.3.* Devil tempts Christ. Attempts to persuade
Christ to throw himself from temple tower. <u>Alonso</u>:
Pt. I, Ch. III 1213a.

G303.9.7.2.1.* Devil advises youth to surrender to local
authorities. He bribes constable and frees youth. He
later steals bribe money from the officer. <u>Diablo</u>:
Tranco X 1677a.

K331. Goods stolen while owner sleeps.

G303.9.9.22.* Devil causes curious woman to physic herself.
He sweetens dish of wood-lye soup and woman eats all of
it. <u>Manzanares</u>: Ch. X 65.

J1803.1.1.* Adulteress does not understand words
of confessor.

G303.22. The devil helps people.

H1561.21.* Student wins fencing contest.

G303.24.1.6. Devil writes down all idle words spoken in church.
His parchment is not long enough and he has to stretch it.
<u>Alonso</u>: Pt. I, Ch. III 1211b.

G308.1.1.* Man fights sea-monster. Both are killed.
<u>Marcos</u>: Bk. III, Descanso XIX 1073b.

G500 - G599. OGRE DEFEATED

G510. <u>Ogre killed, maimed, or captured</u>.

G512.3.3.1.* Gunpowder as fuel for burning giants' guards.
Guards are burned while sitting on ground covered with
gunpowder. They think the fire has come out of the earth.
<u>Marcos</u>: Bk. III, Descanso XXII 1080b.

       K812.1.2.* Men blow up giants' cave with gunpowder.

G514.3.1.* Ogres (giants) caught in trap and killed. Men
fell trees and make trap into which giants fall, or on
which they trip themselves. <u>Marcos</u>: Bk. III,
Descanso XXII 1079a.

H. TESTS

H0 - H199. IDENTITY TESTS: RECOGNITION

H50. **Recognition by bodily marks or physical attributes.**

H51. Recognition by scar. Actor identifies former actress by scar on cheek. She is posing as rich widow. <u>Teresa</u>: Ch. XVII 1411b.

>K1954.7.2.* Sham rich woman exposed.

H80. **Identification by tokens.**

H82. Identifying tokens sent with messenger. Man identifies daughter of dead mother by producing half-chain and half-parchment to match those of daughter. <u>Fregona</u>: p. 170a.

>H242. Credential tests. H242.2.* Half-chain and half-parchment as credential test.

H90. **Identification by ornaments.**

H92. Identification by necklace. Long-lost daughter returns home from captivity and identifies herself by producing necklace with crucifix which father had given her. False daughter is banished. <u>Teresa</u>: Ch. XIV 1394a.

>K1926.1.* False daughter

H94.12.* Son identified by ring and mother's letter. Abandoned as an illegitimate baby, he returns as a young man to his parents who are now married. <u>Píndaro</u>: Bk. II, Ch. XXI 360b.

>T96. Lovers reunited after many adventures.

H200 - H299. TESTS OF TRUTH

H210 - H239. TESTS OF GUILT OR INNOCENCE

H210. **Test of guilt or innocence.**

H210.2.* Guilt or innocence tested at man's table. If the man is honest, the sudden appearance of officers at his

table will not upset him; if guilty, he will reveal his
guilt by blushing or by other acts. <u>Periquillo:</u>
Discurso IX   1885b.

H240. <u>Other tests of truth</u>.

H242. Credential tests.

H82. Identifying tokens sent with messenger.

H242.2.* Half-chain and half-parchment as credential test.
Man identifies daughter of dead mother by producing
half-chain and half-parchment to match those of daughter.
<u>Fregona</u>: p. 170a.

H82. Identifying tokens sent with messenger.

H300 - H499. MARRIAGE TESTS

H310 - H359. SUITOR TESTS

H310. <u>Suitor tests</u>.

H315.2. Suitor contest: bride offered to suitor giving the
token of the greater love. His love was as warm as a
chestnut roasting in a fire. <u>Trapaza</u>: Ch. XV 1510a.

H551.3.* Wealthy widow gives self to lackey who
indicates in poetry that she had formerly been a
chestnut vendor. She rejects other suitors.

H331.5.1.1. Apple (golden) thrown in race with bride. Distracts
girl's attention, and she stops to pick it up, suitor
passes her (Atalanta). <u>Justina</u>: Bk. II, Pt. II, Ch. II
791b.

K11. Race won by deception.

H335.0.2.3.* Suitor task: to remain silent for two years.
Selfish woman asks suitor to prove love by being silent
for two years. Task is performed, but man later marries
a princess. <u>Harpías</u>: pp. 152ff.

H387.2.* Man tests hoped-for bride's constancy by threat of
death. Council of men decree death to woman for refusing
love and money. She remains constant. <u>Necio</u>: Ch. VI 301.

    M57.* Decree that woman must be killed for refusing
love and money.

H400 - H459. CHASTITY TESTS

H410. <u>Chastity test by magic objects or ordeals</u>.

H425.2.1.* Horns will be placed over youth's door some day.
Blind man predicts that youth will become a cuckolded
husband. <u>Lazarillo</u>: Tratado I 89a.

    M345.1.2.* Prophecy: Youth's future wife will be
unfaithful.

H490. <u>Other marriage tests</u>.

H493.1.* Virility test for lover. Man forces procuress to
"try" him when latter says that he is reputed to be
impotent. She will report him favorably to his intended
courtesan. <u>Lozana</u>: Mamotreto XXXVII 131.

H500 - H899. TESTS OF CLEVERNESS

H500. <u>Tests of cleverness or ability</u>.

H501.2.1.* Wise fool answers many questions in examination of
his wisdom. Servants as disguised learned men ask fool
questions to entertain their master. <u>Necio</u>: Ch. III 240ff.

    J1250. Clever verbal retorts - general.

H504.1.3. Contest in lifelike painting: grapes and curtain.
First artist paints a bunch of grapes so realistically
that it attracts the birds. The second artist paints a
curtain which deceives the first artist. He wins.
<u>Alonso</u>: Pt. II, Ch. IX 1315b.

    J1792.2.* Birds see painted grapes and peck at them.

H504.3.* Contest in pot washing. A soldier and a kitchen scullion argue over which is the better pot washer. The scullion wins, and the soldier breaks a pot over his head. <u>Estebanillo</u>: Bk. II, Ch. I 1781a.

W121.3.4.* Cowardly soldier's honor not tarnished by beating.

H508.3.* Royal Council tests university professors. The Council asks if standard weights and measures should be adopted throughout the country. Mathematician and theologian team up to supply an affirmative answer. <u>Torres</u>: Trozo VI 2003a.

H509.4. Tests of poetic ability.

Q91.3.1.* Judges reward erudite obscure poem.

H509.4.1.2.* Devil and student win poetry contest. They are elected officers of the academy. <u>Diablo</u>: Tranco IX 1670b.

H509.6.* Test of letter-writing ability. Count's letter is better than king's, and is chosen to send to the Pope. <u>Pindaro</u>: Bk. I, Ch. VI 286b.

J613.3.* Count exiles himself from court after winning over king in letter-writing contest.

H530 - H899. RIDDLES

H551.3.* Wealthy woman gives self to lackey who indicates in poetry that she had formerly been a chestnut vendor. She rejects other suitors. <u>Trapaza</u>: Ch. XV 1510a.

H315.2. Suitor contest: bride offered to suitor giving the token of the greater love.

H580. <u>Enigmatic statements</u>.

H588. Enigmatic counsels of a father.

J555.1.1.* Spend with prudence.

H600. <u>Symbolic interpretations</u>.

H619.6.* Symbolic interpretation of jai-alai game. The ball
is Reason and the rackets are men's tongues which bounce
Reason back and forth. Reason has escaped to heaven when
the ball is lost. Players store the interpreter.
<u>Periquillo</u>: Discurso V 1869b.

  Z100. Symbolism.

H619.7.* Symbolic interpretation of glove shop. Merchant
is the world (society). The poor people who are buying
expensive gloves as gifts for judges, lawyers, etc. are
pretenders for jobs or favors. <u>Periquillo</u>: Discurso VI
1873a.

  Z100. Symbolism.

H630. <u>Riddles of the superlative</u>.

H659.7.3.1.* What is the greatest and the smallest? --
Humility, because it rises from its own smallness.
(Various other answers.) <u>Periquillo</u>: Discurso IX 1887a.

H659.27.* Who is the most left-handed (sinister)? Grandmother
wills property to the most left-handed relative. Legacy
is claimed by various persons, but a woman relative wins.
She is Eve who came from Adam's left side and who gave
him the apple with her left hand. <u>Guadaña</u>: Ch. III 1688b.

  J1179.15.* Woman is the most left-handed (sinister).

H659.28.* Riddle: Which animal has the most poisonous bite?
Answer: The slanderer or the flatterer. <u>Marcos</u>: Bk. I,
Descanso XIX 985b.

H660. <u>Riddles of comparison</u>.

H664.* Riddle: Which is better, hope or possession?
Answer: Hope, because it borders on happiness; possession
is followed by disillusionment and sadness. <u>Guzmán</u> (Luján):
Pt. II, Bk. II, Ch. VI 631a.

H665.* Why do women use harsher words with each other than
men do? Answer: Women fight with words; men use hands
and swords. Flora: p. 374.

H666.* Why do doctors marry more readily than other men?
-- They have in their hands the means of becoming widowers.
Flora: p. 375.

H675.* Who is greater than the Israelites? -- The Senate and
the Roman people. Banners of Jewish children ask the
above question of conquering Romans. Children of the
latter retaliate with banners reading SPR. Lozana:
Mamotreto LII 169.

H770. Riddles of explanation.

H775.* Why are women usually wandering around? -- Man sends
her to look for rib which he has lost. (Various other
answers.) Justina: Bk. II, Pt. I, Ch. I 752a.

H775.1.* Riddle: What meat item first has its skin cut
rather than the meat? -- Gizzard of a fowl. Justina:
Bk. II, Pt. I, Ch. I 759a.

H775.2.* Riddle: What thing when over-loaded is less burdened?
-- A man filled with food. Justina: Bk. II, Pt. I,
Ch. I 759a.

H775.3.* How far is it to Hat Island (men's island) where one
harvests and to Cloth Island (women's island) where one
is tarnished? -- Hats are harvested in Badajoz (Clapper
Town) and one is tarnished in Putasí (Whore Town - pun
for Potasí). Justina: Bk. II, Pt. III, Ch. IV 850a.

H775.4.* Why do men carry wooden swords in a certain region?
-- To use against adulterous women who live on Cuckold
Island. It is not honorable to fight women with steel.
Justina: Bk. II, Pt. III, Ch. IV 850a.

H775.5.* Riddle: Why do men carry scythes? -- To mow down
gold to satisfy evil women. <u>Justina</u>: Bk. II, Pt. III,
Ch. IV 850a.

H775.6.* Riddle: Why don't Asturian men have a crest at back
of neck? -- Two men's heads have been split down the
middle and united smoothly; there is no crest. <u>Justina</u>:
Bk. II, Pt. III, Ch. IV 850b.

H775.7.* Why do Asturians go barefooted? -- They have heard
that gold and barrels of wine would come down the river,
and they want to be ready to wade. <u>Justina</u>: Bk. II,
Pt. III, Ch. IV 850b.

H775.8.* Why do Asturians always talk as if asking questions?
-- Since they err so often in speech, a statement in
form of a question is not an error. <u>Justina</u>: Bk. II,
Pt. III, Ch. IV 850b.

H775.9.* Why do officers and judges hate thieves so much?
-- They want to be the only thieves. <u>Buscón</u>: Bk. I,
Ch. I 1093a.

H775.10.* Riddle: Why doesn't Spain produce lions? -- Because
every man in Spain is a lion, and men and native lions
could not co-exist. <u>Peregrinación</u>, p. 42.

H840. <u>Other riddles</u>.

H871.2.* Riddle: What four things are worthless unless shared?
-- Pleasure, knowledge, money, and a woman's vagina.
<u>Lozana</u>: Mamotreto LXI 200.

H871.3.* What are three things courtesans do not want to
know? -- Color of men's genitalia, to read what they
already know, and to be lost. <u>Lozana</u>: Mamotreto LXII 203.

H872.* Riddle: How can a person cover seven holes with one, or one hole with seven? -- By putting a flute down one's throat. Justina: Bk. II, Pt. I, Ch. I 751b.

H876.* What are the three reasons for which women make love? -- (1) Gifts and interests;(2) they see that a man is subject to them; and (3) persistent urging. Justina: Bk. IV, Ch. IV 879b.

H900 - H1199. TESTS OF PROWESS: TASKS

H900 - H999. ASSIGNMENT AND PERFORMANCE OF TASKS

H900 - H949. ASSIGNMENT OF TASKS

H910. Assignment of tasks in response to suggestion.

H911.2.* Rivals assign themselves task of finding another woman similar to the one who appears to be dead. Urdemalas: 112ff.

Q53.3.2.* Maiden marries rejected lover who rescues her from grave. T86.1.1.* Rivals kill each other over woman for whom they are searching. Urdemalas: 112ff.

H915.2.* Courtesan has man copulate twice with her to test his boast. He "can swim the river twice." He copulates once with her while she sleeps, and again when she is awake. Lozana: Mamotreto LIII 174.

P665. Boasting of sexual prowess. W117.2.* Man "can swim the river twice."

H919.7.* Task assigned servant at suggestion of master. The servant undertakes to win the affection of his master's scornful lady-love by posing as a rich man. Necio: Ch. III 224.

K1917.5.2.* Man wins scornful woman's love by pretending to wealth.

H950 - H999. PERFORMANCE OF TASKS

H970. **Help in performing tasks.**

H983.1.* Unfinished portrait of Virgin finished while artist
slept. <u>Guzmán</u>: Pt. II, Bk. II, Ch. I 437a.

> N810. Supernatural helpers.

> H1000 - H1199. NATURE OF TASKS

> H1010 - H1049. IMPOSSIBLE OR ABSURD TASKS

H1020. **Tasks contrary to laws of nature.**

H1024.4. Task: teaching an ass to read. Trickster starves
ass for two days, then puts barley between pages of book.
Ass "reads" as he turns pages of book seeking food.
<u>Lozana</u>: Mamotreto LXV 209.

> N57.* Wager: to teach donkey to read.

> H1050 - H1089. PARADOXICAL TASKS

H1050. **Paradoxical tasks.**

H1072. Task: give sheep good care but do not let it fatten.
(Sheep fed but kept near wolf where it is afraid and
does not fatten.) <u>Guzmán</u>: Pt. II, Bk. III, Ch. VIII 567b.

H1150. **Tasks: stealing, capturing, or slaying.**

H1151.4. Task: stealing ring from finger. <u>Necio</u>: Ch. II 222.

> K1581.6.1.* Man employs trickster to steal diamonds
> given to mistress.

H1180. **Miscellaneous tasks.**

H1194.0.1. Task: causing silent person to speak. King offers
reward if anyone can cure muteness of his daughter's
suitor. The man had promised a former fiancée to remain
silent for two years. At the end of the period, he
speaks, and the former fiancée must witness his marriage
to the princess. <u>Harpías</u>: Estafa IV 152ff.

> H335. Tasks assigned suitors. H335.0.2.3.* Suitor
> task: to remain silent for two years.

H1200 - H1399. TESTS OF PROWESS: QUESTS

H1250 - H1399. NATURE OF QUESTS

H1370. **Miscellaneous quests.**

H1381.3.1.2.1. Quest for unknown woman whose picture has aroused man's love. Man determines to find original of the portrait he has stolen. <u>Trapaza</u>: Ch. XIV 1497b.

   T11.2. Love through sight of picture.

H1400 -H1599. OTHER TESTS

H1550 - H1569. TESTS OF CHARACTER

H1550. **Tests of character.**

   P361.7.1.* Captain must obey general's order not to kill his enemy.

H1552.3.* General orders captain to mock enemy but not to kill him when he passes ambush. <u>Guzmán</u>: Pt. I, Bk. I, Ch. IV 261b.

H1557.0.1.* God commands Abraham to sacrifice his son Isaac. <u>Alonso</u>: Pt. II, Ch. II 1277a.

H1561.2.1.* Student wins fencing contest. Friends of defeated champion attack student. The latter and the devil escape from officers, taking the officers staffs with them. <u>Diablo</u>: Tranco VI 1658a.

   G303.22. The devil helps people.

J. THE WISE AND THE FOOLISH

J0 - J199. ACQUISITION AND POSSESSION
OF WISDOM (KNOWLEDGE)

J10. <u>Wisdom (knowledge) acquired from experience.</u>

J11.2.* Old blind man advises his guide to stay free of ropes.
They are bad victuals which choke one without eating them.
<u>Lazarillo</u>: Tratado I   89a.

J18.1.* Wisdom acquired from beating. <u>Lazarillo</u>:   Tratado I
86a.

      K1043.3.* Child induced to listen to noise inside
      stone statue.

J21.7.1.* Do not cross a bridge while cattle are crossing.
Man ignores the advice and is battered by the animals.
<u>Marcos</u>: Bk. I, Descanso VIII 949b.

J21.19.1.* Do not start your travel (flight) on the Sabbath
or in the winter. Counsel proved wise by experience.
<u>Alonso</u>: Pt. I, Ch. IV 1216a.

      C631.1. Tabu: journeying on Sabbath.

J21.46.1.* Give money to contentious soldier. Captain advises
complaining host to give money to contentious soldier.
This will stop his impossible demands. <u>Alonso</u>: Pt. I,
Ch. II, 1205b.

      J1563.2.3.* Soldier makes impossible demands on
      host (peasant).

J21.52.10.* Flight from one's home into a strange house may
lead to disaster. Young girl falls into a well and
drowns when she runs to a neighbor's house. A cat,
likewise, fleeing from a dog is clubbed to death in a
neighbor's house. <u>Periquillo</u>: Discurso XVI 1912a.

J21.52.11.* Never give food to people from whom you want
favors. Food does not last, and there is no tangible
reminder of the giver. Necio: Ch. IV 266.

J80. Wisdom (knowledge) taught by parable.

J91.1.* Wind, Water, and Modesty. On leave-taking, Wind and
Water give their addresses. Modesty says that it will
be impossible to find her again, if she ever leaves.
Guzmán: Pt. I, Bk. III, Ch. VIII 366a.

    Z139.6. Modesty personified.

J91.2.* Advice aids Love only in the chase, never in caging
the quarry. Opportunity escapes from Love when the
latter turns to Advice for help in caging her. Justina:
Bk. II, Pt. I, Ch. II 768a.

J130. Wisdom (knowledge) acquired from animals.

J134.2.* Mouse traps himself in bird's cage by overeating.
This incident teaches man to eat moderately. Marcos:
Bk. III, Descanso XI 1057a.

    K1022.1.2.* Mouse overeats in bird's cage and
    cannot escape.

J150. Other means of acquiring wisdom (knowledge).

J152.7.* Philosopher illustrates how gratitude is lacking.
He keeps two boxes: one for troubles, the other for
thanks from people for favors he has done them. When
he opens the boxes, the one for troubles is always full;
the one for gratitude is empty. Guzmán: Pt. II, Bk. III,
Ch. IV 528a.

J153.3.* Sleep-talking hermit explains God's "goodness." God
lets the rich eat partridge; the poor, cow's hoof He
provides donkeys, otherwise the poor would have to transport

the rich. <u>Manzanares</u>: Mamotreto VII 41.

J157.1.1.* Woman acquires wisdom from dream. She dreams that
an old man rescues her from a snake (temptation). She
decides to follow and old servant's advice and give up
her paramour. <u>Marcos</u>: Bk. I, Descanso IV 936b.

> F1068.2.3.* Woman dreams that a snake bites her
> while she is picking an apple.

J157.4.* Man dreams that priest has died. He "sells" his
dream to a procuress who sells it to a solicitor. Dream
is true, and solicitor receives position. He rewards
procuress with a cloak. <u>Lozana</u>: Manotreto LIII 171.

J166.3.* Bible teaches man to honor the doctor. He is God's
creation, and all medicine comes from the hand of God.
<u>Alonso</u>: Pt. I, Ch. VI 1241b.

> P424. Physician.

> J200 - J1099. WISE AND UNWISE CONDUCT

> J200 - J499. CHOICES

J200. <u>Choices</u>.

> J1341.9.1.* Hungry boy chooses large grapes.

J210. <u>Choice between evils</u>.

> J1280. Repartee with ruler (judge, etc.).

> J1293.2.1.* Better to be hanged first, then sent
> to galleys.

J210.2.* Woman chooses the long, expensive lawsuit rather than
the "easy way" which a lawyer suggests. <u>Justina</u>: Bk. III,
Ch. II 855b.

J211.2. Town mouse and country mouse. Latter prefers poverty
with safety. <u>Periquillo</u>: Discurso VIII 1882a.

J215.1. Don't drive away the flies. Beggar covered with
sores refuses to have the flies driven away since they

are now sated and their places will be taken by fierce
and hungry flies. <u>Periquillo</u>: Discurso V 1871b.

J215.1.2.1.* Man asks gossiper to stop praising him. He
wants to be slandered so that he will feel as honorable
as the men who are being slandered by the gossiper.
<u>Justina</u>: Bk. II, Pt. I, Ch. I 757b.

J229.1.1.* Choice: staying at home with thieving maidservant
or moving to another neighborhood and dismissing her.
Man avoids neighbors' censure by moving and dismissing
servant. <u>Guzmán</u>: Pt. II, Bk. III, Ch. IV 535a.

J230 - J299. REAL AND APPARENT VALUES

J240. <u>Choice between useful and ornamental</u>.

J241.1.1.* Assembly of trees chooses olive tree to be helpmate
for Prince Laurel. Because of its virtues, the olive is
chosen over many other trees. <u>Peregrinación</u>: p. 57.

J260. <u>Choice between worth and appearance.</u>

J261. Loudest mourners not greatest sorrowers.

K2000. Hypocrites. T231.6.* Faithless widow puts
dead husband in her bed at night in order to feign
discovery of his death the next morning.

J261.1.* Hypocritical fox goes to bed when his wife dies.
This makes his "grief" seem more intense, and he avoids
going to the funeral. <u>Peregrinación</u>: p. 4.

K2000. Hypocrites.

J264.1.* Apparent affluence may be deceiving. On-lookers
are skeptical of lawyer's ostentatious retinue. <u>Alonso</u>:
Pt. I, Ch. I 1203a.

U110. Appearances deceive.

J330 - J369. GAINS AND LOSSES

J340. <u>Choices: little gain, big loss</u>.

J346.1.* Better small gambling loss than trying to recoup and
lose everything. <u>Alonso</u>: Pt. I, Prologue 1199b.

    N9.1.1.* Gambler loses much of his wife's dowry.

    J400 - J459. CHOICE OF ASSOCIATES

J410. <u>Association of equals and unequals</u>.

    P682.1.1.* Greeting in God's name angers nobleman.

    Q395.1.* Captain's disrespect punished. W165.3.*
Nobleman exiles himself because of false pride.

J411.9.2.* Jupiter reprimands crow for jesting. Crow calls
woodpecker a "cart of bad news." When the woodpecker
complains to Jupiter, the latter says that truths
should not be said as jokes. <u>Justina</u>: Bk. II, Pt. II,
Ch. IV 820b.

J411.11.* "Only one dog to one wolf." Knight-errant dog
rebukes two mastiffs for fighting one wold. He kills
the other animals, scares away the shepherds, and occupies
their cabin. <u>Peregrinación</u>: p. 28.

    K335.0.4.4.* Frightened shepherds abandon cabin
to vicious dog.

J414. Marriage with equal or with unequal.

    J445.1.1.* Foolish youth tricked into marrying old
woman. J445.1.3.* No logic in marriage.

J414.4.* Old man marries pious old virgin. As a virgin martyr
she was like Sara; her dark skin and wrinkles resembled
a Saracen (pun on Sara). <u>Manzanares</u>: Mamotreto XII 80.

J440. <u>Association of young and old</u>.

    J1737.2.* Foolish lover ignorant of wife's flaws
until a relative points them out.

J445.1.1.* Foolish youth tricked into marrying old woman.
She had posed as a young wealthy widow, and the youth
married her for her money. Castigo: p. 1629b.

J414. Marriage with equal or with unequal.

J445.1.2.* Foolish youth marries an ugly old woman. Must
wait for wife's death to free him. Alonso: Pt. II,
Ch. VI 1303a.

J1737.2.* Foolish lover ignorant of wife's flaws
until a relative points them out.

J445.1.3.* No logic in marriage. "There are eyes that are
in love with rheum," commented a man when a youth married
an ugly old woman. Alonso: Pt. II, Ch. X 1322b.

J414. Marriage with equal or with unequal.

J450. Association of the good and the evil.

J451.4.1.* Whitewasher's work spoiled by charcoal-maker.
The two men lived together. Guzmán (Luján): Pt. II,
Bk. I, Ch. IV 596a.

J451.5.* Youth of Rome corrupted by associating with Catiline.
The latter invited youths to orgies at his home. Guzmán
(Luján): Pt. II, Bk. I, Ch. IV 596a.

J455. Harm of association with flatterers.

J2337.1.* Trickster flatters dupe as great Latin
scholar. J2337.1.1.* Trickster flatters ugly wife
of innkeeper and gets good food and lodging.
J2337.2.* Trickster tells dupe that a man would
give 200 ducates just to see him at his home.

J480. Other choices.

J482.4.* Better to spend life with honor in jail than in a
dishonorable marriage. Man refuses to marry a woman who

has falsely accused him of breaking his promise to marry
her. Guadaña: Ch. XII 1719a.

J482.5.* Better to spend one's life in chains and in the galleys
than to marry. Cynic advises men against marrying.
Periquillo: Discurso XVII 1916a.

J494.1.* Young thief prefers revenge and death to life. On
pushing his enemy over precipice, the young thief falls
with him. He kills the older thief and is subsequently
hanged. He would have been willing to give ten lives
for such revenge. Alonso: Pt. II, Ch. I 1273a.

  K1685. The treasure finders who murder one another.

  J500 - J599. PRUDENCE AND DISCRETION

J510. Prudence in ambition.

J513.1. Birds seeking richer lands are nearly all killed.
Survivers advise their friends to let well enough alone.
Guzmán: Pt. II, Bk. III, Ch. IX 573a.

J514.5.1.* Greedy man, dissatisfied with recovering stolen
cloak, sues thief. He loses cloak in payment for lawsuit.
Guzmán: Pt. II, Bk. II, Ch. III 446b.

  W151.9.1.* Greedy man sues imprisoned thief to force
  him to tell from whom he has bought stolen cloak.

J514.7.* Greedy artist wants more money for painting of horse.
He had painted details of scenery in addition. Buyer
buys the painting of another artist who had concentrated
on painting a good picture of a horse. Guzmán: Pt. I,
Bk. I, Ch. I 240b.

  Q338. Immoderate request punished.

J550. Zeal - temperate and intemperate.

J551.1.2.* Servant tells master of wife's infidelity. Master
kills him in order to keep the affair secret. Marcos:

Bk. III, Descanso VI 1046a.

J815. Unpleasant truths must be withheld from the great.

J553.1.1.* The abbot and the unbent bow. Criticized for allowing monks to play on convent grounds, the abbot strings a thin bow and explains how relaxation is good for humans. <u>Alonso</u>: Pt. I, Ch. X 1268a.

J555.1.1.* Spend with prudence. Father asks university-bound son to spend his money with prudence. Son wastes his money on a girl named Prudence. <u>Alonso</u>: Pt. I, Ch. I 1204b.

H588. Enigmatic counsels of a father. J2460. Literal obedience.

J570. <u>Wisdom of deliberation</u>.

J571.4.3.* The child is not to blame. Man is advised not to kill servant who has fathered a child by man's sister. Send sister to a convent and place child in safe-keeping. The child is not to blame. <u>Guadaña</u>: Ch. XII 1717b.

J600 - J799. FORETHOUGHT

J610 - J679. FORETHOUGHT IN CONFLICTS
WITH OTHERS

J610. <u>Forethought in conflict with others - general</u>.

J611.1.* Six o'clock too early for duel. Man sends word to challenger that he never does anything of great importance to him before noon. Besides, why should he want to get killed so early in the morning? <u>Marcos</u>: Bk. I, Descanso I 927a.

J612.2.* Aristotle abandons plan to censure Plato when a pebble falls on his thumb. "A finger that has been stoned cannot throw stones well." <u>Justina</u>: Introduction 718a.

J1050. Attention to warnings.

J613.3.* Count exiles himself from court after winning over king in letter-writing contest. He fears that he will be in disfavor for being wiser than the king. Píndaro: Bk. I, Ch. VI 286b.

H509.6.* Test of letter-writing ability.

640. Avoidance of other's power.

J641.0.1.* Youth flees town after accosting girl. He fears that she may tell her relatives and that they will reveal his conduct to his master. Torres: Trozo II 1939a.

J2160. Other short-sighted acts.

J647.3.* Do not sleep if you have enemies. Man drops big rock on sleeping dog which previously has bitten him. Guzmán: Pt. II, Bk. II, Ch. VIII 483a.

J652.4.3.* Soldier warns captain that peasants will revolt. Warning unheeded, and captain is killed in ensuing fight. Alonso: Pt. I, Ch. II 1207b.

J652.4.4.* Woman repeatedly warns town counselmen of danger of storing gunpowder in tower. Lightening strikes the tower, causing disastrous explosion. Píndaro: Bk. II, Ch. XXV 368a.

J700 - J749. FORETHOUGHT IN PROVISION FOR LIFE

J700. Forethought in provision for life (general).

J701.3.* "Prayer no good." Youth writes a "prayer" which will cure maid's toothache. It is a love-letter, which the maid tears up and returns to sender. Fregona: p. 166a.

D1766.1.4. Pain stopped by prayer. D2161. Magic healing power. D2161.3.12.* Toothache magically cured.

J706.2.* Fiscal expert proposes self-denial days for all
vassals of king between ages 14-60. Money "saved" to be
given to king. Coloquio: p. 231b.

J706.3.* Information requested on receipt of money. Female
trickster who has robbed "husband" writes a letter
requesting him to inform her when he received 6,000 more
ducates. Castigo: p. 1637a.

J710. Forethought in provision of food.

J1314.1.* Koran has nothing to say about wine for
the dead.

J712.2.* Dying man wants food and wine placed in his tomb.
The trip to paradise will be a long one. Urdemalas: p. 4a.

J730. Forethought in provision for clothing.

X653.* Artist paints a naked man to represent
Spaniard.

J732.* Prejudice against tapistries. Discarded drapes are
given as clothing to the poor. Woman does not like
tapistries for this reason. Justina: Bk. II, Pt. III,
Ch. IV 849a.

J740. Forethought in provision for shelter.

J741.2.* Flattery of innkeeper's wife wins shelter for the
night. Marcos: Bk. I, Descanso XIII 968a.

J750 - J799. FORETHOUGHT - MISCELLANEOUS

J758.3. Fish refuse fox's invitation to live on dry land and
thus escape danger of fishermen. Justina: Bk. I,
Ch. I 725b.

A2433.3.1.2.* Fox puts curse of coldness on
unborn kittens.

J759.* Threats after the event valueless. Master, robbed of

jewels, threatens punishment for run-away servant. The
latter is now in a different country. <u>Alonso</u>: Pt. II,
Ch. II 1279b.

J800 - J849. ADAPTABILITY

J810. <u>Policy in dealing with the great</u>.

J811.1.1. Lion divides the booty. Ajudges the whole deer to
himself. <u>Guzmán</u>: Pt. II, Bk. III, Ch. V 548a.

J811.2.1.* Fox refuses to mediate between lion and lioness.
Lion asks dog if his breath is bad. The dog says "yes"
and is killed. The lion says that the dog should learn
from the fox who cannot smell anything. <u>Manzanares</u>:
Ch. XVIII 119.

J811.2.2.* Fox refuses to mediate between lion and lioness.
Latter is seeking a divorce because of lion's bad breath.
Wolf, bear, and fox are brought as witnesses. The lion
kills the wolf and bear for saying that his breath is
bad. Fox says that he has a bad cold and cannot smell
anything. <u>Alonso</u>: Pt. I, Ch. IX 1263a; <u>Periquillo</u>:
Discurso V 1871a.

J814.6.* Man secures position in nobleman's house through
flattery. <u>Marcos</u>: Bk. II, Descanso V 1009b.

J815. Unpleasant truths must be withheld from the great.
          J551.1.2.* Servant tells master of wife's infidelity.
          Master kills him.

J816.1.0.1.* King brought to sense of duty by feigned conversation of mallows. Queen tells king that the mallows along
the road would tell him that he is acting badly, if they
spoke for the road. The king's errors are common
knowledge, and stones and mallows proclaim them. (Pun is
on <u>malvas</u>: "mallows," or "you go evilly.")

<u>Justina</u>: Introduction, p. 710b.

J816.3.1.* Judge brought to sense of duty by discreet man.
After dining, a judge decides to have an honorable man
flogged. The latter suggests that the judge get some
information on him. After hearing two witnesses, the
judge's head clears, and he abandons his rash plan.
<u>Marcos</u>: Bk. III, Descanso XXIII 1082a.

J817.1. Man called a rogue by a nobleman makes a joke of the
insult. (It was not said directly to him.) He thus
avoids trouble. <u>Marcos</u>: Bk. I, Descanso I 926b.

J817.1.1.* Honored to be head of your profession. Captain
is amused when rogues call him a rogue. <u>Marcos</u>: Bk. I,
Descanso I 927a.

J829. Dealing with the great - miscellaneous.

W121.8.2.* Peasant becomes ill with fear when
summoned before Inquisitor.

J829.4.* Frightened peasant digs up pear tree and sends it
to the Inquisitor when he learns that the latter's
summons is related to buying pears. The peasant does not
want another summons. <u>Lazarillo</u> (Luna) : Pt. II,
Prologue 115b.

J829.5.* Justice is too high. Peasant abandons his suit against
mayor of town when he sees a statue of Justice seated
high on a pillar of the chancery. It is useless to hope
that she will stoop to help him, and he cannot reach her.
<u>Guzmán</u>: Pt. I, Bk. I, Ch. I 245a.

J829.6.* Only one student raises hat when mayor passes by.
Other students fail to uncover and are arrested for disrespect. <u>Marcos</u>: Bk. I, Descanso XII 965a.

Q395.2.* Students are arrested for failing to raise hats when officer passes by.

J830. Adaptability to overpowering force.

J836.* Cats do not molest strong bands of mice. Prudence dictates that they leave the mice alone. Peregrinación: p. 17

J850 - J899. CONSOLATION IN MISFORTUNE

J860. Consolation by a trifle.

J861.1.1.* Dupe is consoled when woman trickster shows him a real pot of honey. She had sent him to get a pot of "honey buns" which was a chamber pot of excrement, and he had spilled it on himself. Justina: Bk. II, Pt. III, Ch. IV 846a.

K1044.2.* Dupe sent back to inn to get "honey buns" which woman had left under bed.

J861.2.1.* Man on sinking ship eats much food. He fears that the water which he is about to drink may hurt him. Lazarillo (Luna): Pt. II, Ch. II 118a.

J861.2.2.* Man on storm-tossed ship eats much food and drinks much wine. If he is to die, he wants to die satiated. Estebanillo: Bk. I, Ch. II 1735a.

J862.* Consolation found in sexual relations. Alonso: Pt. I, Ch. IV 1219a.

T256.0.2.* Husband and wife quarrel by day, but sleep together at night.

J865.1.1.* Attorney will try to right the wrong done to condemned man about to be hanged. The sentence is unjust, but it cannot be changed, and the condemned man should take his hanging quietly. Guzmán: Pt. II, Bk. I, Ch. VIII 430b.

J865.2.* Reconciliation will be sweet. Woman consoled by
another woman after bully lover had beaten her severely.
Rinconete: p. 188b.

    Q382.* Punishment for suspected thievery.

J865.3.* The mountain slope is not eternal. Muleteer tells
mule which is rolling down the mountain that his fall
will have an end. Alonso: Pt. I, Ch. IV 1219a.

J865.4.* "I might as well talk now because I'm known." Fool
follows instructions to keep silent while courting girl.
She calls him a fool, and he decides that she has discovered his stupidity anyway. Alonso: Pt. II, Ch. VII
1307a.

    J2350. Talkative fools.

J865.5.* Book will be protected from malicious readers. Author
finds consolation when one of his books is put on censored
list. Torres: Trozo V 1978a.

J865.6.* Still carrying wealth. Shipwrecked merchant loses
all his gems, but saves his life by floating ashore on
a board. He comments that he is still carrying wealth
to the harbor of his disillusionments. Necio: Ch. I 175.

J880. Consolation by thought of others worse placed.

J881.0.1.* "Christ endured more." Friends offer consolation
to man being flogged. Manzanares, Ch. I 6.

J890. Consolation in misfortune - miscellaneous.

J893.2.* Exiled man comforted and aided by enemies abroad.
His friends at home offer only advice. He is grateful
for having been given the chance to make such good
friends elsewhere. Guzmán: Pt. II, Bk. I, Ch. VIII 431b.

J894.* Victim of theft is not consoled when thief is exiled.

Judicial decision to banish thief fails to console victim. <u>Guzmán</u>: Pt. II, Bk. I, Ch. VIII 430b.

J900 - J999. HUMILITY

J910. <u>Humility of the great</u>.

J914.2.* King weeps with mother of condemned youth. He cannot pardon the boy, and tears of sympathy are all he can give the mother. <u>Alonso</u>: Pt. I, Ch. V 1231b.

> J1288.1.* King can give only tears.

J914.3.* Alexander gives beloved concubine to Apelles. He humbles himself to please God. <u>Alonso</u>: Pt. I, Ch. X 1267b.

J950. <u>Presumption of the lowly</u>.

J951.1.1.* Ass in lion's skin detected by long ears. Master beats him and strips him of the false skin. <u>Guzmán</u>: Pt. II, Bk. I, Ch. VIII 426a.

J951.1.2.* Ass in lion's skin unmasked when fox sees his hooves. <u>Marcos</u>: Bk. I, Descanso V 941a.

J951.6.* Lapdog bites larger dog. It is brave because its mistress is near. <u>Coloquio</u>: p. 232a.

> W121.2.7.* Lapdog bites larger dog while mistress is near.

J953. Self-deception of the lowly.

> K1955.11.* Sham physician could rid the world of sickness, if only he had a mule for traveling.

J953.2.2.* Bad painter is reprimanded. He talks of having his house whitewashed before he paints it. Friends suggest the opposite. <u>Guzmán</u>: Pt. II, Bk. II, Ch. III 449a.

> P482.1.* Bad painter is advised to paint house first, then whitewash it.

J957.1.* Presumptuous man asks university to postpone examination of candidates for faculty position until he receives
his degree. His pretended qualifications are false, and
he is discredited. <u>Torres</u>: Trozo VI 2001b.

    Q338. Immoderate request punished.

    J1000 - J1099. OTHER ASPECTS OF WISDOM

J1040. <u>Decisiveness of conduct</u>.

    M291.1.* Ruffian cannot slash merchant's narrow face.

J1040.3.* "Hate a man, hate his lackey." Ruffian cannot
slash merchant's narrow face. He slashes merchant's
lackey instead. <u>Rinconete</u>: p. 192b.

J1041.2. Miller, his son, and the ass: trying to please
everyone. Miller blamed when he follows his son on foot;
when he takes the son's place on the ass; when he takes
the son behind him; and when he puts the son in front
of him. <u>Alonso</u>: Pt. I, Ch. IV 1224a.

J1041.3.* Man at theatre cannot please everyone. People ask
him to move to the left or right. He finally decides
to stand where he wishes. <u>Guzmán</u>: Pt. II, Bk. I,
Ch. I 392b.

J1050. <u>Attention to warnings</u>.

    J612.2.* Aristotle abandons plan to censure Plato
when a pebble falls on his thumb.

J1050.0.1.* Man warned by prostitute's physical condition.
Her feverish hands, thin arms, offensive breath, and bad
odor warn him that she is diseased. <u>Guzmán</u> (Luján):
Pt. II, Bk. III, Ch. I 655a.

J1050.0.2.* Man warned by enemy's painted tapistries. "A man
who buys so many painted men to delight him will seek
live one to avenge him." <u>Justina</u>: Bk. II, Pt. III,
Ch. IV 849a.

J1060. <u>Miscellaneous aspects of wisdom</u>.

J1062.2.2.* Sick man runs away from unsuccessful doctors. He
gets well. <u>Torres</u>: Trozo IV 1967a.

J1074.1.2.* Monk is silent about faults of others. He either
did not listen to the parishioners' faults as confessed,
or he immediately forgot them. <u>Marcos</u>: Bk. I, Descanso V
940a.

J1075.1. Woman tests enduring power of gossip by having a
servant ride through streets on a flayed ass (on a horse
loaded with water jugs). By the third day he has ceased
to attract attention. She concludes that it will be the
same way in connection with her intended marriage.
<u>Alonso</u>: Pt. II, Ch. V 1296a.

J1100 - J1699. CLEVERNESS

J1100 - J1249. CLEVER PERSONS AND ACTS

J1110. <u>Clever persons</u>.

J1111.7.* Clever veiled woman gives advice to conceited man.
She censures his extravagant dress and his foolish deeds.
She wants him to be a real man. <u>Píndaro</u>: Bk. II,
Ch. I 323b.

J1112.6.* Clever wife advises husband to plant lettuce
between cabbage plants for double profit.
<u>Lozana</u>: Mamotreto LIV 175.

J1112. Clever wife.

J1112.7.* Clever widow placates jealous lover. She explains
her "errands" to various business men. She pretends
anger and makes lover atone for his suspicions.
<u>Manzanares</u>: Ch. VI 33.

J1112.8.* Innkeeper's wife gives man second jar of cold water
in presence of witnesses. If the man dies, the witnesses

will know what killed him. <u>Marcos</u>: Bk. III, Introduction 1034b.

J1114.2.* Man deceived by servant who writes verses to maid
in his account book. <u>Fregona</u>: p. 164b.

J1114.3.* Servant deceives master with polite phrase: "May
God subtract from my days and add them to yours." Caught
in a blinding snowstorm, the servant tells his master
that days like this one are the ones he means. <u>Alonso</u>:
Pt. I, Ch. IX 1260a.

> J1649.* God asked to subtract and add days.
> K475.4.* Lineage descended from royal house.

J1115.1. Clever gambler.

> N1. Gamblers.

J1115.1.1.* Youths win muleteer's money with marked cards.
Tricksters defend themselves successfully when victim
tries to retake money by force. <u>Rinconete</u>: p. 179a.

J1115.1.2.* Youth wagers his mule by quarters. When he loses
the four quarters, he wagers the tail as the fifth
quarter and wins all the money. <u>Fregona</u>: p. 167b.

> N1. Gamblers.

J1115.1.3.* Gambler wins at cards with help from confederate.
Latter fingers buttons on his jacket to give information
about opponents' cards. <u>Guzmán</u>: Pt. II, Bk. II, Ch. III
452a.

J1115.1.4.* Trickster induces merchants to gamble for ring
"found" by fountain. His confederate wins ring and much
money from merchants. <u>Marcos</u>: Bk. I, Descanso XIII 967a.

J1115.1.5.* Gambler deceives opponents by reference to Mohammed's age. On looking at his cards trickster muttered,
"Mohammed's age." Other gamblers raised their bets, but
trickster won with 55 points. Objector: "Mohammed was

only 48 years old." Trickster: "Oh, I thought that he was older." <u>Marcos</u>: Bk. II, Descanso VI 101la.

J1115.2.3.* Clever physician rebukes careless boasting rival. Declares that boaster can teach all the medicine he knows in six days instead of six months. <u>Alonso</u>: Pt. I, Ch. VI 1241a.

W117.3.* Boastful doctor.

J1115.4. Clever tailor.

W116.2.2.* Tailor erects showy coat of arms over door.

J1115.6.1.* Clever peasant sows wheat for soldiers. "One for God, one for us, and one hundred for the soldiers." <u>Alonso</u>: Pt. I, Ch. II 1207b.

J1115.8. Clever prostitute.

T453. Getting advice from a woman in bed.

J1115.8.1.* Clever prostitute advises man to eat sage with his fiancée in order to get her to love him. <u>Lozana</u>: Mamotreto XXIV 90.

J1115.8.2.* Prostitute heals four men by incantation. She puts her hands on them one at a time and predicts their future occupations. <u>Lozana</u>: Mamotreto LXIV 207.

J1115.8.3.* Procuress melts wax in plugged keyhole and opens door for couple in brothel. After disporting, they pay her well. <u>Lozana</u>: Mamotreto LXI 199.

J1115.8.4.* Clever procuress sells beauty lotion at high price to another courtesan. Latter does not want rival to buy it. <u>Lozana</u>: Mamotreto LVII 187.

J1115.8.5.* Prostitute forces procuress to name her rival. She has bought beauty lotion destined for rival, but she will not conclude transaction unless rival is named. <u>Lozana</u>: Mamotreto LVIII 191.

J1115.8.6.* Prostitute chooses more expensive dress materials
when admirer offers to pay for them. Harpías: Estafa IV
140ff.

J1115.8.8.* Old prostitutes sell well-known names to young
beginners. Receive used clothing in exchange. Diablo:
Tranco III 1648a.

J1115.9.1.* Clever shepherd-alderman gets monopoly on dough-
nuts. Sets the legal price so low that competitors
withdraw. Later, he restores the higher price and has
a monopoly. Guzmán: Pt. I, Bk. I, Ch. III 257a.

J1115.11.* Clever student disarms police force. He persuades
them to hide their swords while they slip up on thieves
inside a public house. Trickster's confederate runs off
with the swords. Buscón: Bk. I, Ch. VI 1109b.

J1118.2.* Clever thrush helps king regain stolen treasure.
Servant teaches thrush to say that the prime minister
stole the money. The king seizes the minister and exacts
a confession. Marcos: Bk. II, Descanso XII 1025b.

J1130 - J1199. CLEVERNESS IN THE LAW COURT

J1140. Cleverness in detection of truth.

J1141.1. Guilty person deceived into gesture (act) which
admits guilt. Told that a bell will ring when thief
touches bottom of designated bowl in a dark room, thief's
clean hands reveal that he did not touch the bowl.
Marcos: Bk. I, Descanso XVI 980a.

J1141.1.4. Guilty man's stick will grow during night. Guilty
man chops end off stick. (He is apprehended when he
returns the shortened stick.) Alonso: Pt. II, Ch. III
1286a.

J1141.1.13.* Mistress tricks maid into confessing false
accusation of manservant. The mistress tells the maid
that she has selected a rich husband for her. Periquillo:
Discurso II 1860a.

K2114.1.* False tokens of man's unfaithfulness.

J1144.1.0.1.* Theft of wine detected. Blindman's guide
inserts straw into wine jug; later, he drinks from hole
bored in bottom of jug. He is detected. Lazarillo:
Tratado I 87b.

K333. Theft from blind person.

J1144.1.0.2.* Theft of wine detected when imbiber falls under
weight of wineskin. Hired to fill a wineskin, the trickster secretly drinks so much that he falls under weight
of filled wineskin when he attempts to carry it.
Estebanillo: Bk. I, Ch. IV 1757a.

J1144.1.0.3.* Theft of brandy detected when drunken trickster
receives blow to his stomach. He disgorges the brandy
in the face of his assailant. Estebanillo: Bk. II
Ch. V 1830b.

J1144.1.1.* Eater of stolen sausage detected. Boy vomits up
sausage when blindman rams his nose into boy's throat.
Lazarillo: Tratado I 89ff.

K333. Theft from blind person.

J1144.1.2.* Eater of stolen bread detected. Key to pantry,
hidden in culprit's mouth, makes hissing noise while he
is snoring. Lazarillo: Tratado II 95b.

K317.0.1.* Thief copies key by making wax impression.

K420. Thief loses his goods or is detected.

J1144.1.2.1.* Stolen bread found beneath culprit's bed.

Searcher pricked head on a nail on which bread was impaled
and discovered the bread. The culprit fled. <u>Marcos</u>:
Bk. III, Descanso XV   1066b.

K420. Thief loses his goods or is detected.

J1144.1.3.* Eaters of sugar lumps detected. Stomachs swell,
thus revealing their guilt. <u>Marcos</u>: Bk. II, Descanso
VII   1013a.

K420. Thief loses his goods or is detected.

J1160. <u>Clever pleading</u>.

J1161.9.1.* Fool will help king in his war by drying up sea
with sponges. He will then sink sea to keep it from
filling again with water. <u>Buscón</u>: Bk. II, Ch. I   1112a.

J1161.12.* The arch-chicken of chickens. Officer rebukes
cowardly soldier for running away during battle. Soldier:
"Others may be archpriests of priests, but I am arch-
chicken of chickens." His clever remark saved him from
further abuse. <u>Estebanillo</u>: Bk. II, Ch. III   1813a.

W121. Cowardice.

J1162.5.* Peacemaker will need large income to pay fines.
While acting as peacemaker at public brawls, a barber is
successively fined for shouting "peace," "death," and
"war." He asks judge what he should do or say when he
sees men fighting. He will need much money to pay fines.
Judge laughs and frees him. <u>Alonso</u>: Pt. I, Ch. V   1232a.

J1170. <u>Clever judicial decisions</u>.

J1170.1.1.* Wise judgments of judge from other world. Aided
by Death, Deceit, and Truth, judge settles many complaints
of people in city. <u>Manzanares</u>: Ch. XVIII   119ff.

N819.5.* Death, Deceit, and Truth help judge
from other world.

J1174.1.1.* Youth in court for intercourse with farmer's
daughter. Father of girl alleges rape. Judge dismisses
the case when he learns that the girl is 21 years old and
the boy, 23. One man's strength cannot prevail against
an unwilling woman. Guzmán: Pt. II, Bk. III, Ch. II 513a.

T470. Illicit sexual relations - miscellaneous.

J1174.3. The girl screams when she is robbed. Accuses young
man of raping her. When he tries to rob her of money, she
summons help. Decision: if she had shouted as loud before,
the man could not have raped her. Youth acquitted.
Guzmán: Pt. II, Bk. III, Ch. II (in James Mabbe, The
Rogue, London: Tudor Translations, IV 116-122).

T470. Illicit sexual relations - miscellaneous motifs.

J1179.5.1.* Soldiers would not have left any sheep. Farmer
complains to captain that soldiers have stolen eight of
his seventeen sheep. Captain says that his soldiers
would not have left any. Alonso: Pt. I, Ch. II, 1205a.

J1179.15.* Woman is the most left-handed (sinister). Judge
rules that she wins legacy left to the most left-handed
heir. Eve came from Adam's left side and gave him the
apple with her left hand. Furthermore, all men know
that a woman never does anything "right." Guadaña:
Ch. III 1688b.

H659.27.* Who is the most left-handed (sinister)?

J1180. Clever means of avoiding legal punishment.

J1181.4.* Man escapes arrest by saying he is a "grandee" of
Spain. His name is Juan Grande. Guadaña: Ch. XII 1718b.

K602. Escape by assuming an equivocal name.

K1951.5.1.* Tailor says that he is a "grandee" of
Spain. Escapes arrest.

J1184.1. Adulteress hurled from high rock escapes injury; she
may not be punished again. <u>Alonso</u>: Pt. II, Ch. XI 1323a.

    K2112.0.1.* Woman slandered as adulteress saved
from death by Virgin.

J1190. <u>Cleverness in the lawcourt - miscellaneous</u>.

J1192.1.3.* Bribed judge justifies unjust decision. Case will
be carried to a higher court where justice will be done.
<u>Guzmán</u>: Pt. II, Bk. II, Ch. III 447a.

J1193.3.* The gallant goes free. Abused judge promises
friendly courtesan that he will grant freedom to a gallant,
if he should be in her house. The gallant walks out of a
closet and escapes. <u>Guadaña</u>: Ch. IV 1692b.

    M202.3.* Abused judge promises friendly courtesan
that he would grant freedom to a gallant.

    P421. Judge.

    J1210 - J1229. CLEVER MAN PUTS ANOTHER

    OUT OF COUNTENANCE

J1210. <u>Clever man puts another out of countenance</u>.

    K1271.2.1.* Nude priest comes to couple's bed.

J1210.1.* Man reveals priest's incontinence. Man, seeking to
be identified, recalls to priest how the latter came nude
to his and his wife's bed while feigning to be frightened
by goblin. Priest identifies man to silence him.
<u>Lazarillo</u> (Luna): Pt. II, Ch. VII 124a.

J1211.4.* Professor seeking appointment to university
criticizes rival candidate's habit of gambling. The
defamed professor admitted that he knew how to gamble,
and he requested that only the students who knew how to
gamble would vote for him. He won all the votes.
<u>Alonso</u>: Pt. I, Ch. IX 1262a.

J1224.3.* Poet puts hotel guests out of countenance. They reprimanded him for yelling "Fire, Fire" while he was working on "Troy Ablaze." Poet: "You should be glad that I was not working on "Darkness of Palestine" in which there is a collision of planets." Diablo: Tranco IV 1652a.

J1224.3.1.* Poet writes a play about Noah's Ark in which all parts are played by animals. How will he stage it? Parrots, thrushes, and magpies would take the talking parts. Monkeys would be used for farcical interludes. Buscón: Bk. II, Ch. II 1115a.

J1224.4.* Exiled philosopher puts enemies out of countenance. He refuses to accept their offer to revoke his unjust sentence in order to shame them for their unjust persecution. Guzmán: Pt. II, Bk. I, Ch. VIII 431b.

J1250 - J1499. CLEVER VERBAL RETORTS (REPARTEE).

J1250. Clever verbal retorts - general.

H501.2.1.* Wise fool answers many questions in examination of his wisdom. T251.4. Socrates and Zanthippe: "After thunder rain."

J1251. Baffling malice with ready answers.

U62.* Poor philosopher rebukes rich ruler.

J1251.1.1.* Not the one who reveals secrets. Jealous woman slaps lover at masked ball for flirting with another woman. She had asked him not to reveal the secret of their relationship. Lover: "I am not the one who reveals secrets so quickly." Garduña: Bk. II 1556b.

J1252.1.* Questions and quibbling answers. E.g., "Where are you going?" - "To old age." "What road are you taking?" - "None, the road is taking me." "What is the land of your birth?" - "I wasn't born on the land, but in a hayloft." Marcos: Bk. III, Descanso XV 1065a.

J1260. <u>Repartee based on church or clergy</u>.

J1261.1.6.* "My God will be the one who can save me from this
danger." In a storm at sea a man is rebuked for praying
to Saint Telmo, the name of a light. Names do not matter
so long as his God saves him. <u>Píndaro</u>: Bk. II, Ch.
XXIII 363b.

> J1741.2.3.* Man prays to Saint Telmo (a light),
> thinking that it is a god.

J1261.1.7.* Man worships the cross first, instead of God, on
entering church. He explains to his questioner that in
the cross he sees everything that there is in heaven.
<u>Periquillo</u>: Discurso XVII 1915a.

J1261.2.0.1.* Talkative man at mass fails to observe order
of service. Finally asks a neighbor if the priest has
lifted up the Host. <u>Alonso</u>: Pt. I, Ch. X 1266a.

J1261.2.2.1.* God's help is too late. Unobservant man steps
in hole and falls. His companion says, "May God help you."
Prone man: "It's too late now." <u>Marcos</u>: Bk. II
Descanso VI 1011a.

J1261.7.1.* Judgment Day a long way off. Traveler, robbed
of money, tells thief that he will be punished on Judgment Day. Thief takes all of the man's money, since he
will have such a long period of grace. <u>Alonso</u>: Pt. II,
Ch. II 1279a.

J1261.9.* Moor is reluctant Christian. He asks for forgive-
ness every time one of his children receives Christian
sacraments. "Forgive me, Mohammed, for I cannot do
otherwise under penalty of fine." <u>Justina</u>: Bk. III,
Ch. III 860a.

J1261.11.* Friday is day of fasting. Priest shows women some scourges in monastery and asks if they would like a "benefice." One woman replies that she fasts on Friday. (Pun is on colación, "benefice," or "lunch.") Justina: Bk. II, Pt. III, Ch. I 827b.

J1261.12.* Infidel not bothered by priest's preaching. Priest complains that what he says goes in one ear and out the other of his audience. An old Moor replies that it neither goes in nor out. Alonso: Pt. II, Ch. I 1274b.

J1262.10.* Spaniard calls Protestants "heretics." "Many are taken (caught) but few are called, because they do not come to the hands of the Pope." He rebukes the Protestant who had said, "Many are called but few are chosen (taken)." Marcos: Bk. III, Descanso III 1039b.

J1262.11.* Each Samson gets what he needs. Criticized for depicting Samson drinking wine instead of water (as in the Bible version), the artist replies, "Don't you see the providence of the Lord who gives to each Samson what he needs?" Alonso: Pt. II, Ch. IX 1316a.

J1263.1.3.2.* Priests rush through Mass either to go to a wedding feast, or to finish before noon. Justina: Bk. II, Pt. I, Ch. I 754b.

J1263.1.5.* "It would be a miracle to see a scribe in heaven." Priest excoriates scribes as the worst of sinners. Guzmán: Pt. I, Bk. I, Ch. I 243b.

    P425.2.* Scribes are the worst of sinners.

J1263.1.6.* Priests are censured for saying "hallelujah" at requiem Mass. Excuse: "It is between Passover and Easter." (The deceased was probably a converted Jew.) Marcos: Bk. I, Descanso XIII 971a.

J1265.4.* Seminarian tells prelate that the latter is better qualified than he for priestly robes. The student asks: "Would you know how to endure a stupid prior?" Manzanares: Ch. XV 100.

J1269.9.1.* "If I were not a Christian I would get revenge on you." Saint Christopher restrains himself when assailant boxes him on ears. Guzmán: Pt. I, Bk. I, Ch. IV 262a.

   V441.2.* Saint forgives man who has assailed him.

J1269.9.2.* Vengeance cannot be justified. Saint Bernard rebukes his brethren who urge him to avenge himself on an assailant. "It is not right for us to avenge the wrong done us by others, because we spend the day on our knees praying for pardon of our own offenses." Guzmán: Pt. I, Bk. I, Ch. IV 262a.

   V441.2.* Saint forgives man who has assailed him.

J1269.14.* "When is the rich man coming?" Avaricious parishioner, impressed by priest's sermon against the Antichrist and his wealth, wants to know when the rich man will arrive. Alonso: Pt. II, Ch. III 1283b.

   M363.1.2.* Antichrist to bring much wealth to people who will follow him.

J1269.15.* Would need an ever-present confessor. Drunken soldier, scratched in a sword skirmish, calls for a confessor. Observing that the wound is slight, the priest remarks that the man needs an ever-present confessor because of his sins. Estebanillo: Bk. II, Ch. V 1825b.

J1270. Repartee concerning the parentage of children.

J1275.* Why she feels so Jewish (confused, upset). Pregnant

Christian woman, wife of a converted Jew, complains that
she has never felt so _judía_ (Jewish, upset) in all her
life. Woman friend answers: "No wonder; you have a
little Jew inside you." _Guzmán_: Pt. II, Bk. III, Ch. I
504a.

J1279.5.* Such things should not be said. Adulteress commends
son for hitting another boy who called him a whore-son.
Mother: "Even if such things are true, they should not
be said." _Buscón_: Bk. I, Ch. II 1094b.

J1280. _Repartee with ruler (judge, etc.)_.

J1293.2.1.* Better to be hanged first, then sent
to galleys. J1675.3.1.* Fool says that the Holy
Trinity is criticizing king. K2245.1.* Treacherous
judge: has deflowered many maidens.

J1281.1.* Not proper for king to avenge wrongs of a duke.
Upon becoming king of France, the Duke of Orleans is
advised to take vengeance on a former assailant. He
refuses saying, "It is not fitting for the king of
France to avenge the wrongs of the Duke of Orleans."
Guzmán: Pt. I, Bk. I, Ch. IV 263b.

J1281.2.* Prince must be above complaining about food.
Emperor dissimulates feelings when bad salad is served
by cook. _Guzmán_ (Luján): Pt. II, Bk. II, Ch. II 616b.

J1287.* Magistrate will take care of "small expenses."
Censured after election for extravagant spending, magistrate explains that he finds the small expenses at the
butcher shop every Saturday. (Pun on word _menudos_ -
"small expenses" or "giblets.") _Guzmán_: Pt. I, Bk. I,
Ch. III 257a.

J1805.1.2.* Magistrate promises to take care of

menudos ("small expenses," "giblets.").

J1288.* He feels no wounds or injury. Constantine the Great
forgives enemies who have stoned his picture. Guzmán:
Pt. I, Bk. I, Ch. IV 262b.

   V441.3.* Constantine the Great forgives his
   enemies who have stoned his picture.

J1288.1.* King can give only tears. Cannot pardon condemned
youth; he can only weep with the youth's mother.
Alonso: Pt. I, Ch. V 1231b.

   J914.2.* King weeps with mother of condemned youth.

J1289.1.1.* Not blushing because of guilt. Maid accused of
theft turns red before judges. They accuse her because
she blushes. She explains that her color change is
caused by fear of judges. Manzanares: Ch. VIII 52.

J1289.2.1.* Judge silences loud-praying priest by telling
him to pray at night. Priest: "Could I by praying
tonight fulfill my obligations for tomorrow?" Judge:
"If I owed you money... would you accept payment the
evening before due?" Priest: "Yes, of course."
Judge: "God is a good payer; He pays in advance, too."
Marcos: Bk. III, Descanso XV 1064b.

J1289.4.1.* "What would I have done if I had heard him?"
Philosopher is enraged on reading Demosthenes' oration
against him. Lozana: Argumento, p. 14.

J1289.6.1.* The judge's excuse: His judicial orders did
not include chastity. Censured for being fond of women,
judge tells critics that his orders did not mention
chastity. Guzmán: Pt. II, Bk. III, Ch. V 548a.

J1289.21.* King's children must eat like men. King writes
rules of etiquette for eating so that royal children

will eat like humans instead of eating like animals.
Guzmán (Luján): Pt. II, Bk. II, Ch. II 616b.

J1289.22.* Ruler rebukes critics. They censure him for risking
his life to rescue a drowning man. "You do not know what
it is to love a servant well," he replies. Guzmán (Luján):
Pt. II, Bk. II, Ch. III 619b.

P360. Master and servant.

J1289.23.* Rain should come from heaven. Woman throws down
hot water on lover in street. He had called her an
angel and her house heaven. She thought that rain
should come from heaven since there was so much noise
below. Justina: Bk. IV, Ch. II 874a.

J1289.24.* Prince rebukes majordomo for criticizing servants.
The majordomo is the "impertinent" one. The lazy
servants please and honor the prince; other paid-
servants seem to think they are honoring the prince by
serving him. Marcos: Bk. I, Descanso VI 945a.

J1290. Reductio ad absurdum of question or proposal.

J1291.5.* "How are you?" - "How better to answer than to show
urine or feel pulse?" Man has a trained monkey produce
a glass of urine when visitor asks about his health.
Necio: Ch. I 181.

J1293.2.1.* Better to be hanged first, then sent to the
galleys. Judge gives man a choice of paying a heavy fine
or serving ten years in the galleys followed by public
hanging. Guzmán: Pt. II, Bk. II, Ch. III 448b.

P210. Choice between evils. J1280. Repartee
with ruler (judge, etc.).

J1293.6.* If king depends on him for victory, he has already
negotiated his account. Captain proposes that cowardly
soldier fight and die defending the faith, or give the
king a victory. Estebanillo: Bk. I, Ch. VI 1777a.

W34.3.1.* Captain tells cowardly soldier to die
defending the faith, or give the king a victory.

J1300. Officiousness or foolish questions rebuked.

J1301.1.* How can she become pregnant? Woman pilgrim asks
procuress how she can become pregnant. Answer: Take
an unbroken friar's sheet, a virile priest's skirt, and
bind them on hips with finger nails of a sexton.
Lozana: Mamotreto LXIII 205.

J1307.* Why are men's testicles of different sizes and shapes?
Foolish answers relating to their association with old or
disease-laden women are given for men with one testicle,
and swallow-like or dove-like testicles. Only the hen-
egg size testicles are the good ones. Lozana: Mamotreto
LXV 206.

J1308.* Why are servants better in bed than their masters?
Answer: Fine dress is good for holidays and appearance,
but a strong man in bed is a woman's delight.
Lozana: Manotreto LXIII 206.

J1309.4.* Does a dying swan sing? Man replies that he has
never heard a swan sing, but that it is a candid bird
and might do so. Periquillo: Discurso VII 1880a.

B752.1. Swan song. Swan sings as she dies.

J1310. Repartee concerning wine.

J1314.1.* Koran has nothing to say about wine for the dead.
Dying Moor wants wine placed in his tomb. Urdemalas: p. 4a.

J712.2.* Dying man wants food placed in his tomb.

J1319.2.* Prisoner wins freedom by clever remark. While
pleading his case before a duke a prisoner is given a
small-mouth glass of wine. Prisoner: "This is adding
trouble to trouble. Bring me a kettle, for if it may not
be full, it does have a bottom." The man's wit frees
him. Estebanillo: Bk. II, Ch. I 1784b.

J1319.3.* "What kills some, cures others." Doctor replies
to man who says that his broken arm was cured by the
large amount of wine which he has drunk. Estebanillo:
Bk. II, Ch. VI 1842a.

F953.2.* Broken arm marvelously cured in two weeks.

J1320. Repartee concerning drunkenness.

J1321.1.1.* To return favors received. Drunkard is annoyed
by children in street. He picks up rocks and tells them
that he will return favors received, if they continue.
The children flee. Guzmán: Pt. II, Bk. II, Ch. IV 460b.

J1326.* More wine than blood from gored drunkard. Drunken
lackey gored and killed at bullfight. Hija: p. 901a.

J1330. Repartee concerning beggars.

J1331.1.* Persistent beggar receives "alms." Irritated man
says, "Extend your cape to receive alms." He throws
contents of stool pan into cape. Guadaña: Ch. I 1684a.

P160. Beggars. Q383.2.* Punishment for persistent
begging.

J1335.* Begin with me. Beggar: "If you haven't given anything yet, begin with me; if you have given to someone
else, give to me, too." Guzmán (Luján): Pt. II, Bk. II,
Ch. III 620b.

J1340. Retorts from hungry persons.

1341.7.1.* Hungry student asks if black peas are in mourning?
Stingy schoolmaster breaks tooth on "pea" in soup. Careless cook had broken rosary and black beads had fallen
in soup. Buscón: Bk. I. Ch. III 1099b.

W152.18.* Stingy schoolmaster.

J1341.9.1.* Hungry boy chooses large grapes. Accustomed to
eating the small grapes of his native region, boy at
first refuses the large grapes of his new home. When he
learns that there are no small grapes he says, "Mother,
give me those, for I now eat fat ones." Guzmán: Pt. II,
Bk. III, Ch. IV 528b.

J200. Choices.

J1341.9.2.* Hungry nobleman's son would prefer to be a peasant
and eat well. Impressive geneology cannot take the place
of food. Alonso: Pt. I, Ch. IV 1226a.

J1341.10.1.* Hungry student wants to pay respects to a man's
sister who is serving a dinner. The man invites the student
to dinner after the latter had interested him in a fabri-
cated story about the man's girl friend. Buscón: Bk. III,
Ch. II 1130b.

J1341.13.* Hungry student sees no reason to give thanks. He
slaps table when head-master indicates offering of thanks.
"Silence, gentlemen. I don't know what I have to be
thankful for, nor why you should give thanks." Guzmán:
Pt. II, Bk. III, Ch. IV 533a.

J1341.14.* No need for toilets. Old student tells new boy
that there are no toilets. Students are served so little
food that they do not need to evacuate themselves.
Buscón: Bk. I, Ch. III 1098a.

W152.18.* Stingy schoolmaster.

J1342.1.* Hungry servant prays that the sick will die. He
always eats well at funerals. Lazarillo: Tratado I 92b.

J1343.3.* "Sponging" guest departs after eating. Criticized
for her haste she replies, "You should thank me, because
I usually stay three days." Justina: Bk. II, Pt. II,
Ch. IV 819a.

J1345.1.* Employee explains why he was late for work. He had
to go a long distance to an inn where they knew his diet:
heavy meats for winter and lighter ones for summer.
Guzmán: Pt. II, Bk. III, Ch. V 542b.

J1347.* Satiated trickster offers to let innkeeper stab him
in payment for meal. Trickster and his servant are
arrested. Manzanares: Ch. XIV 91.

J1348.* "Give him saddlebags, too." Servant places guest's
chair backwards at table. Since the food is plentiful,
the guest remarks that he is poorly saddled and should
be given saddlebags. Estebanillo: Bk. II, Ch. I 1785b.

J1350. Rude retorts.

J1351.3.* Many women deserve the same punishment. Male witness to adulteress' execution observes that many female
on-lookers deserve the same punishment. Guzmán: Pt. II,
Bk. II, Ch. IV 454b.

Q411.0.3.* Husband beheads adulteress.

J1352.3.* "Not enough barley for so many asses." Courtesan
refuses to copulate with four men who stop her.
Lozana: Mamotreto VII 28.

J1352.4.* Town crier calls youth an ass. Greedy crier proclaims
reward for any man who has never been in love, instead of
a reward for the finder of a lost ass. When a youth

claims the reward for never having been in love, the crier takes him to the owner of the ass. "Give me the reward; here is your ass." Guzmán: Pt. II, Bk. I, Ch. II 397b.

J1352.5.* Woman insinuates that her displeasing lover is an ass. He has something in common with her donkey which keeps looking at him. "Blood boils without fire." Justina: Bk. II, Pt. II, Ch. IV 819b.

J1352.6.* There are more asses now. Student taunts monk for riding on a donkey, saying that in the time of Saint Francis the monks rode on horses. Friar: "Brother, it was because then there were not as many asses as there are now." Justina: Bk. II, Pt. II, Ch. IV 820b.

J1365.* A horse's neighing sounds sweeter. King has no appreciation for singer's music. Guzman (Luján): Pt. II, Bk. II, Ch. VII 333a.

X145.2.* A horse neighs better than the singer sings.

J1366.* Two kinds of crazy people. One is inwardly crazy, sad and calm; the other, outwardly mad, happy and noisy. Young theologian says that the older student, who had called him a crazy man, is the introverted madman. Torres: Trozo III 1950a.

J1369.6.* Cart full of dung. Philosopher on seeing parade of triumphant emperor: "What a lot of dung this cart carries." Guzmán: Pt. II, Bk. II, Ch. VII 477a.

J1369.7.* "Did you expect to find a pearl?" Master rebukes maidservant for picking nose and looking at extraction. Periquillo: Discurso XVI 1912b.

J1380. Retorts concerning debts.

W153.10.1.* Dead miser owes many debts to his body.

J1385.* Man is stingy with creditors, but generous with others.
His explanation: To pay obligations is the way a tax-
payer pays; to give where no duty demands, is the way a
nobleman acts. Justina: Bk. II, Pt. I, Ch. II 770a.

J1390. Retorts concerning thefts.

J1391.1.1.* Thief steals shirts because he is hungry. He
wants to sell them to buy food. He is flogged and banished
from city. Guzmán: Pt. II, Bk. II, Ch. IV 460a.

J1391.3.2.* The hogs entered without knocking. Student kills
two hogs which wandered into his house. "Since they
entered without knocking, I thought they were ours."
Buscón: Bk. I, Ch. VI 1106b.

J1391.5.1.* Gluttonous foxes explain to other animals that
their bellies are swollen from hunger and cold. They
had pillaged henhouse after condemning cats for stealing
meat. Peregrinación: p. 11.

U129.1. Thieving nature of the fox will show itself.

J1391.9.* Tablecloth to cure stomach-ache. Owner catches
thief with tablecloth wrapped around his stomach. Thief
says that doctor has advised him to use new tablecloth
on his stomach to cure sickness. Master retrieves cloth.
Alonso: Pt. II, Ch. II 1280b.

K420. Thief loses his goods or is detected.

J1391.10.* They were taking the officer's trunk to his ship.
Officer returns home just as his servant and another
thief are carrying his trunk out of the house. They
explain that they were taking the trunk to the officer's
ship. The officer dismisses his servant, saying, "I
don't want such a punctual servant." Estebanillo:
Bk. I, Ch. II 1739a.

J1391.11.* Had to take sanctuary. Thief runs away with
master's money and hides in a church. When found by
master he says that he has taken sanctuary because he
wounded a man. Estebanillo: Bk. I, Ch. V 1764b.

J1392.6.* Owner helps thief pick up stolen coins. Thief drops
coins on removing them from man's pocket. Thief pulls
out his own handkerchief while dropping other coins.
The owner of the stolen money helps the thief recover
all of it. Guzmán: Pt. II, Bk. III, Ch. VI 555a.

J1399.1.1.* "It is risen; it is not here." Youth steals
purse from cabinet in uncle's house and leaves a note
stating that the purse has risen. Necio: Ch. II 208.

K341.9.2.* Youth persuades uncle that thieves
are downstairs.

J1399.2.* Mayor's house harbors two thieves: father and son.
Thieving soldiers, formerly quartered in town, give it
a reputation for harboring thieves. Guzmán: Pt. I,
Bk. II, Ch. IX 331b.

F709.3.1.* Town of thieves.

J1399.3.* "Gentlemen thieves, we are all here." Owner hidden
in money sack frightens away thieves when he speaks to
them. Diablo: Tranco II 1645a.

K335.1.6.4.* Man hidden in large money sack
frightens robbers.

J1430. Repartee concerning doctors and patients.

J1431.1.* "You are really sick." Patient tells doctor that
he cannot eat or drink, and that he has not slept in a
month. Doctor tells patient that he is really sick.
Alonso: Pt. II, Ch. VII 1309b.

J1435.* Church no sanctuary from doctor. In order to get
more fees from recovered patient, doctor follows him to
church. The patient exclaims, "I perceive that this holy
place cannot give me sanctuary from you." Guzmán:
Pt. I, Bk. I, Ch. IV 259b.

P424. Physician.

J1436.* Doctors were the only devils possessing man. Unable
to cure a sick man, doctors say that he is possessed of
a devil, and they order him to be exorcised. The invalid
thinks that the doctors are the devils. Torres:
Trozo V 1986b.

J1439.* Doctor's fee too high. Patient refuses to pay,
stating, "What silk or cloth did you give me, or what
merchandise did you bring from your house to justify
taking my property?" Alonso: Pt. I, Ch. VI 1239b.

J1440. Repartee - miscellaneous.

J1441.1.* Courtesan cannot describe her seducer. She has
seen him only naked. Lozana: Mamotreto LI 167.

J1442.1. The cynic wants sunlight. King (to cynic): "What
can I do for you?" - "Get out of my sunlight.
Guzmán (Luján): Pt. II, Bk. I, Ch. VIII 611b.

J1442.1.2.* Cynic rebukes bold and reckless soldier. "It
is very important to know what you think little of -
life or virtue." Guzmán (Luján): Pt. II, Bk. III,
Ch. XI 701b.

J1442.2.1.* Cynic does not need drinking glass. He sees a
girl dip water with her hand, and he throws away his
drinking glass. Nature has provided a means, and the
glass is superfluous. Guzmán (Luján): Pt. II, Bk. I,
Ch. VIII 611b.

J1442.3.1.* The cynic and his wealth. Cynic puts all his
gold and jewels in a bag and throws them into the sea.
Better to drown his riches than to have his riches
drown him. Guzmán: Pt. II, Bk. III, Ch. III (in James
Mabbe, The Rogue, London: Tudor Translations, IV 145).

J1442.7.1.* Whoever is hit by stone deserves to be hit.
Fool throws stones at people while shouting, "Watch out,
watch out; it cannot fall amiss." Guzmán: Pt. II,
Bk. I, Ch. I 389b.

J1442.7.2.* The cynic and his assailant. Philosopher refuses
to prosecute man who has slapped him. "Wouldn't it be
foolish of me to have a beast called into court?"
Guzmán: Pt. I, Bk. I, Ch. IV 263b.

J1442.8.1.* The cynic and the astrologers. "Consider how
these men spend their lives. They cannot see the fish
in the river when they are at the river bank, but they
appear to see those which are in the sky at a great
distance." Guzmán (Luján): Pt. II, Bk. III, Ch. IV 666a.

J1442.12.1.* Cynic: No age is good for marrying. When one
is a youth, it is too early; when old, it is too late.
Marcos: Bk. I, Descanso V 940b.

J1442.14.* Cynic: A bad commodity - mothers-in-law. Cynic
reads sign on shop, "Here are sold deceits for the
deceived." He sees many old women in the shop, and he
thinks that they must be mothers-in-law. Periquillo:
Discurso VI 1875b.

J1442.15.* The woman deserves a statue. A group of men censure
a woman for refusing a man's love and money. One man
suggests, however, that she should have a statue erected
to her, since this is the first time such an offer has

been rejected. <u>Necio</u>: Ch. VI 305.

J1454.1.* The butcher and the statue. Butcher refuses to
revere statue of Venus made from a chop-block. "Since
I knew you as a chop-block, I cannot have respect for
you." <u>Justina</u>: Bk. IV, Ch. IV 881a.

 U121.6.1.* Butcher cannot revere statue of Venus
 made from chop-block.

J1459.* One cannot escape his fate. At public hanging,
woman tells thief that he was fated to be hanged. He
slaps her, saying that she was fated for such treatment.
<u>Alonso</u>: Pt. I, Ch. IV 1220a.

 N101.5.* Thief fated to be hanged.

J1463.1.* A long beard necessary for monk to become a
superior. Religious order refuses to make a monk a
superior if he does not have a beard. <u>Lazarillo</u> (Luna):
Pt. II, Ch. XV 142a.

J1464.* Cynic: "Cut the hawk-like claws of the rich instead
of the nails of the poor." Cynic advises woman that she
will need cloth shears for the rapine claws of the rich.
<u>Periquillo</u>: Discurso XVI 1913b.

J1469.* Time and place for jokes. First comedian: "What if
the king summons us and asks us to tell jokes?" Second
comedian: "... The only thing we could tell him is that
they aren't cooked up yet." (Pun on the word "fritas.")
<u>Guzmán</u>: Pt. II, Bk. I, Ch. II 395a.

J1484.1.* Skinning or shaving? Customer to unskilled barber:
"If you are skinning me, you are doing a fine job; but
if you are shaving me, you are making a mess of it."
<u>Marcos</u>: Bk. II, Descanso VI 1010b.

 P446. Barber.

J1484.2.* Howling dog must be getting a free haircut. An
apprentice barber cuts student's face and pulls his hair
as he gives him a free haircut. A dog starts howling
upstairs, and the master barber calls out to ask what is
the matter with the dog. Student: "They must be giving
him a free haircut. Alonso: Pt. I, Ch. VI 1245b.

P446. Barber.

J1491.1.* Grief of parents cannot be painted. Artist paints
face of dead girl and faces of some members of the funeral
group, but he leaves blank the faces of the girl's
parents. Guzmán: Pt. I, Bk. I, Ch. VIII 284a.

J1494.1.* Young monks would eat too much. King refuses
Franciscan general's offer of 22,000 friars for his army.
Lazarillo (Luna): Pt. II, Ch. IX 128b.

J1500 - J1649. CLEVER PRACTICAL RETORTS

J1510. The cheater cheated.

J1510.1.* False inheritor robbed of money by prospective
bride. False heir robbed and abandoned by prospective
bride after humiliating treatment. Lazarillo (Luna):
Pt. II, Ch. XVI 145a.

J1786.1.1.* Would-be husband cheated. K778.4.
Attack made on groom after he has been invited to
female apartments to have meal with bride.

J1510.2.* Sham rich soldier robbed of possessions by sham
rich bride. She deserts him, leaving him with a disease.
Casamiento: p. 196b.

K306.3. Man is robbed of gold chain while with
prostitute. K1954. Sham rich man.

J1510.3.* Thieving innkeeper hands stolen money at night to
guest instead of wife. Guest returns the money to owners.

<u>Marcos</u>: Bk. I, Descanso XIII   969a.

  N630. Accidental acquisition of treasure or money.

J1511. A rule must work both ways.

  K1510.2.1.* Wife of suspected philanderer decides
  to get revenge by having an affair herself.

J1521.2. The old man nods "Yes." Dying hermit answers "Yes"
  to all questions. Trickster asks him if he is to inherit
  all his property. Hermit nods "Yes," and the hermit's
  house and property are given to trickster.

  <u>Lazarillo</u> (Luna): Pt. II, Ch. XV 140b.

  K1923. The false heir. K1938. Rascal pretends to
  be dead man's heir and receives money.

J1530. <u>One absurdity rebukes another</u>.

J1532.2.* Unfaithful to one husband, unfaithful to another.
  Lover refuses to marry adulteress after her husband dies.

  <u>Teresa</u>: Ch. XVII 1411a.

  M205.0.2.* Lover refuses to marry adulteress
  after her husband dies.

J1540. <u>Retorts between husband and wife</u>.

J1541.1.2.* Husband's affectionate words mask mistreatment
  of his wife. In a loud voice the husband speaks sweet
  words to his wife while pinching her severely. The
  neighbors think that he is kind, but that his wife is
  terrible. <u>Alonso</u>: Pt. II, Ch. VI 1299b.

J1545.3. Fault-finding husband nonplussed. The wife has
  cooked so many dishes that when he complains she can
  always supply another. <u>Alonso</u>: Pt. II, Ch. VI 1301a.

J1560. <u>Practical retorts: hosts and guests</u>.

J1561.4.1.1.* Hostess serves youth rotten scrambled eggs.

He could feel the baby chicks' bones as he swallowed.
Guzmán: Pt. I, Bk. I, Ch. III 256a.

J1561.4.3.* Servant refuses to defend stingy master a second
time. He has not been repaid for personal losses in
former defense of master. Guzmán: Pt. I, Bk. II,
Ch. V 314b.

    P360. Master and servant. W152.12.5.* Stingy
master refuses to repay servant for personal losses
incurred while defending him.

J1562.3.1.* Lover hides meat in trousers while he consorts
with woman. Dog drags trousers into street, and lover
is exposed when officer breaks into room. Coloquio: p. 215a.

J1563.2.1.* Soldier makes demands on host. Latter gives
money to soldier, but he stays to dinner. Servants ignore
his requests for wine or give him watered wine. He leaves.
Guzmán: Pt. I, Bk. III, Ch. X 374b.

J1563.2.2.* Unwelcome guests are tricked into insulting each
other's dyed beard. Host's servant says, "Both have
told the truth and have lied by their beards." Guzmán:
Pt. II, Bk. I, Ch. III 406a.

J1563.2.3.* Soldier makes impossible demands on host (peasant).
Captain advises the host to give money and the soldier
will be satisfied. Alonso: Pt. I, Ch. II 1205b.

    J21.46.1.* Give money to contentious soldier-guest.

J1563.2.4.* One soldier in a group demands money of hostess.
Woman's husband and friends chase soldiers from house.
Alonso: Pt. I. Ch. II 1209a.

J1563.2.5.* Soldier makes exaggerated food demands for
quartered troops. Host: "If servants' table needs so
much food, there will not be enough wealth in the town

to supply the master's table." <u>Estebanillo</u>: Bk. I,
Ch. VI 1775a.

    K170.2.* Soldier gets much food through deceptive
partnership with host.

J1563.6.1.* Servant ties uninvited guest's leg to chair.
When the inebriated guest attempted to rise, he fell on
his face, injuring himself. <u>Guzmán</u>: Pt. I, Bk. III,
Ch. X 374a.

J1563.9.* Priest "absolves" parasitic guest. Uninvited guest
has promised Saint Francis to eat with his friars on
feast days. Priest says that he has a bull from the
saint for the absolution of this vow. <u>Alonso</u>: Pt. II,
Ch. I 1275a.

    M273.* Trickster promises Saint Francis to eat
with friars on feast days.

J1564.3.* Incessant talker silenced by man who out-talks
him. Talker is interrupted constantly and finally leaves.
<u>Marcos</u>: Bk. I, Descanso XVIII 982a.

J1577.2.* Artist receives a false invitation to a king's
banquet. With a piece of charcoal he paints on a wall
the portrait of the trickster who has invited him. All
recognize the man. <u>Alonso</u>: Pt. II, Ch. XIII 1337b.

J1580. <u>Practical retorts connected with almsgiving</u>.

J1581.1. Poem for poem: all for all. The poet gives the
emperor (prince) a poem, hoping for reward. The emperor
(prince) later **gives** the poet a poem in return. The
poet thereupon **hands** the emperor two pennies (one penny),
saying that this is all the money he has. The emperor
(prince), seeing that he is defeated in the exchange,
laughs and becomes the poet's friend. <u>Guzmán</u>: Pt. II,

Bk. I, Ch. III 402b.

J1600. Practical retorts - miscellaneous.

J1606.2.* A tired man can rest, a hungry man eats, and a sleepy
man sleeps. Friend cures another man who complains that
he cannot rest, eat, or sleep, by taking him on a long
hike in search of a special herb. Marcos: Bk. III,
Descanso XIII 1060b.

J1619.* "The kinship is too sudden." Innkeeper becomes
furious when traveler addresses him as "brother," and
refuses to serve wine to him. The traveler takes out
his sword, and the innkeeper gets wine for the guest.
Píndaro: Bk. II, Ch. VII 334a.

J1629.* Treatment for fainting. Man throws basin of water
on friend who falls asleep while he is telling story.
The man explains that he thought that his friend had
fainted. Necio: Ch. II 223.

J1638.1.* Franciscan drops Dominican in mid-stream. Tired
from carrying the heavy Dominican, the Franciscan asks
him if he has any money. On hearing "Yes," the Franciscan
drops him in the water. "It's against the rules of our
order to carry money." Alonso: Pt. II, Ch. II 1278a.

     K1268. Man carried and dropped in mid-stream.

J1649.* God asked to subtract and add days. Servant explains
to his master that the days which he wants God to subtract from his life and add to his master's are the days
of difficulty and peril. Alonso: Pt. I, Ch. IX 1260a.

     J1114.3.* Servant deceives master with polite
     phrase: "May God subtract from my days and add
     them to yours."

J1650 - J1699. MISCELLANEOUS CLEVER ACTS

J1664.1.1.* Which is the most fortunate man? First man: The man who has married a good woman. Second: The man who has quickly lost a bad wife. Third: The man who has never had a good or bad wife. Guzmán: Pt. II, Bk. III, Ch. IX 572b.

J1664.2.* Which is the greatest invention? Members of a group debate the merits of many inventions. A man stops the debate by stating that the needle is the greatest invention. One can mend clothes with a needle, for which all other inventions are useless. Marcos: Bk. III, Descanso XIV 1062b.

J1671.1.* Clever donkey driver uses soft speech and a goad to make donkey run. Angry speech of brother is ineffective. Marcos: Bk. I, Descanso VII 948a.

J1675. Clever dealing with a king.

J1280. Repartee with ruler (judge, etc.).

J1675.3.1.* Fool says that the Holy Trinity is criticizing king. When pressed to tell who is criticizing the king for dismissing a minister, the fool replies: "The Holy Trinity. Now see which one you want to punish." Guzmán: Pt. II, Bk. I, Ch. II 396b.

J1280. Repartee with ruler (judge, etc.).

J1675.5.1.* King influenced by music. His musicians can excite him to dress for battle by singing or playing music. Likewise, they can quiet him with music. Guzmán (Luján): Pt. II, Bk. II, Ch. VII 632b.

D1275.1. Magic music.

J1700 - J2799. FOOLS (AND OTHER UNWISE PERSONS)

J1700 - J1729. FOOLS(GENERAL)

J1700. Fools.

J1705.1.1.* Stupid peasants refuse to change route of procession. Prefer to walk through water and mud rather
than to change route. Alonso: Pt. I, Ch. I 1202b.

J1710. Association with fools.

J1714.4.1.* Man has two reasons for writing autobiography.
(1) If it is worth money, he deserves it more than
someone else. (2) He wants his merits known now so
that people will not find new virtues and make him a
saint after he is dead. Torres: Introduction, p. 1925b.

J1714.4.2.* Author loses faith in books. He sees people
buying and praising the ones he has written. He knows
that he is ignorant and that his books are worthless.
Torres: Trozo I 1932a.

J1730 - J1749. ABSURD IGNORANCE

J1730. Absurd ignorance.

J1734.2.* Urine analysis to diagnose illness of community.
Stupid doctor pours all urine specimines together in
order to diagnose the illness of a community.
Lozana: Mamotreto LIX 194.

    K1955.2. Sham physician pretends to diagnose
    entirely from urinalysis.

J1737.2.* Foolish lover ignorant of wife's flaws until a
relative points them out. Alonso: Pt. II, Ch. VI 1303a.

    J445.1.2.* Foolish youth marries an ugly old woman.

J1741.2.1.* Deum de Deo. Ignorant man interpreted the phrase
to mean "Give wherever you will give." Coloquio: p. 206b.

J1741.2.2.* Ignorant cleric thinks that <u>Corpus Christi</u> is a
saint. He has seen his name on a calendar and would
wager that he has been canonized. <u>Buscón</u>: Bk. II,
Ch. II 1115a.

J1741.2.3.* Man prays to Saint Telmo (a light), thinking that
it is a god. In a storm at sea sailors see the strange
light called Saint Telmo. A terrified man prays to this
"saint." <u>Píndaro</u>: Bk. II, Ch. XXIII 363b.

> J1261.1.6.* "My God will be the one who can save
> me from this danger."

J1749.3.* Ignorant innkeeper thinks that "angles" are birds.
He will have his wife cook them for the mathematician.
<u>Buscón</u>: Bk. II, Ch. I 1113b.

> J1750 - J1849. ABSURD MISUNDERSTANDINGS
>
> J1750 - J1809. ONE THING MISTAKEN FOR ANOTHER

J1750. <u>One animal mistaken for another</u>.

J1758.0.1.* Lion mistaken for cat. Children mistake artist's
picture of lion for cat. Artist: "'Cat' isn't so bad;
I'm getting close to painting a lion." <u>Alonso</u>: Pt. II,
Ch. IX 1315b.

J1761.5.1.* Mule's leg bone thought to be log of wood. Stench
from bone makes students ill. <u>Marcos</u>: Bk. I, Descanso
XII 964b.

J1762.10.* Ram's butting at door mistaken for woman's knock.
Conceited man thinks that a woman is knocking at his
door at night. In the darkness he puts his hands on
ram's horns and thinks that it is the devil. <u>Guzmán</u>:
Pt. II, Bk. I, Ch. V 600b.

J1765.3.* Man mistaken for sea monster. Cast-away swimming
toward shore frightens man away from his food. Cast-

away eats the food. <u>Marcos</u>: Bk. III, Descanso X 1055a.

J1765.4.* Man mistaken for hog and beaten. Hogs had entered
room where man was sleeping and had covered him with
filth. When the swineherd comes to drive out the hogs
he beats the man, thinking that he was a hog. <u>Marcos</u>:
Bk. III, Descanso XV 1066a.

J1766.2.* Devil and student mistaken for king's emissaries.
They are honored by local authorities until devil begins
to explain his "mission." <u>Diablo</u>: Tranco VI 1660a.

J1772.9.2.* Excrement thought to be stone. Trysting lover
at night picks up excrement to throw at barking dog. He
hits his fingers against wall and thrusts them into his
mouth to ease pain. His subsequent gagging and spitting
break up his amorous conversation. <u>Guzmán</u>: Pt. II,
Bk. III, Ch. I 508a.

J1772.15.* Youth mistakes jar of laxative syrup for honey.
He consumes all and befouls himself in his sleep.
<u>Manzanares</u>: Ch. IV 18.

J1772.16.* Drunken soldier mistakes wax candles for radishes.
He asks why the leaves have been removed. After store
owner hits him for upsetting all candles, soldier slashes
candles. <u>Estebanillo</u>: Bk. II, Ch. I 1789b.

J1772.17.* Make-believe castle mistaken for real. Foolish
man details ways to blow up a make-believe castle at
fiesta. Thus, the Moors will be defeated in battle with
Christians. Moors learn of man's proposals and try to
kill him. <u>Estebanillo</u>: Bk. II, Ch. VI 1836a.

J1780. <u>Things thought to be devils, ghosts, etc</u>.

J1781.4.* Sleeping boy dreams that "hot-foot" treatment is
devil carrying him away. His screams terrify his master.

Guzmán (Luján): Pt. II, Bk. I, Ch. IV 596a.

> K2250.2.* Treacherous servants give new boy a
> severe "hot-foot" treatment.

J1781.5.* Puppet thought to be devil. Tricksters throw
horrible-looking puppet through doctor's window at night.
Doctor's wife thinks it is the devil. Guadaña: Ch. XII
1718a.

J1785.5. Cat mistaken for devil.

> K335.0.12.1.* Owner frightened by thief who brings
> forth "devil" to tell him where stolen money is
> located.

J1785.5.1.* Servant mistakes cat for devil. He steps on cat
in dark, is scratched, and thinks that the devil is
carrying off his soul. Guzmán: Pt. I, Bk. II, Ch. VI 317a.

J1786. Man thought to be devil or ghost.

> K673.* Entrapped lover sets fire to house...

J1786.1.1.* Would-be husband cheated. He is blackened by
prospective bride and her friends and thrown into street.
When he entered a church, the monks thought that he was
the devil. Lazarillo (Luna): Pt. II, Ch. XVI 145a.

> K302.1.1.* Courtesan-"wife" runs away with man's
> goods.

J1786.1.2.* Men dressed as devils thought to be devils. They
enter man's room and toss him in a blanket until he
loses consciousness. Guzmán: Pt. I, Bk. III, Ch. I 340b.

J1786.1.3.* Disguised servants thought to be devils. They
rush out and punish men who enter their master's house
without knocking. Necio: Ch. I 173.

> K1838.2.* Servants disguise as devils.

J1786.2.1.* Servant and mistress mistake each other for ghosts.
They meet on stairs at night as each goes to scare away
fighting cats. <u>Guzmán</u>: Pt. I, Bk. II, Ch. VI 317a.

J1786.5.1.* Officer thinks man lifting up fellow officer is
devil. He flees. <u>Guadaña</u>: Ch. VII 1705b.

    K1269.* Officer lifted into air by pulley and
    dropped.

J1789.3.* Monkey throws tiles from housetop at night. Passers-
by think that the place is haunted. <u>Marcos</u>: Bk. I,
Descanso V 943b.

J1790. <u>Shadow mistaken for substance</u>.

J1791.1.1.* Numskulls think companion has swallowed the moon.
Cloud hides moon just as a man begins drinking from a
stream. Companions beat the man, thinking that he has
swallowed the moon. <u>Periquillo</u>: Discurso XIII 1904b.

J1792.2.* Birds see painted grapes and peck at them.
<u>Alonso</u>: Pt. II, Ch. IX 1315b.

    H504.1.3.* Contest in life-like painting: grapes
    and curtain.

J1796.2.* Drunken hermit mistakes moonlight for swollen
river. Removes his clothes in order to cross it.
<u>Manzanares</u>: Ch. VII 40.

J1800. <u>One thing mistaken for another - miscellaneous</u>.

J1801.1.* Not the picture he ordered. Patron sees upside-
down painting of horse and thinks that artist has
painted a horse wallowing instead of running. Artist
turns picture into proper position and patron is satisfied.
<u>Guzmán</u>: Pt. II, Bk. III, Ch. IX 570b.

J1803.1.1.* Adulteress does not understand words of confessor.
He asks her concerning her lechery (<u>lujuria</u>) and her

wood-lye (<u>lejía</u>). She later makes some wood-lye and
drinks it, the devil having sweetened it. <u>Manzanares</u>:
Ch. X 65.

G303.9.9.22.* Devil causes curious woman to physic
herself.

J1803.2.1.* Doctor's elegant language wins him great reputation among uneducated. <u>Manzanares</u>: Ch. X 64.

J1803.2.2.* Sick man does not understand doctor's learned
expressions. He sends doctor away. <u>Marcos</u>: Bk. I,
Descanso IV 937b.

J1803.3.* Executioner's words misunderstood. Son returns to
place where father is being flogged; he wants to see the
"other men." The executioner says, "This is the punishment which our lord the king orders for these men who
are thieves." <u>Manzanares</u>: Ch. I 5.

J1803.4.* Man thinks mathematical terms are insults. Ignorant
bully thinks that mathematician is insulting him when he
uses the words "obtuse angle." <u>Buscón</u>: Bk. II, Ch. I
1114a.

J1805.1.1.* Similar-sounding words confuse sick woman. Mid-
wife has come to give sick woman medicine for her womb
(<u>madre</u>), but the sick one thinks that the medicine is
for her mother (<u>madre</u>). <u>Lozana</u>: Mamotreto XXIII 84.

J1805.1.2.* Magistrate promises to take care of <u>menudos</u>
("small expenses," "giblets"). After election, when
censured for extravagant spending, he explains that
he receives the <u>menudos</u> (giblets) every Saturday at the
butcher shop <u>Guzmán</u>: Pt. I, Bk. I, Ch. III 257a.

J1287.* Magistrate will take care of "small expenses."

J1805.1.3.* Countryman mistakes card terms. He says that he

has a "flux" when he means a "flush." <u>Guzmán</u>: Pt. I,
Bk. I, Ch. V 264b.

J1805.1.4.* Soldier receives chamber pot instead of service
papers. Innkeeper mistakes soldier's demand for return
of his service papers and brings him a chamber pot.
(Pun on "servicios.") <u>Buscón</u>: Bk. II, Ch. III 1119b.

J1805.2.2.* Ignorant youth misinterprets word "contrapás"
("dance step") to mean "poorly clothed." He becomes
angry with serenader who has used it in song. <u>Fregona</u>:
162a.

J1805.2.3.* Courtesan misinterprets foreign word "mancha"
("tip") to mean "blemish." She is insulted, thinking
that tavern-keeper is referring to a blemish on her face
when he is asking for a tip. <u>Lozana</u>: Mamotreto XIII 46.

J1805.2.4.* Woman thinks that man is accosting her when he
is offering food. She does not understand his dialect.
<u>Justina</u>: Bk. II, Pt. II, Ch. IV 807a.

J1805.2.5.* Woman berates man who proposes to take her to a
shrine. She thinks that the dialectical word for shrine
is an obscenity. <u>Justina</u>: Bk. II, Pt. II, Ch. IV 817a.

J1805.2.6.* Master asks servant to take a letter to the
general delivery (post) of Aragón. Servant takes the
letter to a prostitute so named. Unexpected results
follow. <u>Necio</u>: Ch. II 213.

J1805.2.7.* Officer misinterprets thief's unusual word.
Thinks that thief is an astrologer and asks for his
help in catching robber. (Pun on word <u>efemerides</u>, "diary"
and "astronomical almanac.") <u>Urdemalas</u>: p. 6b.

J1810. <u>Physical phenomena misunderstood</u>.

J1812.6.* Numskull mistakes companions' flatulence in chamber
pot for thunder. Odor causes him to start a fight with
companions. <u>Buscón</u>: Bk. III, Ch. IV 1134a.

J1820. <u>Inappropriate action from misunderstanding</u>.

J1820.0.1.* Officers arrest men engaged in foot race. They
think runners are fugitives from a crime. <u>Marcos</u>:
Bk. III, Descanso XII 1058a.

J1820.0.2.* Running harder because of echo. Foxes think
that dogpack has increased when they hear the echo of
barking dogs. <u>Peregrinación</u>: p. 8.

J1823.1.5.* Brothers misinterpret sister's vow before statue
to mean she will become a nun. They expect to inherit
her property. She has vowed to leave home; and she
does, with stolen jewels. <u>Justina</u>: Bk. III, Ch. I 854b.

J1823.1.6.* Passer-by raises hat to Holy Sacrament and feels
insulted when youths in church door lift their hats in
response. They explain that they raise their hats to
honor him. <u>Marcos</u>: Bk. II, Descanso VI 1010b.

J1833.1.3.* Soldier misinterprets noise in convent at night
as arrival of police. He escapes from an upstairs window.
Later, he discovers that noise was caused by arrival of
wounded man seeking sanctuary. <u>Píndaro</u>: Bk. I,
Introduction, p. 275a.

J1839.* Man thinks snake has two heads. One is frog's head
sticking out of serpent's mouth. Snake disgorges frog
when man strikes it. <u>Marcos</u>: Bk. III, Descanso XIV 1064a.
B15.1.2.1.1.1.* Two-headed serpent.

J1840.* Woman misinterprets hand-kissing custom. She thinks
man is trying to seduce her, and she hits him with skillet.
<u>Estebanillo</u>: Bk. II, Ch. VI 1831a.

P618.* Hand-kissing as greeting custom.

J1849.1.2.* Maidservant panics when she hears actor reciting lines about a furious bear. She drops dishes and flees into street. Buscón: Bk. III, Ch. IX 1149b.

J1850 - J1999. ABSURD DISREGARD OF FACTS

J1850 - J1899. ANIMALS OR OBJECTS TREATED AS IF HUMAN

J1860. Animal or object absurdly punished.

J1864.1.* Night revelers attack stone statues, thinking that they are men. Urdemalas: p. 190b.

J1900. Absurd disregard or ignorance of animal's nature or habits.

J1908.2. Cat transformed to maiden runs after mouse. Alonso: Pt. II, Ch. VI 1302a.

D342. Transformation: cat to person.

J1908.4.* Ass transformed to man dances and turns head around whenever he hears an ass bray. Justina: Bk. II, Pt. III, Ch. I 830b.

D332.1. Transformation of ass (donkey) to person.

J1909.8.* Pedantic teacher uses Latin phrases to incite cocks at fight. Cocks ignore him, while by-standers ridicule him. Marcos: Bk. I, Descanso VII 948a.

J1930. Absurd disregard of natural laws.

J1944.2.* Numskull expects to get dates from newly-planted date palm. He waits for it to produce fruit. Marcos: Bk. I, Descanso VI 945a.

J2066. Foolish waiting.

J1960. Other absurd disregard of facts.

J2066.11.* Doctor waits two years for wife to give birth.

J1972.1.* Adulteress asks observers to keep secret the slashing she received on her face. She does not want her husband to know that she has been disfigured by a rival. Guzmán: Pt. II, Bk. I, Ch. VI 418a.

J1978.* Drowning sailor is advised to go to Santiago. There he will be absolved for failing to go to the shrine of Our Lady of Loreta. Lazarillo (Luna): Pt. II, Ch. II 118a

J2000 - J2049. ABSURD ABSENT-MINDEDNESS

J2010. Uncertainty about own identity.

J2012.7.* Black child frightened when he sees black father. His mother and half-brother are white. Lazarillo: Tratado I 85b.

J2020. Inability to find own members, etc.

J2021.2.* Starving student cannot find his mouth. Having gone without food so long, the student tries to put crusts of bread into his eyes. Buscón: Bk. I, Ch. III 1098a.

W152.18.* Stingy schoolmaster.

J2040. Absurd absent-mindedness - miscellaneous.

J2041.2.* "Sleeping" actor in Passion Play takes food from time to time. Judas rebukes Saint John, saying, "Either be Saint John or not be Saint John. If you are Saint John, sleep and don't eat; if you are not, eat and let another take your place." Alonso: Pt. I, Ch. VII 1250a.

J2050 - J2199. ABSURD SHORT-SIGHTEDNESS

J2060. Absurd plans. Air-castles.

J2062.0.1.* As much an ass as is my father. Third man intervenes in dispute of two men over whether a new-born foal of a mare is an ass or a mule. Guzmán: Pt. II, Bk. II, Ch. V 462b.

       J2211.0.2.* Man declares that mare's foal is an
       ass instead of a mule.

J2066. Foolish waiting.

       J1944.2.* Numskull expects to get dates from newly-
       planted date palm.

J2066.10.* Impoverished nobleman expects son to become wealthy.
He must wait for grandmother and other relatives to die.
Marcos: Bk. I, Descanso VI 945a.

J2066.11.* Doctor waits two years for wife to give birth.
Mistakes stomach swelling for pregnancy. Alonso:
Pt. I, Ch. VI 1243b.

       J1960. Other absurd disregard of facts.

J2070. Absurd wishes.

J2072.7.* Partially-blind man wishes to become totally blind
in order to get revenge on enemies. He has been exiled
from town because he was not a blind beggar. Alonso:
Pt. I, Ch. V 1227b.

J2080. Foolish bargains.

J2083.6. Selling more yards of goods for the money than they
received. Marcos: Bk. III, Descanso XXII 1078a.

       K173.2.* Deceptive bargain: linen priced according
       to the measuring stick.

J2083.6.1.* Selling more sausage by lengthening measure.
Weasel persuades merchant cat to lengthen his span,
which measures sausage, by clipping his claws and lining
them up. Weasel gets more sausage for his money.
Justina: Bk. II, Pt. III, Ch. IV 844b.

J2100. Remedies worse than the disease.

J2102.1.1.* Sleeping with a bundle of herbs soaked in vinegar
to get rid of mosquitoes. Trickster attracts more

mosquitoes than ever to his victim. <u>Guzmán</u>: Pt. I,
Bk. III, Ch. VII 364a.

     K1010.2.* Remedy for mosquitoes.

J2103.1.2.* Foxes and cats are invited into man's pantry to
exterminate mice. They eat more in one day than the mice
do in a year. <u>Peregrinación</u>: p. 6.

J2130. <u>Foolish disregard to personal danger</u>.

J2131.2.2.* Scorpion stings numskull. Doctor tells him he
will suffer for 24 hours. When the clock strikes the
quarter hour, the fool says, "Praise God! I have only
23 hours and 45 minutes left." <u>Alonso</u>: Pt. II,
Ch. VII 1309a.

J2133.8.1.* Ruler falls into ditch while gazing at stars.
Woman by-stander: "How do you think that you can reach
the things in the sky, if you don't see what is before
your eyes?" <u>Guzmán</u> (Luján): Pt. II, Bk. III, Ch. IV 666a.

J2133.15.* Pimp falls into privy trying to avoid rat.
<u>Lozana</u>: Mamotreto XXXIII 116.

J2136. Numskull brings about his own capture.

     J2173.1.1.* Servant puts stolen honeycomb in his
        pocket. W121.3.5.* Cowardly soldier insults enemy.

J2136.2.1.* Thieving servant's hand gets caught in chest.
He cannot remove hand from small opening before master
arrives. He is punished. <u>Guzmán</u>: Pt. I, Bk. III,
Ch. VII 363a.

J2160. <u>Other short-sighted acts</u>.

     J641.0.1.* Youth flees town after accosting girl.

J2161.4.* Man wears foreign costume, hoping to impress people.
He is stoned as a fool when he tries to talk to his
former mistress who does not recognize him.
<u>Estebanillo</u>: Bk. II, Ch. VI 1839b.

J2173.1.1.* Servant puts stolen honeycomb in his pocket.
Is detected when body heat causes honey to run down his
legs. Guzmán: Pt. I, Bk. III, Ch. VII 362a.

J2136. Numskull brings about his own capture.

J2174.5.* Condemned man wants wine and cards before hanging.
The wine to drown his sorrow; the cards to help him pass
the time, since he has finished praying. Guzmán: Pt. II,
Bk. III, Ch. VIII 563a.

J2174.6.* Condemned man shows bravado on gallows. He places
noose around his neck and tells priests to stop their
services, because he does not want to take too long.
Buscón: Bk. I, Ch. VII 1110b.

Q413.1. Hanging as punishment for theft.

J2175.1.2.* Sleepwalking man beats wife. Upon waking he
comforts her. It is anticipatory punishment for when
she might need it. Diablo: Tranco II 1647a.

J2175.1.3.* Mother punishes children in advance. Nightly
whippings are to remind them to be good when they get
too big for her to punish them. Alonso: Pt. II,
Ch. XIII 1336a.

J2183.0.1.* Hunter decides to pacify fighting servants before
rescuing fettered women. When he returns, they are gone.
Hija: p. 910a.

Q434. Fettering.

J1299.2.1.* Soldiers pour stolen honey into powder horns.
They are unable to defend themselves later. Alonso:
Pt. I, Ch. II 1208b.

J2199.4. Short-sighted economy.

W153.10.1.* Dead miser owes many debts to his body.

J2200 - J2259. ABSURD LACK OF LOGIC

J2210. Logical absurdity based upon certain false assumptions.

J2211.0.1.* Builder can drink from watering trough; therefore, all animals can reach it. Guzmán: Pt. II, Bk. II, Ch. V 462b.

J2211.0.2.* Man declares that mare's foal is an ass instead of a mule. "It is as much an ass as is my father." Guzmán: Pt. II, Bk. II, Ch. V 462b.

    J2062.0.1.* As much an ass as is my father.

J2212.10.* Larger canvass needed to paint picture of lion. Artist sees large paw of dead lion and tells patron that he needs a larger canvass to paint picture of such a large animal. Periquillo: Discurso XIII 1904a.

J2213.5.2.* Servant swears that his master is 800 years old instead of 80. He misunderstands master's instructions. His testimony was given to serve God and his lord the count. Guzmán: Pt. II, Bk. II, Ch. VII 475a.

J2214.13.* Cobbler's son thinks that someone is ruining the business. He finds excrement in basket which he is taking to his father. Justina: Bk. I, Ch. II 735a.

    J2260 - J2299. ABSURD SCIENTIFIC THEORIES

J2280. Other absurd scientific theories.

J2285.2.* A short man can grow tall. Dupe believes statement concerning interpretation of comet: "The tall will decrease and the short will grow." Tricksters gull him into thinking that he has grown taller. Marcos: Bk. I, Descanso XXIII 996b.

J2286.* Foolish interpretation of physical appearances. Man claims ability to judge a person by looking at him. He judges Socrates to be stupid and crude because his foreneck is fleshy. _Guzmán_ (Luján): Pt. II, Bk. III, Ch. IV 664a.

U110. Appearances deceive.

J2300 - J2349. GULLIBLE FOOLS

J2300. **Gullible fools.**

K1966.2. Alchemist secures payment for his "secret."

J2310. **Nature of gullibility.**

J2311.1.6.* Short man believes that he will grow taller. He performs special rituals for three days and thinks that he has grown two inches. Tricksters have lowered the measuring device by two inches. _Marcos_: Bk. I, Descanso XXIII 996b.

J2285.2.* A short man can grow tall.

J2323.1.* Numskull is tricked into marrying ugly woman. He had fallen in love with the picture of a beautiful woman and thought he was marrying her. _Diablo_: Tranco II 1647a.

K1915.4.* Ugly woman substituted for beautiful one whose picture dupe had seen. T11.2. Love through sight of picture.

J2325.2.* Gullible rich man made to believe that urine from red-haired boy is an essential ingredient for making gold. He pays dearly for urine, because boy's mother thinks that the man is mad. _Garduña_: Bk. II 1570b.

K1966.2. Alchemist secures payment for his "secret."

J2337.1.* Trickster flatters dupe as great Latin scholar. Trickster orders food for the "scholar" and eats it himself. _Marcos_: Bk. I, Descanso IX 957b.

J455. Harm of association with flatterers.

K455.1.1.* Supper won by flattery.

J2337.1.1.* Trickster flatters ugly **wife** of innkeeper and gets good food and lodging. <u>Marcos</u>: Bk. III, Descanso XV 1065a.

    J455. Harm of association with flatterers.

    K455.1.1.* Supper won by flattery.

J2337.2.* Trickster tells dupe that a man would give 200 ducates just to see him at his home. The flattered dupe discovers that the man is blind. <u>Marcos</u>: Bk. I, Descanso IX 958a.

    J455. Harm of association with flatterers.

J2342.1.1.* Husband refuses to believe that wife is unfaithful even after discovering her lover's picture. Husband is deceived when town crier announces a "lost" picture. <u>Teresa</u>: Ch. XVII 1408a.

    J2301. Gullible husbands. K1543.1.* The lover's picture in the wife's sleeve.

J2342.1.2.* Husband refuses to believe that wife is unfaithful, although he shares her with archpriest. <u>Lazarillo</u>: Tratado VII 110b.

    V465.1.1. Incontinent monk (priest).

J2349.1.1.* Dupe is made to believe that mule speaks Greek. He speaks to it in Italian and is kicked. "No more dealing with Greek mules. They speak from behind." <u>Guadaña</u>: Ch. III 1690a.

    B211.1.3.2. Speaking mule.

      J2350-J2369. TALKATIVE FOOLS

    J865.4.* "I might as well talk now because I'm known." J2461.9.1.* Numskull is silent while courting girl.

J2353.1.1.* Foolish boast about cook's remarkable ability gets man into trouble. Woman asks for food samples, always praising food sent and asking for more. Finally the man, who has no cook, says that the cook has died. Necio: Ch. IV 267.

    X1005. Lie: remarkable cook.

J2359.* Widower's grief too exaggerated. Constable rebukes him: "Console yourself, brother, and don't go to those extremes; and since God has taken her away, to the devil with you!" Manzanares: Ch. XVII 114.

J2362.1.* Talkative visitors impede wounded man's recovery. So many relatives visit him and ask about his health that he almost dies. Guzmán (Luján): Pt. II, Bk. II, Ch. VII 633b.

    J2400 - J2449. FOOLISH IMITATION

J2410. Types of foolish imitation.

J2413.1. Ass tries to caress his master like the dog. He is driven off. Alonso: Pt. II, Ch. VIII 1311b.

J2415.1.3.* The two presents to the emperor: two speaking birds. First bird was taught to say "May God save you, victorious Augustus Caesar." The bird's owner was richly rewarded. Another man had a stupid bird which did not talk, but which heard its owner often wail, "I have wasted my work and money." On another occasion when Caesar refused to reward owners of talking thrushes, the stupid bird screamed, "I have wasted my work and money." Caesar was amused and rewarded the owner. Alonso: Pt. II, Ch. VIII 1313a.

    B211.3. Speaking bird.

J2420. <u>Foolish imitation - miscellaneous</u>.

J2421.0.1.* Boy seriously wounds another with blows. "Here, take these blows," the boy says, imitating what his father said when he scourged him. <u>Manzanares</u>: Ch. II 9.

J2450 - J2499. LITERAL FOOLS

J2450. <u>Literal fool</u>.

D1275.2.2.* Realistic song overcomes serenader.

J2460. <u>Literal obedience</u>.

J555.1.1.* Spend with prudence.

J2461.1.2.2.* Literal numskull asks woman to stab him. While singing, "Break the veins of my heart," he asks woman to stab him. <u>Marcos</u>: Bk. III, Descanso V 1043a.

D1275.2.2.* Realistic song overcomes serenader.

J2461.9.1.* Numskull is silent while courting girl. He has been told that he can hide his stupidity by talking little. Girl calls him a fool. "I might as well talk now because I'm known." <u>Alonso</u>: Pt. II, Ch. VII 1307a.

J2350. Talkative fools.

J2469.1.1.* Unappetizing food seems best to maidservant. Innkeeper instructs maid to buy the food which seems best to her. He scolds her when she returns with poor-quality food. <u>Justina</u>: Bk. I, Ch. III 740b.

J2469.5.3.* Literal obedience: "Master says that he is not at home." Servant repeats literally master's instructions when visitors knock at door. <u>Necio</u>: Ch. I 171.

J2470. <u>Metaphors literally interpreted</u>.

J2483. The house without food or drink. Young boy hears woman on street mourning for dead husband: "He goes to the place where there is darkness and nothing to eat or drink." The frightened boy rushes home and tells his master that

they are bringing a corpse to their house. <u>Lazarillo</u>:
Tratado III 102b.

J2486.* Numskull rings bells "quickly." Master tells servant
to ring church bells quickly to announce that a woman was
in labor. The bells ring so fast that townspeople think
there is a fire and rush to the woman's house to save
her. She gives birth in the street. <u>Necio</u>: Ch. II 200.

J2486.1.* Numskull rings church bells "merrily." Master tells
servant to ring church bells "merrily" when a prominent
man died. The fool played dance tunes on the bells, since
the man had been fond of dancing. The family of the
deceased man objected. <u>Necio</u>: Ch. II 201.

J2490. <u>Literal fool - miscellaneous</u>.

J2495.6.* Don't say Pontius Pilate again. Boy is punished
for calling Pontius Aguirre "Pontius Pilate." Thereafter,
in saying the Credo, the boy repeated, "He suffered
under Pontius Aguirre." <u>Buscón</u>: Bk. I, Ch. II 1095a.

J2500 - J2549. FOOLISH EXTREME

J2500. <u>Foolish extreme</u>.

J2501.* Foolish lover spends all of his money on a gold chain
and a cloak to give to his beloved. <u>Manzanares</u>:
Ch. XIII 82.

J2600 - J2649. COWARDLY FOOL

J2600. <u>Cowardly fool</u>.

J2627.1.* Cowardly sailor hides in tavern when he hears ships
firing at each other. He fears that a cannon ball might
hit him if he stays outside. <u>Estebanillo</u>: Bk. II,
Ch. II 1798a.

J2650 - J2699. BUNGLING FOOL

N300. Unlucky accidents.

J2650. <u>Bungling fool</u>.

J2661.5.* Importunate lover falls from horse in presence of
fiancée. He has rented a horse from a lackey whose
master is in church. Master comes to claim the horse
and berates the sham horseman. Fiancée's relative
suspects that the would-be lover is his former servant.
<u>Buscón</u>: Bk. III, Ch. VII 1143a.

N300. Unlucky accidents.

K. DECEPTIONS

K0 - K99. CONTESTS WON BY DECEPTION

K10. **Athletic contest won by deception.**

K11. Race won by deception.

> H331.5.1.1. Apple thrown in race with bride.

K80. **Contests in other physical accomplishments won by deception.**

K82.2.1.* Man wins drinking contest with help of confederate. He pours some of his brandy in a confederate's boot when opponent is not watching. Estebanillo: Bk. II, Ch. V 1820a.

K90. **Other contests won by deception.**

K92.4.* Servant wins conserves by deception. Master wagers that servant may have a second cask of conserves if he can steal one. He has already stolen one, and he wins a second cask when he produces the stolen one. Guzmán: Pt. I, Bk. III, Ch. VIII 366b.

> N1. Gamblers.

K100 - K299. DECEPTIVE BARGAINS

K110 - K149. SALE OF WORTHLESS ARTICLES

K110. **Sale of pseudo-magic objects.**

K112.4.* Sale of pseudo-magic powdered herbs. Student tricks companions into buying herb powder which will improve their memory, if snuffed into nostrils. Estebanillo: Bk. I, Ch. I 1728a.

K130. **Sale of worthless animals.**

K134.3. Trickster grooms master's old mule and then sells him back without detection at huge profit. Coloquio: p. 227a.

> K258. Stolen property sold to its owner.

K134.3.1.* Trickster grooms owner's mean mule and tries to sell it back to him. Owner detects fraud and recovers mule. Marcos: Bk. I, Descanso XVI   978a.

K1810. Deception by disguise.

K134.7.1.* Men sell meat from dead horse. They make meat pies and sell them. Manzanares: Ch. IV   17.

K134.9.* Butcher sells donkey meat. The son sees his father weighing the donkey in the butchershop, and reveals this to customers. Justina: Bk. I, Ch. III   742a.

K140. Sale of other worthless objects.

K142.1.* Sale of worthless ashes. Trickster receives money from people who want some of the ashes from his cremated father. Estebanillo: Bk. I, Ch. V   1765b.

K143.2.* Servant sells cow's bone encased in dough as rabbit meat pie. Master discovers the deception and dismisses servant. Guzmán: Pt. I, Bk. II, Ch. VI   319a.

K144.4.* Hay sold for barley. Trickster is killed by irate customer. Justina: Bk. I, Ch. III   744b.

K1600. Deceiver falls into own trap.

K150. Sale of worthless services.

K154.1.* Trickster feigns ability to influence viceroy. Sells his services to others. He merely recites the "Ave María" to the viceroy, and when the latter discovers the fraud, he punishes the trickster. Guzmán (Luján): Pt. II, Bk. I, Ch. VIII   612b.

K170. Deception through pseudo-simple bargain.

K170.2.* Soldier gets much food through deceptive partnership with host. He agrees to tell quartered troops that host is poor so that host can save money on food. Soldier's deceit is detected and he is punished. Estebanillo: Bk. I, Ch. VI   1775b.

J1563.2.5.* Soldier makes exaggerated food demands for quartered troops.

K173.1.* Deceptive bargain: as many preserves as he can eat
at one sitting. Trickster steals half of the preserves
from jars, stuffing the bottom of jars with brown paper.
Master gives servant the preserves when he discovers
the trick. Guzmán: Pt. I, Bk. III, Ch. IX   369a.

K173.2.* Deceptive bargain: linen priced according to measuring stick. Trickster produces a longer measuring stick
and cheats sellers. Marcos: Bk. III, Descanso XXII   1078a.

> J2083.6. Selling more yards of goods for the money
> than they received.

> K200 - K249. DECEPTION IN PAYMENT OF DEBT

K200. Deception in payment of debt.

> K455.4.0.1.* Money has been left with innkeeper.
> Z131.1.* Falsehood tries to get free meal through
> false credit.

K230. Other deceptions in the payment of debt.

K231.2.2.* Trickster gives barber coin of little value for
extensive services. Posing as a rich man, trickster
had promised to reward barber well. When barber asks
for more pay, he is tossed in a blanket. Trapaza:
Ch. IV 1442b.

K231.2.3.* Contestants in story-telling of personal danger
are denied reward. Diamond ring will go to the virgin
of second man's story who slept chastely with the man
all night. She ran the greatest danger. Guzmán: Pt. II,
Bk. I, Ch. IV 408a.

> K444.4.* Diamond ring as reward for story of
> great personal danger.

K231.6.2.1. Trickster returns a bottle of water instead of

the bottle of rum (wine) he has just purchased.
Codicia: Ch. VII 1178a.

K231.6.2.3.* Thieves get wine by trickery. Fill wine skin
one-fourth full of water and then have barmaid fill skin
with wine. On tasting the wine, they complain of its
poor quality and have barmaid withdraw the amount she
put in. They later sell their diluted wine.
Codicia: Ch. VII 1178a.

K233.0.1.* Woman trickster escapes without paying man for
work. He carries a box from her house to a cart, but
when he asks for pay, she knocks him unconscious.
Lazarillo (Luna): Pt. II, Ch. IX 127b.

K233.0.2.* Priest escapes without paying man for work. He
said, "God bless you," and disappeared. Lazarillo (Luna):
Pt. II, Ch. IX 128b.

K233.3.1.* Trickster escapes with several pairs of shoes.
He tells several cobblers that a gentleman wants to buy
shoes of a certain size. He asks to take one shoe back
from the various cobblers for the gentleman to try on.
He leaves town. Codicia: Ch. IV 1171b.

K246.1.* Arrest feigned to avoid paying debts at inn. Man
has himself arrested and carried away by pretended
agents of the Inquisition. Buscón: Bk. III, Ch. VI 1139b.

K250. Other deceptive bargains.

K254.3.* Trickster receives double portion of food on pretense
of taking some to other unfortunates. When other beggars
find him eating the double portions they flog him.
Buscón: Bk. III, Ch. II 1132a.

Q458.0.4. Flogging as punishment for imposture.

K258. Stolen property sold to its owner.

K134.3. Trickster grooms master's old mule and
then sells him back without detection at huge profit.

K258.0.1.* Thief robs people on highways and later sells their
own goods back to them. Guzmán: Pt. I, Bk. II, Ch. X   335a.

K258.0.2.* Servants steal household supplies and sell them
to owner. Buscón: Bk. I, Ch. VI 1107a.

K258.3.* Stolen cup sold to owner. Servant steals silver cup,
has it cleaned, and sells it back to distraught owner.
Guzmán: Pt. I, Bk. II, Ch. V 310b.

K258.4.* Maidservant sells stolen household supplies to
owner. Guzmán: Pt. II, Bk. III, Ch. IV 534a.

K282.2.* Trickster sells borrowed jewel to silversmith. Later
he successfully gets back the jewel, claiming that the
silversmith has stolen it from him. Guzmán: Pt. I,
Bk. II, Ch. X 335b.

   K405. Thief successfully claims that stolen goods
   are his own.

K282.3.* Thief sells house tiles to mason. Thief reports to
woman owner that someone has sold objects taken from her
unoccupied house. When mason comes for the tiles, the
owner prevents him from getting them, and forces him to
pay for missing doors which the thief has already sold.
Guzmán: Pt. II, Bk. III, Ch. VI 554a.

   K346.7.* Thief trusted to guard woman's unoccupied
   house.

K282.4.* Trickster sells load of barley which is not his.
Innkeeper's wife pays him in advance, and he absconds.
When the owner of the barley delivers it, the landlady
refuses to pay; but she does when the man threatens her
life. Urdemalas: p. 20a.

K300 - K499. THEFTS AND CHEATS

K300. **Thefts and cheats - general**.

K302.1.1.* Courtesan "wife" runs away with man's goods. She
sends him to newly-rented house to receive goods which
will be delivered. She and accomplices steal man's
possessions from his old house and escape. **Castigo**:
p. 1633b.

> J1786.1.1.* Would-be husband cheated.

K302.1.2.* Courtesan steals slain lover's carriage. Disguises
it and uses different horses, posing as rich lady.
Harpías: Estafa I 28ff.

K302.1.3.* Courtesan dupes egotistical courtier into giving
her expensive gifts. She pretends that her male confederate is a jealous rival. **Urdemalas**: p. 190b.

K302.2.* Woman steals meat from basket carried by dog. The
dog did not bite her because he did not want to put his
filthy mouth on her clean white hands. **Coloquio**: p. 205a.

> B211.1.7. Speaking dog.

K302.3.* Female thief advises enamoured man to hide his
treasure in garden. She and confederates steal the
treasure while owner is away from home. **Garduña**: Bk. I,
1548a.

> K343.0.3.* Female thief advises man to leave home.
> N511.1.8.1.* Gold coins buried in cask; silver,
> in six money bags.

K305.4.* Youth slashes traveler's suitcase and removes
contents. He sells shirts, a watch, and a book.
Rinconete: p. 179b.

K305.5.* Youth steals cleric's purse and silk handkerchief.
Rinconete: p. 181a.

K306. Thieves steal from each other.

K343.6.* Cheat induces dupe to go get jewels reported found, and steals clothes while owner is away.

K306.2. Highjacking. Thief robbed of his booty. Other thieves, posing as officers, frighten chicken thief at night and take the stolen chickens. Guzmán: Pt. II, Bk. I, Ch. III 402a.

K306.3. Man is robbed of gold chain while with prostitute. Casamiento: .p. 196b.

J1510.2.* Sham-rich soldier robbed by sham-rich bride.

K307. Thieves betray each other.

K314.4.* Young man feigns being pursued by armed ruffians and rushes into woman's house.

K307.3.* Thief entrusted with merchant's money absconds with it. Merchant walks ahead of thief and latter disappears with money. Guzmán: Pt. I, Bk. II, Ch. VII 322b.

K307.4.* Thief entrusted with another's stolen goods cheats him. Trickster hides stolen bags inside carcass of dead pig. Put under torture, trickster confesses and loses stolen bags and pig. Guzmán: Pt. II, Bk. III, Ch. VIII 564b.

K420. Thief loses his goods or is detected.

K307.5.* Thieves betray hiding place of other thieves. All but one betrayed thieves are executed. One escapes jail dressed as a woman. Garduña: Bk. III 1594b.

R211.11.* Male thief escapes from prison dressed as a woman.

K307.6.* Thieving soldier steals horse entrusted to him by another soldier. Latter hopes to steal a better horse from supply convoy. On discovering his loss, he reports

that he has lost his horse in battle. Estebanillo:
Bk. II, Ch. IV 1814b.

K346. Thief trusted to guard goods.

K310 - K439. THEFTS

K310. Means of entering house or treasury.

K310.1.* Thieves enter upstairs rooms by means of rope ladder.
Codicia: Ch. VII 1177a.

K311.2.1.* Thieves disguised as statues. Confederates place
"statues" in church where sculptor was to leave real ones.
Thieves take money intended for sculptor. Manzanares:
Ch. XII 79.

K311.9.1.* Thief disguised as rich gentleman. He has four
maidservants who steal for him at night by handing out
costly things through the windows of the houses in which
they work. Periquillo: Discurso VIII 1883b.

K311.12.1.1.* Thief disguised as owner's lackey. Steals
horse and sells it. Thief is apprehended and punished,
and his horse is given to victim. Trapaza: Ch. VIII 1462b.

K420. Thief loses his goods or is detected.

K311.14.1.* Thief disguises as fisherman's helper. He robs
fish from nets and throws them to confederate who hides
them in sand. They later dig up the fish and sell them.
Estebanillo: Bk. I, Ch. V 1764a.

K311.18.* Thieves disguise as lackeys to steal. Enter houses
where night festivals are held and walk out with capes.
They also rob capes at night from pedestrians.
Codicia: Ch. VII 1177a.

K312.1.1.* Thief hidden in trunk is carried into house. Is
apprehended when he tries to come out at night.
Codicia: Ch. VIII 1181b.

K420. Thief loses his goods or is detected.

K312.1.2.* Thief hidden in box is carried into house by
confederate. He throws things out of window to confederate in the street. Night watchman captures confederate.
Codicia: Ch. XII 1192b.

K314.1.* Woman trickster feigns being carried off to unwanted
marriage. She receives sanctuary in rich man's house.
Harpías: Estafa I 33ff.

K314.2.* Woman trickster feigns danger to her life and gains
admittance to rich man's estate. Garduña: Bk. I 1540a.

K314.3.* Woman thief feigns being murdered to obtain entrance
to monastery. She knows that the hermit there stores
money and goods for robber band. Garduña: Bk. III 1574b.

 K1961.1.5.6.* Sham holy man is ally of robber band.

K314.4.* Young man feigns being pursued by armed ruffians and
rushes into woman's house. He plans to rob her to avenge
his master, but he falls in love with her. The woman and
the young lover betray the youth's master to the police.
Garduña: Bk. IV 1596b.

 K307. Thieves betray each other.

K315.0.2.* Thieves dig tunnel under man's bed and steal hams
hidden there. Miser has put hams in a sack and hidden
them in a hole under his bed. Estebanillo: Bk. II,
Ch. III 1805a.

K317.0.1.* Thief copies key by making wax impression. Steals
bread from priest's pantry. He is later detected.
Lazarillo: Tratado II 95b.

 J1144.1.2.* Eater of stolen bread detected.

 K420. Thief loses his goods or is detected.

K317.0.2.* Thief copies keys to trunks by making wax impressions.

While companion arranges with man to transport trunks,
thief makes wax impressions of trunk keys. <u>Guzmán</u>:
Pt. II, Bk. I, Ch. VIII 426b.

K317.1.1.* Thieves enter home with master key. Force owner
to give them keys to money box, and they steal all the
money. <u>Trapaza</u>: Ch. IV 1441a.

K317.2.1.* Entrance gained into wine cellar under pretense
of getting water for mule. Servant draws a pail of wine
and has to give it to mule because mistress is watching.
Mule becomes intoxicated and mistress pays veterinarian
to cure him. The veterinarian splits fees with servant.
<u>Trapaza</u>: Ch. XIII 1496a.

K317.2.2.* Servant fills pail with wine instead of barley
when he goes to feed master's mule. Master arrives and
servant gives the wine to the mule. Tricksters "cure"
mule's illness by spraying cold water on him. Rogues
are arrested and imprisoned. <u>Manzanares</u>: Ch. XV 97.

K317.2.3.* Woman thief gains entrance into sick woman's pantry
when "doctor" (confederate) prescribes poultice of bacon
grease. Tricksters eat their fill. <u>Justina</u>: Bk. II,
Pt. III, Ch. II 836a.

    K1983. Trickster poses as helper and eats woman's
stored provisions.

K317.2.4.* Female thief offers to take gift of food to another
person. She gets pantry key, steals much food, and keeps
it for herself. <u>Justina</u>: Bk. II, Pt, III, Ch. III 843a.

K325.1.* Thief pretends to be wounded and confederate gets
sanctuary for both of them in convent. During the night
they steal 50 chickens and escape. <u>Píndaro</u>: Bk. II,
Ch. XIII 345b.

K330.   Means of hoodwinking guardian or owner.

      K1213.4.* Tricksters terrorize lovers by shouting "fire."

K330.1.1.* Man gulled into stripping off his clothes. He strips and leaves clothes by door when he enters to visit his mistress. Thieves steal clothes and yell "Fire!" Lover flees nude into street. Manzanares: Ch. XI 68ff.

K330.1.2.* Man gulled into taking off wet clothes to dry them. Thieves run away with clothes which contain victim's money. Estebanillo: Bk. I, Ch. IV 1755b.

K330.1.3.* Man robbed of new clothes while trying them on and is left nude. Merchant's confederate uses a fishing line and hook to pull clothes to an upstairs window. Periquillo: Discurso VI 1876a.

K330.2.* Guardian deceived by youths. University-bound youths trick guardian, sell possessions, and escape to distant city. Fregona: p. 152a.

K330.3.* Old would-be lover fleeced by woman and male accomplices. He gives money and gifts to woman. He falls from horse while trying to impress woman with his horsemanship. Urdemalas: p. 41a.

      K1969.5.* Sham horseman.

K331.   Goods stolen while owner sleeps.

      G303.9.7.2.1.* Devil advises youth to surrender to local authorities.

K331.0.1.* Goods stolen while owner sleeps. Servant gives a "squire" lodging for the night. The "nobleman" left during the night with the servant's money and clothing. Master discharges servant , saying that the latter might admit another guest who would rob him (master). Lazarillo (Luna): Ch. I 117a.

K331.0.2.* Snoring betrays sleeping people. Bandits rob
them at an inn. Guadaña: Ch. VI 1702b.

K331.2.2.1.* Foxes cause peasants to become tired and sleep
while food is stolen. They incite peasants to attack a
snake, and when tired peasants are sleeping, the foxes
eat many rabbits in the town. Peregrinación: p. 21.

K331.3.1.* Pebbles substituted for candy while miser sleeps,
and tow is put in wine bottle. Later, when awake, miser
breaks a tooth on the "candy," and the tow in wine bottle
keeps him from getting sufficient wine. Buscón: Bk. I,
Ch. IV 1102b.

K331.3.2.* Servant substitutes worn-out cloak for master's
new one. He escapes by night. Estebanillo: Bk. I,
Ch. I 1731b.

K331.3.3.* Servant substitutes fish for meat stew while cook
is gambling. The trickster serves meat stew to his table.
Cook breaks stew pot over trickster's head. Estebanillo:
Bk. I, Ch. II 1736a.

K333. Theft from blind person.

J1144.1.0.* Theft of wine detected. J1144.1.1.*
Eater of stolen sausage detected. J1144.1.2.* Eater
of stolen bread detected. K1610.1.* Blind deceiver
outwitted by boy guide.

K333.6.* Trickster steals food from blind man. Rips open
seam in food sack, takes out food, and resews sack.
Lazarillo: Tratado I 87a.

K333.7.* Trickster steals blind man's money. Blind man's guide
hides coins in his mouth. Lazarillo: Tratado I 87a.

K333.8.* Theft of money by covering eyes of owner. Under
pretense of applying a poultice to woman's face, female

thief covers the woman's eyes and steals money from her
purse. <u>Justina</u>: Bk. II, Pt. III, Ch. II 837b.

K333.9.* Theft of wine through tobacco pipe. Soldier pretends
to sleep beside a wine barrel at night. He inserts his
pipe stem through the bung and sucks out all the wine he
can hold. <u>Estebanillo</u>: Bk. II, Ch. V 1826b.

K335.0.1. Owner frightened from goods by report of approaching
enemy. Woman has would-be lover hide in large jar when
her "brother" comes to door. She and paramour eat the
food brought by hidden lover and enjoy each other.
<u>Guzmán</u>: Pt. I, Bk. II, Ch. VIII 326b.

K1218.1.5.1.* Importunate lover enticed into large jar.

K335.0.4.3.* Shop owner made to believe that swordsman will
kill him. When he drops to the floor behind counter,
the trickster runs his sword through a box of candy and
escapes. <u>Buscón</u>: Bk. I, Ch. VI 1109a.

K335.0.4.4.* Frightened shepherds abandon cabin to vicious
dog. <u>Peregrinación</u>: p. 28.

J411.11.* "Only one dog to one wolf."

K335.0.9.1.* Woman is frightened into giving up her hens.
Trickster tells her that the Inquisition will come for
her unless he can take some hens to propitiate the Holy
Office. <u>Buscón</u>: Bk. I, Ch. VI 1108a.

K335.0.12.1.* Owner frightened by thief who brings forth
"devil" to tell where stolen money is located. At night
the thief throws a cat with lighted firecrackers on the
victim. <u>Castigo</u>: p. 1635a.

J1785.5. Cat mistaken for devil.

K335.1.6.4.* Man hidden in large money sack frightens robbers.
He sticks his head out and says, "Gentlemen thieves, we

are all here." <u>Diablo</u>: Tranco II 1645a.

    J1399.3.* Gentlemen thieves, we are all here."

K336.3.* House "haunted" by servants to drive mistress away.
Man is engaged to discover what causes nocturnal noises.
When he discovers that they come from rascally servants'
quarters, he is so frightened that he advises owner to
abandon the house. <u>Torres</u>: Trozo III 1952b.

K341.2.2.2.* Beggar shams illness in order to fleece guardian.
Conspires with doctors to share their fees for treatment
of his "sore leg." Guardian will pay for the cure.
<u>Guzmán</u>: Pt. I, Bk. III, Ch. VI 357a.

K341.9.2.* Youth persuades uncle that thieves are downstairs.
While uncle investigates, the youth gets key to cabinet
and steals money. <u>Necio</u>: Ch. II 208.

    J1399.1.1.* "It is risen; it is not here."

K341.12.1.* Trickster falsely announces approaching marriage
to relative of family. Receives many valuable gifts
and escapes with them. <u>Guzmán</u>: Pt. II, Bk. II, Ch. VIII
489a.

K341.13.2.* Thieving sister throws silver serving pieces out
of window and yells "thief." He brothers pursue the
girl's lover who runs by at that moment. Sister has
previously stolen jewels, and thus throws suspicion on
the fleeing "thief." <u>Justina</u>: Bk. III, Ch. I 854a.

    K400. Thief escapes detection.

K341.15. One thief distracts attention of owner while other
steals.

    K365.1.1.* Boy confederate feigns madness and is
knocked down by trickster.

K341.15.2.* Thief and confederate rob merchant. Confederate

takes stolen articles to town crier and has him announce
that they have been found and that owner can call at town
hall for them. Confederate escapes with stolen goods.
Codicia: Ch. VIII 1180a.

K2054.2.* Thief pretends honesty to mulct victim.

K341.15.3.* Thief steals woman's jewels while his female
accomplice is telling her fortune. Urdemalas: p. 796ff.

K341.22.1.* Galley thief performs "magic spell" for enamoured
officers. He promises to procure women for them by magic.
He orders captain to enter sack and majordomo to be tied.
Thief escapes from galley, taking officers' properties.
Codicia:. Chs. IX-X 1182b-1189a.

K711.1.1.* Victim tricked into entering sack.

K713.1. Deception into allowing oneself to be tied.

K1200. Deception into humiliating position.

K341.22.2.* Gypsies steal woman's "enchanted" fortune.
Gullible woman brings jewels and money to basement where
Gypsies will disenchant a hidden fortune for her. They
send owner on errand and escape with the fortune.
Alonso: Pt. II, Ch. III 1285a.

K341.28.1.* Miser lured into digging for treasure in garden.
Trickster shows him a skull in a tree, and an accomplice's
voice - that of a "dead Moorish king" - reports that
a treasure is hidden throughout the garden.
Urdemalas: p. 54b.

K341.28.2.* Miser enticed into liberal giving when he fails
to find "hidden" treasure. Tricksters tell miser that
his successors will find the treasure in the garden.
Urdemalas: p. 58a.

K343. Thief advises owner to go away; meantime steals the goods.

K362.0.2.* Trickster presents false "official papers" to owner of chickens.

K343.0.2.* Woman thief asks lover to take her on trip. Robs his house when he goes to take leave of a relative. Harpías: Estafa I 67ff.

K343.0.3.* Female thief advises man to leave home. He shoots a dummy at night thinking it is a man whom he has killed. Later, thieves steal the man's goods. Garduña: Bk. I, 1546b-1548a.

K2152.3.* Dummy set up in front of dupe's window at night.

K343.6.* Cheat induces dupe to go get jewels reported found, and steals clothes while owner is away. Thief's friends rob him during the night. Guzmán (Luján): Pt. II, Bk. I, Ch. I 582a.

K306. Thieves steal from each other.

K344.4.* Servant makes master think that mice have spoiled bread. Master gives him the spoiled pieces to eat. Lazarillo: Tratado II 93b.

K345.5.* Thief steals clothes and mule of priest who has come to comfort dying man. Urdemalas: p. 46.

K346. Thief trusted to guard goods.

K307.6.* Thieving soldier steals horse entrusted to him by another soldier.

K346.2.1.* Shepherds slaughter sheep and tell master that wolf has done it. Shepherds punish their dogs for being "negligent." Coloquio: p. 207b.

K346.7* Thief trusted to guard woman's unoccupied house.

Steals all the doors and hardware and sells them. He sells
tiles to a mason; but when the latter comes for them, the
owner refuses them and forces the mason to pay for the
stolen doors. Guzmán: Pt.II, Bk. III, Ch. VI 554a.

   K282.3.* Thief sells house tiles to mason.

K347. Cozening. Trickster's claim of relationship causes
owner to relax vigilance. Goods stolen. Guzmán: Pt. II,
Bk. I, Ch. VIII 427a.

K347.1.2.* Prostitute claims to be pregnant by man's dead
brother. The man gives her sanctuary until child is born.
Prostitute and a confederate rob the man and flee.
Trapaza: Ch. VII 1458a.

K347.2.* Woman gets lover to replace "lost" ring (jewel).
Maid pretends to search for jewel (diamond ring) which
her mistress "lost" in lover's house. The lover gives
her a jewel (ring) to replace the lost one. Guzmán:
Pt. I, Bk. II, Ch. VIII 327b; Guzmán (Luján): Pt. II,
Bk. I, Ch. VI 602b; and Harpías: Estafa I 40ff.

   T455.1.4.* Woman "loses" a ring when she fakes a
   fall in front of man's house.

K347.3.* Woman cozens lover into buying her some new dresses.
Because of her mother's antagonism, she is unable to
return home to get her clothes, she states.
Harpías: Estafa I 49.

K347.4.* Mistress cozens lover into giving her clothes,
jewels, and money. She needs these things in order to
act in a play. She departs secretly with her gifts.
Harpías: Estafa II 99ff.

K347.5.* Woman tricks priest into advancing money on her
"jewel" box. She makes priest think that she is rich

and will endow chapel. She escapes, leaving priest with box of rocks. Harpías: Estafa III 107-137.

K455.9. Worthless chests offered to obtain credit. K476.2.1.1.* Box of supposed jewels given to help build church. K1954.7.1.* Sham rich woman tricks priest.

K347.6.* Woman cozens lover into paying for her purchases at market. Guzmán: Pt. I, Bk. II, Ch. VIII 328a.

K347.7.* Soldier claims to be run-away husband sought by guardian of convent. He accepts gifts of money and clothes from his "brother-in-law" the guardian, and escapes with loot at night. Píndaro: Bk. I, Ch. V 284a.

K347.8.* Prostitute sells goods entrusted to her and escapes. Soldier leaves all his clothes with woman while he is away on duty. Woman sells clothes and escapes. Estebanillo: Bk. II, Ch. VII 1847a.

K351.0.1.* Actor thief escapes with rich costume he is wearing. Pretends that he is going to change costume. Estebanillo: Bk. I, Ch. II 1741b.

K351.1.1.* Trickster persuades nun to let him sell (raffle off) her handiwork. He escapes with it. Buscón: Bk. III, Ch. IX 1151b.

K351.4.* Woman trickster becomes agent for wool carders. She dampens some of the spun wool, keeps some of it, and returns the correct weight to the carders. Justina: Bk. III, Ch. II 857a.

K400. Thief escapes detection.

K352.1.* Fake doctor steals purse of dying man. He feigns grief, falls upon dying man's pillow, and takes purse from beneath it. Estebanillo: Bk. I, Ch. III 1747a.

K2000. Hypocrites.

K359.2.2.* Thief persuades soldier to say that he (soldier) is the enseign-designee of package which youth is delivering. The package contains handkerchiefs, and the soldier refuses to give thief his part. <u>Buscón</u>: Bk. III, Ch. I 1128a.

K359.3.1.* Mother dupes duaghter's lover into renting room from her. She is the "aunt" from whom girl has escaped. Lover has girl escape to another house. <u>Harpías</u>: Estafa I 49-66.

K359.6.* Thieving servant removes valuables from bag between owner's feet. Trickster pretends to take wine from pail which he has placed on floor. <u>Guzmán</u>: Pt. II, Bk. III, Ch. VIII 564a.

K359.7.* False hermit obtains money to get a soul out of purgatory. The "soul" is a young woman who needs money to pay off debts before eloping with the "hermit." <u>Urdemalas</u>: p. 144a.

    K1961.1.5.7.* Sham ascetic obtains money to get a soul out of purgatory.

K360. <u>Other means of theft</u>.

K361.0.1.* Servant ordered to buy wine keeps the money and sells wine jug. He tells his master that he bought wine, but that he broke the jug, spilling all the wine. <u>Guzmán</u>: Pt. II, Bk. III, Ch. IV 534b.

K361.7.* Servant steals half of master's gifts to mistress. He gives them to his own beloved. He is apprehended and dismissed. <u>Trapaza</u>: Ch. V 1445b.

    K424.1.* Thief (servant) condemned when owner discovers stolen dress materials.

K361.8.* Shepherd entrusted to care for master's sheep steals

many. During the winter 260 of master's sheep "disappear",
killed by wild animals or by cold weather, but none of the
shepherd's sheep are missing. Master: "If the sheep could
talk, they would tell what a big thief you are."
<u>Alonso</u>: Pt. II, Ch. XIII 1334a.

K362.0.2.* Trickster presents false "official papers" to
owner of chickens. While owner is on errand to deliver
papers to designated person, thief steals his hens.
<u>Guzmán</u>: Pt. II, Bk. I, Ch. III 401b.

> K343. Thief advises owner to go away; meantime
> steals the goods.

K362.1.1.* Money for the patent fee. Old students demand and
get "entrance" money from new students. <u>Buscón</u>: Bk. I,
Ch. V 1103b.

K362.7. Theft by forgery: signature used to obtain money.
Woman dupes man into entrusting his money and valuables
with her by producing a forged letter from man's friend.
<u>Marcos</u>: Bk. III, Descanso VIII 1050b.

> K455.8. Credit based on forgery. K1667.1.3.* Man
> retrieves stolen money and valuables.

K362.7.1.* Courtesan forges business man's name to letter
and receives money from stingy lover. <u>Harpías</u>:
Estafa II 83-86.

K362.7.2.* Man writes "postage-due" letters to important
people, forging well-known names. He carries the letters
and collects the postage fees. <u>Buscón</u>: Bk. III,
Ch. I 1128a.

K362.12.* Female thief gets money from lover to bury a "dead"
friend. She sends a false letter to her gullible lover,
stating that a friend has been stabbed to death.
<u>Flora</u>: p. 394.

K365.1.1.* Boy confederate feigns madness and is knocked down
by trickster. Latter robs people who rush to stricken boy.
Guadaña: Ch. I 1683b.

> K341.15. One thief distracts attention of owner
> while other steals.

K365.2.1.* Woman thief pays innkeeper's wife for keeping
donkey's saddle overnight. Thief steals a donkey from
the inn to replace hers which has run away. Justina:
Bk. II, Pt. II, Ch. IV 809b.

K365.2.2.* Thieving guests rob silver pieces from viceroy
while visiting his majordomo. Viceroy dismisses servant
because of the friends' actions. Estebanillo: Bk. I,
Ch. III 1749b.

K366.9.* Self-returning sheep. A sheep is sold to a man,
but returns to seller. It is trained to run away with
seller in pursuit whenever it is sold. Estebanillo:
Bk. I, Ch. II 1734a.

K376.* Officer condones chain gang's theft of pigs. The
gang's commander shares the stolen pigs with the thieves.
Guzmán: Pt. II, Bk. III, Ch. VIII 563b.

K376.1.* Hungry officer continues search for slaughtered hog
after finding it in soldier's trunk. He quietly asks
soldier to send him his share. Marcos: Bk. I,
Descanso XVIII 983b.

K400. Thief escapes detection.

> K341.13.2.* Thieving sister throws   silver
> serving pieces out of window and yells "thief."
> K351.4.* Woman trickster becomes an agent for
> wool carders.

K401.0.2.* Master exposes servant's theft of eggs. It is to prevent detection of food they both have stolen.
Guzmán: Pt. I, Bk. II, Ch. VI 318b.

    K1693.1.* Thief's stolen eggs are broken in his breeches.

K401.0.3.* Thief drinks wine then adds water to refill container. Owner of wine blames wine merchant for adulterating the wine. Necio: Ch. II 199.

K401.0.4.* Theft of food blamed on mice. Servant eats food in pantry and blames the loss on mice. Master gets a cat, but servant prevents cat from entering pantry.
Necio: Ch. II 204.

K401.2.3.1.* Transfer of stolen silver dish to innocent man's room brings condemnation. Guzmán: Pt. II, Bk. III, Ch. IX 573b.

K401.5.1.* Thieves successfully accuse owner of having stolen property they covet. Owner of stolen sword retrieves it and beats up one thief, but other thief makes officers think that the owner has robbed him. He gets money.
Píndaro: Bk. I, Ch. II 278b.

K405. Thief successfully claims that stolen goods are his own.

    K282.2.* Trickster sells borrowed jewel to silversmith.

K405.3.1.* Female thief successfully claims that stolen donkey is her own. The theft was only a "joke" which her servant had taken seriously. Her accuser and servant apologize.
Justina: Bk. II, Pt. II, Ch. IV 815b.

K405.4.* Thief successfully claims that money bags contain his deposits. He has banker's office boy slip notices of ownership and some special coins in each bag.
Guzmán: Pt. II, Bk. II, Ch. VI 467b.

K409.* Stolen horse successfully sold. One thief sells horse in order to pay "debt" to his confederate. Owner of horse later recovers it, but thieves escape. Coloquio: p. 217b.

K417.2.* Thief swallows stolen pearls to avoid detection. Police give him a purgative and recover jewels. Codicia: Ch. XI 1190b.

    K420. Thief loses his goods or is detected.

    K432.3.* Clever woman has police give jewel thief a purgative.

K419.2.1.* Thief escapes detection by turning corner and sitting on stolen box of raisins. He pretends that fleeing thief has stepped on his foot, and he sends officers running after thief. Buscón: Bk. I, Ch. VI 1108b.

K419.2.2.* Thief avoids detection by pretending to search for dropped coins. He stoops over and sneaks out of butcher shop with stolen meat. Estebanillo: Bk. I, Ch. V 1761b.

K420. Thief loses his goods or is detected.

    J1144.1.2.* Eater of stolen bread detected. J1144.1.2.1.* Stolen bread found beneath culprit's bed. J1144.1.3.* Eaters of sugar lumps detected. J1391.9.* Tablecloth to cure stomach-ache. K307.4.* Thief entrusted with another's stolen goods cheats him. K311.12.1.1.* Thief disguised as owner's lackey. K312.1.1.* Thief hidden in trunk is carried into house. K312.1.2.* Thief hidden in box is carried into house by confederate. K317.0.1.* Thief copies key by making wax impression. K417.2.* Thief swallows stolen pearls to avoid detection.

K424.1.* Thief (servant) condemned when owner discovers
stolen dress materials. Servant had given half of the
materials to his mistress instead of giving all of them
to master's mistress. <u>Trapaza</u>: Ch. V 1445b.

> K361.7.* Servant steals half of master's gifts
> to mistress.

K424.2.* Thief condemned when witnesses of theft find stolen
trunks. An accomplice is too frightened to run away with
other thieves and is captured. <u>Estebanillo</u>: Bk. I,
Ch. III 1750b.

> K512.0.2.1.* Executioner persuaded to let condemned
> man go because he has formerly served the duke.

K426.1.* Apparently dead virgin revives when thief tries to
strip off her burial clothes. She scratches out his eyes.
<u>Alonso</u>: Pt. II, Ch. IV 1291a.

> Q212.2.1.* Dead virgin punishes grave robber.

K427.1.1.* Cats betray theft. Catch mice in woman's sleeves
where food is hidden. <u>Teresa</u>: Ch. VII 1368a.

K432.3.* Clever woman has police give jewel thief a purgative.
Later he excretes pearls which he has swallowed.
<u>Codicia</u>: Ch. XI 1190b.

> K417.2.* Thief swallows stolen pearls to avoid
> detection. K420. Thief loses his goods or is
> detected.

K434.1.1.* Thief sneezes, thus betraying hiding place under
bed. He is captured. <u>Codicia</u>: Ch. VIII 1180b.

K439.1.1.* Betrayal through attempt to sell stolen goods to
owner. Thieves are jailed and punished. <u>Buscón</u>:
Bk. III, Ch. III. 1133b.

K439.2.1.* Thief claims that stolen mule is his own, but

owner detects fraud and recovers mule. <u>Marcos</u>: Bk. I,
Descanso XVI 978a.

K439.12.* Nocturnal thief mistakes passer-by for confederate
and gives him bundle of stolen goods. Recipient returns
goods to owner's house. <u>Píndaro</u>: Bk. II, Ch. IX 338a.

K440. <u>Other cheats</u>.

K443. Money acquired by blackmail.

> K1875. Deception by sham blood. K2121.3.* Man
> slandered as having deflowered innocent girl.
>
> K2150. Innocent made to appear guilty.

K443.1.1.* Woman exacts money from thief disguised as hermit.
She says that her officer-lover will come unless "hermit"
pays. <u>Justina</u>: Bk. II, Pt. II, Ch. II 799a.

> K2285. Villain disguised as ascetic or nun.

K443.14.* Marriage broker blackmails innocent young man.
Latter gives broker a ring to stop his efforts to marry
him to an ugly "widow." <u>Manzanares</u>: Ch. XVI 102ff.

K443.15.* Rogue extorts money from Moor after "finding"
incriminating evidence in his store. Rogue has hidden
in the store a box containing a picture of a Moor holding
the Koran. <u>Píndaro</u>: Bk. I, Ch. XXII 319b.

K444.4.* Diamond ring as reward for story of greatest personal
danger. Two men compete for prize. First had been with
woman while her husband slept near-by; second thought
that he was sleeping with woman's husband while the wife
was with lover, but he discovered next day that he had
slept chastely with woman's sister. Donor of ring:
"Take the ring to the girl; she ran the greatest danger."
<u>Guzmán</u>: Pt. II, Bk. I. Ch. IV 408a.

> K231.2.3.* Contestants in story-telling of personal
> danger are denied reward.

K455.1.1.* Supper won by flattery. Trickster flatters dupe as great Latin scholar. <u>Marcos</u>: Bk. I, Descanso, IX 957b.

J2337.1.* Trickster flatters dupe as great Latin scholar. J2337.1.1.* Trickster flatters ugly wife of innkeeper and gets good food and lodging.

K455.1.2.* Supper won by posing as relative of dupe. Latter pays for supper of invited and uninvited guests. <u>Buscón</u>: Bk. I. Ch. IV 110la.

K455.4.0.1.* Money has been left with the innkeeper. Woman alleges that her servant deposited money with innkeeper when her party entered restaurant. Innkeeper denies the allegation, and woman has to pay for meal. <u>Guzmán</u>: Pt. I, Bk. III, Ch. VII 360a.

K200. Deception in payment of debt.

K455.4.0.2.* Falsehood alleges that she has paid debt for food. She asks Truth to verify, but latter remains silent in order not to pay for debts of others. <u>Guzmán</u>: Pt. I, Bk. III, Ch. VII 360b.

Z121.1.1.* Truth is dumb.

K455.4.2.* Tricksters buy chickens, telling farmer that priest will pay. Tricksters tell priest that farmer has come for confession. Thieves escape, and a third person pays the farmer. <u>Codicia</u>: Ch. VII 1178b.

K455.8. Credit based on forgery.

K362.7. Theft by forgery.

K455.8.1.1.* Credit established by false documents. Father-in-law draws up false documents to establish credit of son-in-law. Latter uses these documents to gain release from jail and from creditors. <u>Guzmán</u>: Pt. II, Bk. III, Ch. II 515a.

K455.8.1.2.* Trickster receives special consideration at inn
with false bill of exchange. Confederates leave a worthless bill of exchange for 5,000 crowns for trickster.
Buscón: Bk. III, Ch. V 1137a.

    K1954. Sham rich man.

K455.8.2.1.* Sham dying man writes bogus will leaving "fortune"
to scornful woman. Latter rushes over to his bedside.
Necio: Ch. IV 281.

    K1352. Death feigned to woo maiden.

K455.9. Worthless chests offered to obtain credit. Youth
dupes his uncle with chests filled with pebbles. Uncle
offers youth a distant female relative in marriage.
Guzmán: Pt. II, Bk. II, Ch. VIII 485b.

K455.9.1.* Worthless chest offered to obtain credit. Woman
tricks priest into advancing money on her "jewel" box.
She escapes, leaving priest with rocks. Harpías:
Estafa III 107-137.

    K347.5.* Woman tricks priest into advancing money
    on her "jewel" box. K476.2.1.1.* Box of supposed
    jewels given to help build church. K1954.7.1.* Sham
    rich woman tricks priest.

K455.9.2.* Trickster leaves two chests filled with pebbles
as payment for summer's lodging at inn. Guzmán: Pt. II,
Bk. II, Ch. VIII 489b.

K475.4.* Lineage descended from royal house. Boast is true:
Man's ancestors were servants and "descended" in a basket
from palace wall as they fled. Justina: Bk. I, Ch. II
730b.

    J1114.3.*·Servant deceives master with polite phrase,
    K2319.1.1.* Family had descended from the royal
    house of Aragon.

K476.1.3.* Trickster fleeces gullible man out of costly
rosary. Offers worthless rosary full of special
indulgences. Urdemalas: p. 145b.

K476.2.1.1.* Box of supposed jewels given to help build church.
Woman then borrows an "advance" sum of money from priest.
Harpías: Estafa III 107-137.

    K347.5.* Woman tricks priest into advancing money
on her "jewel" box. K1954.7.1.* Sham rich woman
tricks priest into advancing money on her "jewel" box.

K476.2.1.2.* Money advanced on ring. Woman tricks man into
giving her money for a ring which a jeweler will deliver
later. Guadaña: Ch. VII 1704b.

K476.2.2.* Reward for "philosopher's stone" which makes gold.
Trickster gets much money from rich man and later robs
him of money and jewels. Garduña: Bk. II 1569a.

    K1966.2. Alchemist secures payment for his "secret."

K476.4.2.* Thief substitutes silver-plated candlesticks for
solid silver ones. Confederate sells silver ones and
shares profits with thief. Guzmán: Pt. II, Bk. II,
Ch. IV 458b.

K476.4.3.* Man substitutes gilded chain for solid gold chain.
Receives a large sum of money from a relative. Guzmán:
Pt. II, Bk. II, Ch. VIII 487b.

K476.4.4.* Woman substitutes gilded Agnus Dei for man's golden
crucifix. She then sells the man her purse in order to
keep the Agnus Dei from tarnishing. Justina: Bk. II
Pt. II, Ch. II 792ff.

K477.2.1.* Thieves want to speak privately to intended victims.
Approach victims and rob at dagger point. Codicia: Ch. VII
1177a.

K477.2.2.* Tricksters awaken newly-married druggist by knocking on door at night. They hand him a coin and ask if
it is false. Guadaña: Ch. XII 1717b.

K482. Money received to bury sham-dead person. When trick
is discovered, collector runs off with money. Guzmán
(Luján): Pt. II, Bk. II, Ch. III 621a.

K1860. Deception by feigned death (sleep).

K495.1.* Woman trickster shams sickness in order to get
costly gifts from duped gallant. She "faints" when
suitor's horse rears, and pretends to have a high fever
the next day. Urdemalas: p. 205b (Page is erroneously
numbered 105b.)

K500 - K699. ESCAPE BY DECEPTION

K510. Death order evaded.

K512.0.2.1.* Executioner persuaded to let condemned man go
because he has formerly served the duke. Estebanillo:
Bk. I, Ch. III 1750b.

K424.2.* Thief condemned when witnesses of theft
find stolen trunks.

K515.7.* Thief escapes by hiding among beehives. Pursurers
arouse bees and abandon search. Marcos: Bk. III,
Descanso XV 1067a.

K515.8.* Thieves escape by hiding in outdoor ovens. They
nearly die from the sun's heat. Píndaro: Bk. II,
Ch. XII 344a.

K520. Death escaped through disguise, shamming, or substitution.

K521.2.1. Disguise by shaving off beard so as to escape.
Urdemalas: p. 6a.

K1821.11.* Disguise by cutting off beard.

K521.4.1.1. Girl escapes in male disguise. <u>Marcos</u>: Bk. III,
Descanso XXIII 1081b.

K1236. Disguise as man to escape importunate lover.

K1837. Disguise of woman in man's clothes.

K522.0.2.* Death feigned to escape police. When the latter
enter culprit's room, he is being given last rites by a
"priest" while other companions pray. <u>Buscón</u>: Bk. I,
Ch. VI 1110a.

K522.1. Escape by shamming death. Imprisoned woman escapes
from jailer at a festival when her priest paramour stages
a fight with gypsies. <u>Lazarillo</u> (Luna): Pt. II, Ch. XI
132a.

K531.1.* Ship escapes powerful enemy fleet by flying
enemy's flags. <u>Estebanillo</u>: Bk. II, Ch. VII 1846a.

K540. <u>Escape by overawing captor</u>.

K540.1.* Female rogue's beauty overcomes captor. She promises
him a rendez-vous, but gives false address. <u>Hija</u>: p. 904a.

K547.15.* Trickster makes officer believe that vicious devil
is pursuing him. Frightened officer frees man and flees.
<u>Marcos</u>: Bk. II, Descanso IV 1006b.

K550. <u>Escape by false plea</u>.

K567.0.1.* Escape by pretending to take stolen cloak to
dress-maker for alterations. Thief gulls master of house
who sees him with stolen cloak. <u>Guzmán</u>: Pt. II, Bk. II,
Ch. IV 458a.

K572.1.* Escape from night gangs by clever remark. Youth
does not know answer to gangs' challenge, "Who lives?"
He saves himself twice by clever remarks. <u>Alonso</u>:
Pt. II, Ch. I 1276a.

K579.3.2.* Man escapes from robbers by telling them that a

rich merchant will soon arrive. <u>Marcos</u>: Bk. I,
Descanso XX 987b.

K600. <u>Murderer or captor otherwise beguiled.</u>

K601.3.* Prisoner escapes by posing as a relative of jailer's
wife. He has previously bribed jailer. <u>Buscón</u>: Bk. III,
Ch. IV 1136b.

K602. Escape by assuming an equivocal name. Man says that
he is a "grandee" of Spain. His name is Juan Grande.
<u>Guadaña</u>: Ch. XII 1718b.

> J1181.4.* Man escapes arrest by saying he is a
> "grandee" of Spain. K1951.5.1.* Tailor says that
> he is a "grandee" of Spain.

K620. <u>Escape by deceiving the guard.</u>

> K1821.11.* Disguise by cutting off beard.

K630. <u>Escape by disarming (making pursuit difficult).</u>

K631.1.1.* Student seizes bully's sword and wounds him with
it. Bully flees and reports a fight with 30 ruffians.
Student is admitted into the brotherhood of bullies.
<u>Marcos</u>: Bk. II, Descanso II 1004a.

K640. <u>Escape by help of confederate.</u>

K643.1.* Confederate tells bailiff that "cripple" will pay
to be carried home. Greedy bailiff carries to his
("cripple's") home the fugitive for whom he is searching.
<u>Marcos</u>: Bk. II, Descanso V 1008b.

K649.2.1.* Captain pretends to punish soldier who has
stolen for him. He strikes soldier repeatedly with soft-
soled shoe. Soldier is not injured. <u>Guzmán</u>: Pt. I,
Bk. II, Ch. X 335a.

K650. <u>Other means of escape.</u>

K673.* Entrapped lover sets fire to house and escapes from basement prison in bucket drawn up from well. Servants think he is the devil. <u>Marcos</u>: Bk. II, Descanso III 1005b.

> J1786. Man thought to be devil or ghost.

K675. Sleeping potion given to man who is to pass the night with a girl. While he sleeps, the girl and a confederate rob him. <u>Garduña</u>: Bk. III 1593a.

> K1961.1.5.6.* Sham holy man is ally of robber band.

K700 - K799. CAPTURE BY DECEPTION

K710. <u>Victim enticed into voluntary captivity or helplessness</u>.

K711.1.1.* Victim tricked into entering sack. Galley prisoner promises officer to procure a woman for him. <u>Codicia</u>: Chs. IX - X 1182b-1189a.

> K341.22.1.* Galley thief performs "magic spell" for enamoured officers. K1200. Deception into humiliating position.

K713.1. Deception into allowing oneself to be tied. Galley prisoner tricks officer into allowing himself to be tied. Prisoner promises to get a woman for him. Prisoner escapes from galley ship. <u>Codicia</u>: Chs. IX - X 1182b - 1189a.

> K341.22.1.* Galley thief performs "magic spell" for enamoured officers. K1200. Deception into humiliating position.

K729.* Beggar lured to officer's house by promise of a shirt. Instead, the beggar receives a flogging for being an imposter. <u>Guzmán</u>: Pt. I, Bk. III, Ch. V 354a.

> Q458.0.4. Flogging as punishment for imposture.

K730. <u>Victim trapped</u>.

K730.6.* Horses walk into wolf traps at night. Master and
servant are unable to release horses until trapper comes
next day. One horse dies. <u>Torres</u>: Trozo IV 1960a.

K732.1.* Thief smoked out of chimney. He fails to get
sausages. <u>Alonso</u>: Pt. I, Ch. II 1206b.

K735.1.1.* Wolf falls into covered pit and breaks legs while
chasing lamb. Latter detours around pit because of
dead snake on top. <u>Marcos</u>: Bk. III, Descanso XV 1067b.

K755.1.1.* Capture by fraudulently giving signal of friend's
return. Officers gain entrance to home of falsely-
accused man by using the name of man's friend.
<u>Necio</u>: Ch. VIII 330.

K756.4.* Hunters use songbirds in order to kill wild animals.
When the latter stop to listen to bird songs, hunters
shoot animals. <u>Periquillo</u>: Discurso XIII 1904b.

K765.* Capture by decoys on road or path. Thieves place a
purse, watch, or suitcase on road. When travelers stop
to pick them up, thieves capture and rob them.
<u>Codicia</u>: Ch. VII 1176b.

K770. <u>Other deceptive captures</u>.

K772.0.1.* Girl induced into dancing: captured by students
who make others think that it is part of an act.
<u>Justina</u>: Bk. II, Pt. I, Ch. I 764a.

K778.3.1.* Naked lover captured in courtesan's house. Is
hidden in chest, but shirt cuff on floor betrays his
presence when police raid house. <u>Guzmán</u>: Pt. I, Bk. II,
Ch. VIII 329a.

      K1210. Humiliated or baffled lovers.

K778.3.2.* Capture by luring to women's room, which closes
around man. Latter has to fight the corpse of a man

whom he killed without allowing him to confess.

Píndaro: Bk. I, Ch. XVII 311b.

> Q223.4.2.* Revenant punishes dueler for letting
> him die without confessing.

K778.4. Attack made on groom after he has been invited to
female apartments to have meal with bride.

Lazarillo (Luna): Pt. II, Ch. XVI 145a.

> J1510.1.* False inheritor robbed of money by
> prospective bride.

K778.6.* Veiled women lure man to a secluded spot and flog
him. One was the woman whose diamonds the man had
stolen earlier. Necio: Ch. III 229.

> K1581.6.1.* Man employs trickster to steal
> diamonds given to mistress.

K800 - K999. KILLING OR MAIMING BY DECEPTION

K810. Fatal deception into trickster's power.

K812.1.2.* Men blow up giants' cave with gunpowder. Destroy
huge idol guarding cave. Marcos: Bk. III, Descanso XXI
1077a.

> G512.3.3.1.* Gunpowder as fuel for burning
> giants' guards.

K824.2.* Sham doctor kills feverish man. Accepts the man's
bribe and gives him cold water to drink, which kills him.

Estebanillo: Bk. I, Ch. III 1746b.

K870. Fatal deception by narcotic (intoxication).

K872. Judith and Holofernes: girl from enemy camp chosen to
sleep with intoxicated general kills him in bed.

Alonso: Pt. II, Ch. IX 1317b.

K910. Murder by strategy.

K929.8.1.* Lover slain while eloping with the other man's
fiancée. Fiancé hides near girl's house and kills lover
in the street. <u>Garduña</u>: Bk. I 1542b.

> T92.10. Rival in love killed.

K940. <u>Deception into killing own family or animals</u>.

K940.2.1.* Man is betrayed by servant girl's false report
into killing his wife and faithful servant. Latter has a
letter in his pocket warning the husband about the girl's
desire for revenge on her mistress, but the letter is
found too late. <u>Píndaro</u>: Bk. II, Ch. XXVII 371b.

> K1000 - K1199. DECEPTION INTO SELF-INJURY

K1010. <u>Deception through false doctoring</u>.

K1010.2.* Remedy for mosquitoes. Trickster puts a bundle of
herbs soaked in vinegar at head of victim's bed. More
mosquitoes than ever are attracted. <u>Guzmán</u>: Pt. I,
Bk. III, Ch. VII 364a.

> J2102.1.1.* Sleeping with a bundle of herbs soaked
> in vinegar to get rid of mosquitoes.

K1013. False beauty doctor. Woman trickster gives man salve
to make his beard grow. His face gets covered with sores
and his mistress leaves him. <u>Teresa</u>: Ch. XI 1382a.

K1013.5. False hair restorer injures patient. Trickster
puts turpentine in woman's hair dye. Hair sticks
together and has to be pulled out. <u>Trapaza</u>: Ch. XIII
1495b.

K1020. <u>Deception into disastrous attempt to procure food</u>.

K1022.1.2.* Mouse overeats in bird's cage. Cannot escape.
<u>Marcos</u>: Bk. III, Descanso XI 1057a.

> J134.2.* Mouse traps himself in bird's cage by
> overeating.

K1034.1.* Soldier persuades Jew to descend into deep well for wine. Soldier pulls up ladder, leaving the Jew in the icy well overnight. Victim agrees to pay much money for his freedom. Estebanillo: Bk. II, Ch. I 1789a.

K1040. Dupe otherwise persuaded to voluntary self-injury.

K1043.3.* Child induced to listen to noise inside stone statue. His master shoves child's head against statue to teach him to distrust everyone. Lazarillo: Tratado I 8
    J18.1.* Wisdom acquired from beating.

K1043.4.* Blind man induced to jump into stone pillar. Vengeful guide tells him that he must jump a puddle of water. Lazarillo: Tratado I 90b.

K1044.2.* Dupe sent back to inn to get "honey buns" which woman had left under bed. The woman had left without paying for lodging, and innkeeper's wife makes dupe pay. In a struggle with innkeeper's wife, dupe spills the "honey buns" (chamber pot of excrement) on himself. Justina: Bk. II, Pt. II, Ch. IV 821a.
    J861.1.1.* Dupe is consoled when woman trickster shows him a real pot of honey.

K1044.3.* Dupes induced to eat fritters filled with tow. They get lent stuck between teeth. Justina: Bk. IV, Ch. V 883a.

K1066.1.* Dupe induced to wear incriminating cape. He is severely beaten by servants of man whose cape he is wearing. Buscón: Bk. III, Ch. VII 1144a.

K1067.* Dupe induced to fight and is doubly punished: by other boy and by parents. Torres: Trozo I 1932a.

K1080. Persons duped into injuring each other.

K1081.4.* Blind men duped by devil into fighting. They
have mocked him with their verses. Diablo: Tranco VI
1659b.

N388.1.* Blind poets in confusion knock each other
off platform. Q288. Punishment for mockery.

K1084.2.1.* Trickster brings enmity among three of his enemies.
He tricks a blind man into hawking off a work attributed
to a poet and which maligns a renegrade. The three men
fight each other. Urdemalas: pp. 86a - 91a; 104b - 106a.

K1084.3.1.* Trickster attempts to promote fight between a
fencing master and a constable. Trickster posts a false
notice attributed to the fencing master, defying a
decree of the constable. Urdemalas: p. 164a.

K1086.1.* Women incite men to fight over them. Police
intervene, but are begrimed and beaten by the fighters.
Lazarillo (Luna): Pt. II, Ch. XIV 138a.

K1110. Deceptions into self-injury - miscellaneous.

K1132.1.* New student receives blows at night from older
students who pretend they are being punished, also.
When the new student hides under his bed, another boy
defecates in it, and the new student is covered with
filth when he returns to bed. Buscón: Bk. I, Ch. V 1105a.

K1200 - K1299. DECEPTION INTO HUMILIATING POSITION

K1200. Deception into humiliating position.

K341.22.1.* Galley thief performs magic spell for
enamoured officers. K711.1.1.* Victim tricked into
entering sack. K713.1 Deception into allowing
oneself to be tied.

K1210. Humiliated or baffled lovers.

K335.0.1. Owner frightened from goods by report of

approaching enemy. K778.3.1.* Naked lover captured
in courtesan's house. T320. Escape from undesired
lover.

K1211.2.* Lover drugged, diapered, and suspended in basket
before rich man's house. The rich man finds the "baby"
the next morning. Harpías: Estafa IV 176-178.

K1212.1.* Lover left hiding behind curtains all night while
woman's mother and servants stay in girl's room. The
intruders had been frightened by a storm. The lover
becomes sick from the cold. Píndaro: Bk. II, Ch. IV 329a.

K1213. Terrorizing the paramour (importunate lover).

K2122.* Man falsely accused of rape.

K1213.2.1.* Prostitute's bullies frighten lover. They pretend
to be angry with the woman and lover. The latter wounds
one bully and escapes. Guzmán (Luján): Pt. II, Bk. III,
Ch. III 661a.

K1213.3.* Prostitute terrorizes two lovers - one at a time -
by having "dead" squire's ghost appear. Lovers run away.
Teresa: Ch. XVIII 1415a.

K1833. Disguise as ghost.

K1213.4.* Tricksters terrorize lovers by shouting "fire."
Lovers run naked from the house. Manzanares: Ch. XI
68 - 75.

K330.1. Man gulled into giving up his clothes.

K1213.5.* Adulteress contrives with swordsmen to attack her
unarmed lover. Latter escapes into adjoining room and
drops through a hole into room below. Píndaro: Bk. II,
Ch. V 331b.

R213.3.* Trapped man escapes from woman's apartment by dropping through hole in the floor.

K1214.1.2.* Importunate lover is tricked into paying for
woman's trip. She needs to go to the city to seek
justice against an alleged seducer. She deserts lover.
Lazarillo (Luna): Pt. II, Ch. I 116b.

T70. The scorned lover.

K1218.1.3. The entrapped suitor: tricked into room where he
is left to himself. Alonso: Pt. II, Ch. VIII 1312a.

K1218.1.3.3.* Importunate lovers tricked by prostitutes.
Men are lured into bed, and officers raid rooms, exacting
fines (bribes) from entrapped lovers. Coloquio: p. 214b.

K1218.1.3.4.* The entrapped suitor: tricked into room where
his dagger is stolen. Woman locks him in an adjacent
room. Hija: p. 894b.

K1218.1.3.5.* Importunate lover falls through trap door into
pit. Woman's squire, disguised as ghost, frightens
lover. Teresa: Ch. XVIII 1419b.

K1218.1.5.1.* Importunate lover enticed into large jar.
Courtesan tells man that her angry brother is at the door.
She and the "brother" eat the food brought by importunate
lover and spend the night together. Guzmán: Pt. I,
Bk. II, Ch. VIII 326b.

K335.0.1. Owner frightened from goods by report
of approaching enemy.

K1218.2. Suitor locked in pigsty. Woman tricks would-be
suitor into spending a rainy night in a pigsty.
Guzmán: Pt. II, Bk. I, Ch. V 412b.

K1218.2.1.* Suitor locked in courtyard. Spends night in
the rain. Alonso: Pt. II, Ch. VII 1308b.

K1218.7.1.* Importunate lover carried off by boar. Animal
runs between man's legs, carries him away from woman's
window, and dumps him in a filthy place. Guzmán: Pt. II,

Bk. I, Ch. V 415b.

K1218.9.2.* Importunate lover injured while giving pre-
arranged cat-call. A neighbor stones him. <u>Marcos</u>:
Bk. I, Descanso XXI 990b.

K1218.9.3.* Importunate lover is given a rendez-vous and
pushed into millrace by woman's men friends. Lover
almost drowns. <u>Marcos</u>: Bk. I, Descanso XXI 991b.

K1218.9.4.* Importunate lover falls off roof on way to
woman's window. He falls on a neighboring roof and is
imprisoned as thief. <u>Buscón</u>: Bk. III, Ch. V 1138a.

N300. Unlucky accidents.

K1223.3.1.* Woman substitutes for rival at rendez-vous with
lover. Intercepts note from rival to lover. <u>Trapaza</u>:
Ch. IX 1467a.

N391.2.* Woman intercepts note from rival addressed
to her lover.

K1227. Lover put off by deceptive respite.

T320. Escape from undesired lover.

K1227.1.1.* Lover put off until woman returns from errand.
She steals his money and never returns. <u>Guzmán</u>: Pt. II,
Bk. III, Ch. I 507b.

K1227.4.3.* Girl sends importunate lover to buy a ring. In
the meantime she hides. <u>Justina</u>: Bk. II, Pt. I, Ch. I
757a.

K1227.5.0.1.* Woman has her squire feign death to get rid
of unwanted lover. <u>Teresa</u>: Ch. XVIII 1417a.

K1227.5.2.* Woman keeps importunate lover locked in dark
room until her "uncle" goes to sleep. Woman's squire,
dressed as ghost, frightens away the lover. <u>Teresa</u>:
Ch. XVIII 1418a.

K1833. Disguise as ghost.

K1227.9.1.* Importunate lover left at dining table while
woman goes for more food. She escapes to another room
and kills the man when he breaks into the room.
Alonso: Pt. I, Ch. VII 1251b.

    K2250.1.1.* Treacherous servant murders woman's
    small son in vain hope of seducing the woman.

K1227.10.2.* Girl escapes would-be lover when he falls over
chair while pursuing her. Guzmán: Pt. I, Bk. II,
Ch. VIII 329b.

K1227.11.* Girl escapes from undesired lover by telling him
entertaining stories all night. Justina: Bk. II,
Pt. I, Ch. II 766a.

    T320. Escape from undesired lover.

K1233.1.* Impotent courtier is duped by courtesan. Unknown
to him, a trickster "friend" has sexual relations with
the woman. When she becomes pregnant, she leaves town
so that her generous and duped courtier will not discover
her condition. Urdemalas: p. 206b. (The page is
erroneously numbered 106.)

K1236. Disguise as man to escape importunate lover.

    K521.4.1.1. Girl escapes in male disguise.

    K1837. Disguise of woman in man's clothes.

K1240. Deception into humiliating position - miscellaneous.

K1268. Man carried and dropped in mid-stream. Alonso:
Pt. II, Ch. II 1278a.

    J1638.1.* Franciscan drops Dominican in mid-stream.

K1269.* Officer lifted into air by pulley and dropped. Man
hooks officer to rope and companions pull him upward and
then drop him. It is dark, and officer's companions flee,
thinking that the devil has carried the officer away.

<u>Guadaña</u>: Ch. VII 1705b.

J1786.5.1.* Officer thinks man lifting up fellow officer is devil.

K1271. Amorous intrigue observed and exposed.

J1562.3.1.* Lover hides meat in trousers while he consorts with woman. N777.2.1.* Overturned tub leads to adventures.

K1271.1.4.4.* Lovers exposed when dripping water chases them out of bed. Water spilled in room above falls on woman and priest. They run outside nude and are arrested. <u>Lazarillo</u> (Luna): Pt. II, Ch. V 122a.

N777.2.1.* Overturned tub leads to adventures.

K1271.2.1.* Nude priest comes to couple's bed. He had been "frightened" by goblin in his room. He later enjoys the man's wife. <u>Lazarillo</u> (Luna): Pt. II, Ch. VII 124a.

J1210. Clever man puts another out of countenance.

K1271.2.2.* Lovers observed in intrigue in the garden. They are forced to marry. <u>Alonso</u>: Pt. II, Ch. IX 1314b.

T30. Lovers' meeting.

K1281.2.* Man draws a donkey to him instead of a woman. Donkey enters man's room at night at time of expected tryst with woman. Man is injured when he tries to embrace the animal. <u>Guzmán</u>: Pt. I, Bk. II, Ch. VIII 329b.

K1300 - K1399. SEDUCTION OR DECEPTIVE MARRIAGE

K1310. <u>Seduction by disguise or substitution</u>.

K1315.2.2. Seduction by sham process of retrieving lost gem. <u>Lozana</u>: Mamotreto LXI 201.

K1871.2.1.* Man pretends to extract lost rings from woman's body through sexual intercourse.

K1315.8. Seduction upon false promise of marriage. Seducer

forced by girl's brother and friend to marry girl.
Garduña: Bk. III 1588a.

K1317.7.1.* Woman at night gives passer-by box of jewels and
money intended for her elopement. She sends man away
immediately with treasure. Píndaro: Bk. I, Ch. XIV 304a.

    N391.3.* Woman planning to elope mistakes strange
man at night for her lover and gives him a locked
chest containing letters, pictures, jewels , and
money.

K1315.8.1.* Seduction upon false promise of marriage. Married
man, posing as bachelor, seduces woman. He gives her a
certificate, enjoys her for a night, but never returns.
Urdemalas: p. 33b.

K1330. Girl tricked into man's room (or power).

K1339.3. Woman enticed into man's room by feigned illness.
Man wants her to "heal" his organ. He is trying to get
free love. Lozana: Mamotreto L 165.

K1339.6.1.* Married woman on trip to visit convent is lured
into home of former suitor where seduction takes place.
She is arrested next day when a fire in man's house
exposes her. A faithful maid exchanges clothes with
her, allowing her to escape from prison and return to
unsuspecting husband. Guzmán: Pt. II, Bk. II, Ch. IX
495a.

K1340. Entrance into girl's (man's) room (bed) by trick.

K1342. Entrance into woman's room by hiding in chest.
Lazarillo (Luna): Pt. II, Ch. X 129a.

K1349.1.0.1.* Manservant, disguised as count, invades maid's
room and flogs her. Necio: Ch. III 234.

K1349.1.2. Disguise as madman (woman) to enter girl's room.
Lozana: Mamotreto LV 183.

K1818.7.* Man disguises as serving woman to enter
former fiancée's household.

K1349.1.6.* Man feigns wound from sham battle. Is carried
"unconscious" into woman's house. Trapaza: Ch. XIV
1499a.

K1350. Woman persuaded (or wooed) by trick.

Q252.2.* Prince punished for breaking betrothal.

T455. Woman sells favors for particular purpose.

K1350.0.1.* Rival lover compromises widow's honor by
adjusting his clothes in front of her house in early
morning. She marries him, kills him while he sleeps,
then enters a convent. Her preferred lover enters a
monastery. Guzmán: Pt. II, Bk. II, Ch. VIII 481b.

T92. Rivals in love. T173.2.1.* Hostile bride
kills husband who has compromised her honor before
marriage.

K1352. Death feigned to woo maiden. She shows remorse when
she hears of lover's death. Necio: Ch. IV 281.

K455.8.2.1.* Sham dying man writes bogus will
leaving "fortune" to scornful woman.

K1353.2.* Prince promises to marry woman and give her a large
sum of money for her favors. When he refuses to fulfill
agreement, the court forces him to pay. Guzmán: Pt. II,
Bk. III, Ch. II 513a.

Q252.2.* Prince punished for breaking betrothal.

T455. Woman sells favors for particular purpose.

K1354.4.1.* Judge seduces woman whose husband has been
imprisoned on false charge. Necio: Ch. IV 263.

K1363.2.1.* Doctor adds missing fingers to unborn child. He has a procuress to persuade neighbor's wife to allow him to substitute for absent husband and complete imperfect foetus. Lozana: Mamotreto LXI 201.

K1371.4.3.* Lover substitutes for coachman and drives his beloved's carriage to his house. He keeps the lady locked up, making tests of her constancy. Necio: Ch. V 291 - 293.

> K1831.2. Service in disguise.

K1380. Seductions - miscellaneous.

K1388.2.* Trickster judge gives a husband commission away from home then seduces his wife. When man's property is depleted, judge banishes man and wife from city. Guzmán: Pt. II, Bk. III, Ch. V 548b.

> K2016. Friendship pretended to gain access to girl (wife).

K1397.1.* Noble woman sexually assaulted during siesta hour. Since no one had seen man enter house, he tells woman that she would compromise her honor if she screamed. Fregona: p. 174a.

> K1400 - K1499. DUPE'S PROPERTY DESTROYED

K1410. Dupe's goods destroyed.

K1410.1.* Poet's house destroyed. Trickster has sexton ring church bell and announce that poet's house is on fire. People tear down part of poet's house and soak it with water. Urdemalas: pp. 96a - 106a.

> K1500 - K1599. DECEPTIONS CONNECTED WITH ADULTERY

K1500. Deception connected with adultery.

> Q241. Adultery punished. T481. Adultery.

K1510. <u>Adulteress outwits husband</u>.

K1510.2.1.* Wife of suspected philanderer decides to get
revenge by having an affair herself. <u>Necio</u>: Ch. II 217.

J1511. A rule must work both ways.

K1514. Adulteress gets rid of husband while she entertains
lover. <u>Teresa</u>: Ch. VI 1364b.

K1514.10.1.* Adulteress sets husband to watch for "phantom"
while she entertains paramour. <u>Marcos</u>: Bk. III,
Descanso VI 1045b.

K1551.1. Husband returns home secretly and kills
unwelcome suitor.

K1514.11.1.* Woman feigns illness in order to be taken into
home of her lover. She and paramour enjoy each other
while her husband waits for her to finish her "nap."
<u>Guzmán</u>: Pt. I, Bk. I, Ch. II 248b.

K1514.14.1.* Wife unties mule at night so that husband will
have to chase it. She plans to be with lover while
husband is out of bed. The husband rushes so quickly to
the stable that the wife has to hide in it, and she
receives many of the blows intended for the mule.
<u>Marcos</u>: Bk. I, Descanso III 934a.

K1516.1.1.* Wife hits husband's good eye. He "sees double"
while lover escapes. <u>Manzanares</u>: Ch. V 25.

K1517.1. The lovers as pursuer and fugitive. Mistress is
visited at night by lover who is being pursued by
"enemies." Husband chases a fugitive and is locked out
of house while lover enjoys the wife. <u>Teresa</u>: Ch. VI
1364b.

K1521.6.1.* Wife hides lover behind curtain. While husband
rushes downstairs to chase away "invaders," the paramour

escapes behind him. <u>Píndaro</u>: Bk. I, Ch. XII 298a.

K1525.1.* We're all here. Woman hides a stupid man under her
bed. When her paramour arrives, the simpleton comes out
and exclaims, "We're all here!" <u>Justina</u>: Bk. II, Pt. I,
Ch. I 754a.

K1543.1.* The lover's picture in the wife's sleeve. Husband
sees picture and locks up the **wife**. The latter claims
that she found the picture at church. She arranges to
have the town crier announce a lost picture. Husband is
deceived and apologizes to wife. <u>Teresa</u>: Ch. XVII
1408a.

> J2301. Gullible husbands. J2342.1.1.* Husband
> refuses to believe that wife is unfaithful even
> after discovering her lover's picture.

K1550. <u>Husband outwits adulteress and paramour</u>.

K1550.1.3.* Husband discovers that his wife has a lover.
She is not in bed, and has arranged chairs to topple
and warn her if husband touches them. The next night
he kills the lover. <u>Píndaro</u>: Bk. II, Ch. X 340a.

K1550.1.4.* **Cuckolded** husband overhears two rival lovers
quarreling over the affections of his wife. Outraged,
he decides to kill his wife and writes a note explaining
the reason. He dies of a heart attack while writing the
note. <u>Garduña</u>: Bk. I 1536a.

K1550.1.5.* Husband hides adulterous wife from public
in a rented house with no balcony. Finally, he sends
her back to her guardian. She has had too many "cousins"
visiting her. <u>Estebanillo</u>: Bk. II, Ch. II 1801a.

> K2051.6.* Adulteress pretends sensitivity toward
> certain food.

K1551.1. Husband returns home secretly and kills unwelcome
suitor. Marcos: Bk. III, Descanso VII 1046b.

> K1514.10.1.* Adulteress sets husband to watch for
> "phanton" while she entertains paramour.
>
> Q469.1.1.* Adulterer caused to fall down stairs
> from which steps have been removed. S139.6. Murder
> by tearing out heart.

K1567. Husband tricks wife into riding a mule which has
been denied water. On fording a stream the mule plunges
into the water. Wife drowns. Guzmán: Pt. II, Bk. III,
Ch. IX 573a.

> T255.2.1.* Obstinate wife drowned when thirsty
> mule rushes with her into swollen stream.

K1569.1.1.* Husband approves wife's adultery, if other men
pay well. Disapproves relations with impoverished
paramour, and the latter kills him. Hija: p. 916a.

> K1613.0.2.* Wife tries unsuccessfully to poison
> husband.

K1569.1.2.* Husband pimps for his wife. He collects money
from men who come to visit her. Manzanares: Ch. VI 28.

K1569.10.* Husband stabs wife's ex-paramour. He has abandoned
man's wife for another woman, and gifts have stopped
coming. Guzmán: Pt. II, Bk. III, Ch. V 544a.

K1570. Trickster outwits adulteress and paramour.

K1572.1.* Trickster makes paramour believe that woman's
husband is coming to punish him. The paramour leaves
town. Necio: Ch. III 235.

K1573.1.* Trickster sends his master running after "thieves"
while paramour tries to escape. Trickster explains
that paramour has been frightened by thieves. Husband

invites paramour to remain. <u>Marcos</u>: Bk. I, Descanso
III 932a.

K1577.1.* Jealous lover has door of mistress' house sealed
during night. Exposes judge's illicit relationship with
her. <u>Guadaña</u>: Ch. VII 1706b.

K1580. <u>Other deceits connected with adultery</u>.

K1581.5.3.* Lover "borrows" back dress which he has stolen
from another woman. His deceit is discovered, and
mistress' father is killed in a duel with him.
<u>Garduña</u>: Bk. I 1532b.

K1581.6.1.* Man employs trickster to steal diamonds given
to mistress. Trickster takes rings from woman's fingers
under the guise of having more made for her. <u>Necio</u>:
Ch. II 222.

    H1151.4. Task: stealing ring from finger.

    K778.6.* Veiled women lure man to a secluded spot
    and flog him.

K1581.11.1.* Man takes back the three crowns paid to prostitute when she asks for more. "I serve the king a month
for three crowns, and you will not serve me one night
for them." <u>Lozana</u>: Mamotreto XXXIII 115.

K1592.1.* Paramour unwittingly sends adulteress' husband to
unlock room where husband's wife and sister are concealed.
Wife hides, but husband kills his sister. He sickens
and dies. <u>Teresa</u>: Ch. XVII 1409b.

K1592.2.* Paramour sends constable to unlock room where
lover's mistress is concealed. Constable discovers his
own wife and kills her. <u>Guadaña</u>: Ch. VIII 1708a.

    K1600 - K1699. DECEIVER FALLS INTO OWN TRAP

K1600. <u>Deceiver falls into own trap</u>.

K144.4.* Hay sold for barley. Trickster is killed
by irate customer. K333. Theft from blind person.
K1917. Penniless bridegroom pretends to wealth.
K1917.5.1.* Man wins girl's love by posing as
wealthy Portuguese official. He is detected.

K1606.* Thief's plan for stealing is betrayed by friend.
The latter tells other thieves who rob the schemer of
his stolen chickens by posing as officers. Guzmán:
Pt. II, Bk. I, Ch. III 402a.

K306.2. Highjacking thief robbed of his booty.

K1610. Deceiver falls into his own trap - miscellaneous
incidents.

K1610.1.* Blind deceiver outwitted by boy guide. Latter ate
three grapes at a time when master broke agreement and
ate two at a time instead of one. Lazarillo: Tratado I
88b.

J1510. The cheater cheated. K333. Theft from
blind person. M200. Bargains and promises.

K1611.0.1.* Soldier wearing enemy uniform is wounded by own
men. The enemy uniform is more comfortable than his own.
Soldier is denied service benefits. Estebanillo: Bk. II,
Ch. VI 1822b.

K1611.0.2.* Soldier in foreign costume is captured as spy.
He is taken before a prince who recognizes him and frees
him. Estebanillo: Bk. II, Ch. VI 1842b.

K1613.0.2.* Wife tries unsuccessfully to poison husband.
Latter is killed by paramour hidden in closet.
Hija: p. 918a.

K1569.1.1.* Husband approves wife's adultery,
if other men pay well.

K1619.* Deceiver in card game loses. Man has a deck of marked
cards and is confident of winning. An unknown sharpster
fleeces him. Guzmán (Luján): Pt. II, Bk. III, Ch. VIII
683a.

K1623.1.* Faithless lover tricked into signing his name to a
blank piece of paper. It is a promise of marriage, and
man is forced to marry the woman whom he seduced.
Garduña: Bk. IV 1608b.

    K1816.0.2.1.* Seduced woman disguises as servant
    and gains employment in home of her seducer's
    fiancée.

K1631.1.* The bribed assistant detected by judge. Youth
accepts bribes from prisoners' relatives, but fails to
get prisoners released. Youth and judge fight, and
former is dismissed. Estebanillo: Bk. I, Ch. III 1750a.

    P672. Pulling a man's beard as an insult.

K1641.2.* Trickster planning to sell entrusted cloak is
arrested for theft. To avenge himself on man who has
formerly tricked him, cloak's owner has the man falsely
arrested for theft. Marcos: Bk. I, Ch. IX 958b.

    K2104.1.* Cloak entrusted to man brings false
    accusation of theft.

K1641.3.* Trickster sets ambush for man whom he has cheated.
Armed men seize the victim and beat him. Estebanillo:
Bk. I, Ch. II 1734b.

K1657.1.* Unjust official outwitted by landlady. She shouts
when crafty constable comes to arrest lovers in her
house. Police come and arrest everyone. Coloquio: p. 215b.

K1663.1.* Spying wife disabled by fall on stairway. Trickster
soaps stairway so that wife has a disabling fall and

cannot spy on her husband at a neighbor woman's house.
<u>Trapaza</u>: Ch. XIII 1494b.

K1667.1.3.* Man retrieves stolen money and valuables. Pretends
he wants to cash a check and put the money with other
valuables. Female thief returns stolen money box, hoping
to get more. <u>Marcos</u>: Bk. III, Descanso IX 1052a.

> K362.7. Theft by forgery.

K1676.2.* Students pretend to be sick from constipation in
order to miss school. They are given enemas. <u>Buscón</u>:
Bk. I, Ch. III 1099a.

K1685. The treasure finders who murder one another.
<u>Alonso</u>: Pt. II, Ch. I 1273a.

> J494.1.* Young thief prefers revenge and death
> to life.

K1693.1.* Thief's stolen eggs are broken in his breeches.
Master beats servant, thus breaking eggs, in order to
prevent detection of food they both have stolen.
<u>Guzmán</u>: Pt. I, Bk. II, Ch. VI 318b.

> K401.0.2.* Master exposes servant's theft of eggs.

K1694.* Woman's rotten-egg omelet thrown in her face. Innkeeper's wife serves bad omelet to soldiers. <u>Guzmán</u>:
Pt. I, Bk. I, Ch. IV 260a.

> K1600. Deceiver falls into own trap. K2241.1.*
> Innkeeper's wife serves a rotten-egg omelet to
> soldiers.

K1696.1.* Trickster gives a "found" purse to a priest. The
latter collects alms for the man. Thief's confederate
identifies purse and receives it from the priest.
<u>Guzmán</u>: Pt. II, Bk. III, Ch. VI 555a; and <u>Alonso</u>:
Pt. II, Ch. III 1287a.

K1700 - K2099. DECEPTION THROUGH SHAMS

K1700 - K1799. DECEPTION THROUGH BLUFFING

K1700. **Deception through bluffing**.

T320.3.2.* Woman saves herself from would-be
ravisher by threatening to call her servants.
T320.3.3.* Woman saves herself from would-be
ravisher by telling him that a relative of hers
is sleeping near-by.

K1760. **Other bluffs**.

K1771.4.1.* Sham duel staged by two drunken soldiers. They
"fight" harmlessly with swords until they fall from
exhaustion. A would-be helper is wounded when he stoops
to aid one of the duelers. Estebanillo: Bk. II,
Ch. I 1779b.

K1772.1.* Disguised abductor pretends to be angry with
captive girl. He and other disguised men decree death
to girl for refusing love and money. They are only
testing her constancy. Necio: Ch. VI 301.

M57.* Decree that woman must be killed for
refusing love and money.

K1800 - K1899. DECEPTION BY DISGUISE OR ILLUSION

K1810. Deception by disguise.

K134.3.1.* Trickster grooms owner's mean mule and
tries to sell it back to him. K439.2.1.* Thief
claims that stolen mule is his own, but owner
detects fraud and recovers mule.

K1810.1.4.* Young woman beggar exchanges clothes with old
woman. The latter has to fight off lovers, while the
former receives many alms. Justina: Bk. II, Pt. II,
Ch. IV 812b.

K1810.3.1.* Lover disguised as court jester to gain entrance to girl's home. He accompanies girl and her father on trip and confesses his love to the girl. Garduña: Bk. III 1581b.

K1810.4.* Woman disguises as prostitute, hoping to seduce indifferent lover. Latter discovers her identity and takes her back home. Píndaro: Bk. II, Ch. IX 337b.

K1810.5.* Man escapes creditor by disguise. He wears a patch over one eye, lets his hair down, and speaks a foreign language. Buscón: Bk. III, Ch. II 1129b.

K1816.0.2.1.* Seduced woman disguises as servant and gains employment in home of her seducer's fiancée. She has followed her seducer by means of a picture and a letter which the man had left in bed. Garduña: Bk. IV 1604b.

K1623.1.* Faithless lover tricked into signing his name to a blank piece of paper.

K1816.13.1.* Disguised slave turns out to be master's long-lost friend. Discovery comes when the "Moor" begins to speak Spanish at his confessional. Píndaro: Bk. II, Ch. XXVI 369a.

V23.3.* Moorish slave starts talking Spanish to master in order to confess before he dies.

K1817.1.0.1.* Disguise as beggar to enter house. Lover's servant in disguise enters courtesan's house and verifies that "dead" squire is still alive. Teresa: Ch. XVIII 1417a.

K1817.1.0.2.* Impoverished man disguises as beggar and gains much money. Buscón: Bk. III, Ch. VIII 1146b.

K1817.2.1.* Disguised as pilgrim, offended enemy kills nobleman. Latter's servants flee, taking master's money and jewels. <u>Harpías</u>: Estafa I 26ff.

    K2357.2. Disguise as pilgrim to enter enemy's
camp (castle).

K1817.3.1.1.* Trickster disguises as poet to rob manager of
theatrical troupe. He creates a disturbance in manager's
home, and confederates rob the troupe's money during the
confusion. <u>Garduña</u>: Bk. IV 1616a.

K1817.4.0.1.* Shipwrecked prince disguises as merchant.
He becomes a secretary in duke's home, and jousts so
well in tournament that he is forced to identify himself. He marries a daughter of the duke. <u>Trapaza</u>:
Ch. IX 1464a.

K1817.6.* Man disguised as prostitute. Rushes from sleeping
chamberlain's room when cardinal calls, thus throwing
suspicion on chamberlain. <u>Guzmán</u>: Pt. I, Bk. III,
Ch. VIII 365a.

    K2150. Innocent made to appear guilty.

K1818.0.1.* Lover disguises as sick man to test fickle
woman's love for him. <u>Necio</u>: Ch. IV 279.

K1818.2.1.* Sore neck disguise. Trickster raises blisters
on his neck with poultices, and collects money for cure.
<u>Estebanillo</u>: Bk. I, Ch. V 1766a.

K1818.7.* Man disguises as serving woman to enter former
fiancée's household. He is advised to say that he can
cure "French disease" so that people will think him mad.
He will declare his love to his former fiancée when her
husband is away from home. <u>Lozana</u>: Mamotreto LV 183.

K1821.3.0.1.* Disguise by wearing masks. People enter shop
to buy masks to change their appearance and to get
favors from the public. When masks slip off, the public

repudiates the wearers. <u>Periquillo</u>: Discurso VI 1874a.

K1821.11.* Disguise by cutting off beard. Thief cuts off
beard and covers his head; pursuing officers fail to
recognize him. <u>Urdemalas</u>: p. 6a.

    K521.2.1. Disguise by shaving off beard so as to
    escape. K620. Escape by deceiving the guard.

K1822.2.1.* Soldier disguised as scholar. Is engaged to
teach a youth the difference between right and wrong.
The youth becomes a thief. <u>Justina</u>: Bk. I, Ch. III 743b.

    K1958. Sham teacher. P340. Teacher and pupil.

K1826.2.1.* Trickster disguised as pious hermit (friar)
fleeces victims in card game. <u>Buscón</u>: Bk. II, Ch. III
1119a; and Bk. III, Ch. VII 1142b.

    K1961.1.5. Sham holy man.

K1831.0.1. Disguise by changing name. Moor has two names:
a Christian name for the street and a Moorish name at
home. <u>Alonso</u>: Pt. II, Ch. V 1295b; and <u>Urdemalas</u>:
p. 28b.

    V330. Conversion from one religion to another.

K1831.2. Service in disguise.

    K1371.4.3.* Lover substitutes for coachman and
    drives his beloved's carriage to his house.

    R18. Abduction by rejected suitor.

K1833. Disguise as ghost. Courtesan's "dead" squire returns
at night to frighten two importunate lovers away.
<u>Teresa</u>: Ch. XVIII 1415a.

    K1213.3.* Prostitute terrorizes two lovers.

K1833.1.* Trickster disguises as ghost to frighten critic.
Latter had criticized statue of another man's dead
father. <u>Trapaza</u>: Ch. XII 1487b.

K1836.5.* Man disguises as "fighting nun." People come to
see "her" and give money. <u>Trapaza</u>: Ch. X 1477b.

K1837. Disguise of woman in man's clothes. <u>Marcos</u>: Bk. III,
Descanso XXIII 1081b.

 K521.4.1.1. Girl escapes in male disguise.

 K1236. Disguise as man to escape importunate lover.

K1837.2.1.* Woman disguised as pilgrim goes to shrine to be
cured of "dropsy." She gives birth to baby girl at an
inn and leaves identification tokens. <u>Fregona</u>: p. 170a.

 H82. Identifying tokens sent with messenger.

 H242.2.* Half chain and half parchment as
 credential test.

K1838.2.* Servants disguise as devils. They flog men who
enter their master's house without knocking. <u>Necio</u>:
Ch. I 173.

 J1786.1.3.* Disguised servants thought to be devils.

K1840. <u>Deception by substitution</u>.

 K2241.2.* Innkeeper serves guests mule flesh
 for veal.

K1844.1.2.* Husband has another man substitute for him in
bed. His wife is planning to chloroform him and escape
with her lover. <u>Periquillo</u>: Discurso XI 1895a.

 Q411.0.4.* Husband kills wife and paramour on
 ship. T258.1.1. Husband insists on knowing
 wife's secret.

K1851.2.* Servant substitutes written prayers for lover's
letters. Jealous husband has dropped letters which he
pulled from his wife's blouse, and he asks servant to
pick them up. Husband is mollified when he sees the
prayers. <u>Pindaro</u>: Bk. I, Ch. X 294a.

K1858.1.1.* Substitute specimen in urinalysis. Actress
feigns illness and substitutes white wine for urine
to baffle doctors. The latter prescribe cures and
collect their fees. <u>Teresa</u>: Ch. XVI 1399a.

P460. Other trades and professions. P471.2.*
Actors satirize doctors in a play.

K1858.1.2.* Fake sick man substitutes urine from healthy
youth for his own to test doctors. The latter declare
that the sick man is worse. <u>Necio</u>: Ch. IV 280.

K1860. <u>Deception by feigned death (sleep)</u>.

K482. Money received to bury sham-dead person.

Q591.1. Punishment: death pretended becomes real.

K1870. <u>Illusions</u>.

D1368.2.1.* Magic ring causes illusions.

K1871.2.1.* Man pretends to extract lost rings from woman's
body through sexual intercourse. Husband hears noise
and calls out just as wife asks seducer to bring forth a
bucket and chain. Wife scolds husband. <u>Lozana</u>:
Mamotreto LXI 201.

K1315.2.2. Seduction by sham process of retrieving
lost gem.

K1872.0.1.* Women come daily to the Street of Appearances to
be made up. They receive the kinds of looks they want
to portray all day. <u>Diablo</u>: Tranco III 1647b.

K1875. Deception by sham blood. By stabbing concealed bag
of blood, tricksters make innkeeper think that a man
has been killed. They bargain with innkeeper for
"hush money" to conceal the affair. <u>Píndaro</u>: Bk. XXII
319a.

K1875.1.* Deception by sham blood and cow's intestines.

Dupe is tricked into jumping into bed-sheet stretched over intestines filled with blood. He thinks that he has burst open, and he screams for help. <u>Trapaza</u>: Ch. IV 1444a.

K1875.2.* Deception by bleeding gums. Man removes two false teeth during a fight, makes his gums bleed, and tries to collect damages. His fraud is detected. <u>Guzmán</u>: Pt. II, Bk. II, Ch. III 447b.

K1900 - K1999. IMPOSTURES

K1910. <u>Marital impostors</u>.

K1911.5. Penniless bride pretends to wealth. Day following wedding the borrowed or rented household goods are taken back by owners. <u>Castigo</u>: p. 1632b.

K1915.4.* Ugly woman substituted for beautiful one whose picture dupe had seen. He is tricked into marrying her. <u>Diablo</u>: Tranco II 1647a.

     J2323.1.* Numskull is tricked into marrying ugly woman. T11.2. Love through sight of picture.

K1917. Penniless bridegroom pretends to wealth.

     K1954. Sham rich man.

K1917.5. Man wins girl's love by pretending to wealth and nobility. Deception is discovered and imposter is banished. <u>Trapaza</u>: Ch. XV 1506a.

     N681.1.1.* Fiancé arrives home just as mistress is to marry a sham nobleman.

K1917.5.1.* Man wins girl's love by posing as a wealthy Portuguese official. The fraud is discovered and the man loses his bride-to-be and is punished. <u>Trapaza</u>: Ch. XVI 1516b.

     K1600. Deceiver falls into own trap.

K1917.5.2.* Man wins scornful woman's love by pretending
to wealth. He leaves her in disgust when she begins to
shower him with gifts. <u>Necio</u>: Ch. III 224.

H919.7.* Task assigned servant at suggestion
of master.

K1917.9.* Penniless husband beats wife, steals her jewelry,
and abandons her. <u>Lazarillo</u> (Luna): Pt. II, Ch. VII 125a.

K1917.10.* Husband sells wife's house, steals her jewels, and
abandons her. He feigns need of money for a business
trip. <u>Guzmán</u>: Pt. I, Bk. I, Ch. I 242b.

K1923. The false heir.

J1521.2. The old man nods "yes." K1938. Rascal
pretends to be dead man's heir and receives money.

K1926.1.* False daughter. Woman feigns to be long-lost
daughter of rich man. She is sent away when real daughter
returns and identifies herself. <u>Teresa</u>: Ch. XIII 1390a.

H90. Identification by ornaments. H92. Identification by necklace.

K1930. <u>Treacherous impostors</u>.

K1938. Rascal pretends to be dead man's heir and receives
money. Dying hermit answers "yes" to all questions.
Trickster asks him if he is to inherit all the property.
The hermit says "yes", and the hermit's house and property
are given to the trickster. Lazarillo (Luna): Pt. II,
Ch. XV 140b.

J1521.2. The old man nods "yes." K1923. The
false heir.

K1938.1.* Trickster woman claims to be dead woman's niece
and receives her money. <u>Justina</u>: Bk. III, Ch. IV
862a.

K1950. Sham prowess.

K1951.4.1.* Sham brave man craws under bed to get sword. He
falls asleep. Lozana: Mamotreto XLVI 154.

K1951.5.1.* Tailor says that he is a "grandee" of Spain. He
escapes arrest. His real name is Juan Grande.
Guadaña: Ch. XII 1718b.

> J1181.4.* Man escapes arrest by saying he is a
> "grandee" of Spain.

K1953.2.* Sham brave man fights six ruffians. He overcomes
them and gains a great reputation. Coloquio: p. 216b.

K1953.3.* Sham brave man must remain with lady who has
fainted. He cannot fight man whom he has challenged.
Harpías: Estafa IV 170ff.

K1953.4.* Youth wounds two adversaries the first time he
fights with a sword. He gains fame as a swordsman, and
continues to draw his sword on the slightest provocation.
Alonso: Pt. II, Ch. V 1294a.

K1954. Sham rich man.

> J1510.2.* Sham rich soldier robbed of possessions
> by sham rich bride. K306.3. Man is robbed of gold
> chain while with prostitute. K347.5.* Woman tricks
> priest into advancing money on her "jewel" box.
> K455.8.1.2.* Trickster receives special considera-
> tion at inn with false bill of exchange.
> K1917. Penniless bridegroom pretends to wealth.
> W11.7.2.* Friends' generosity enables impoverished
> lover to entertain his lady and friends.

K1954.3.* Sham rich man pretends to be afraid to go out at
night. He might be robbed. Lazarillo: Tratado III 98b.

K1954.4.* Sham rich man dresses daily with cape and sword.

He hopes to create a favorable impression and receive a
position at court. Women reject him because he cannot
supply food or money. <u>Lazarillo</u>: Tratado III 99a.

K1954.4.1.* Sham rich man stands in front of fine house and
talks with lackey. He appears to be at home talking with
a servant, but he is only asking a question. <u>Buscón</u>:
Bk. III, Ch. II 1131b.

K1954.5.* Sham rich man eats bread and tripe which servant
provides through begging. He joins servant only because
the latter has such grace while eating. <u>Lazarillo</u>:
Tratado III 100b.

K1954.5.1.* Poor proud nobleman hires servant to be go-
between with his lady. Nobleman eats part of bread
which servant has brought home to eat. <u>Trapaza</u>:
Ch. XI 1481b.

K1954.6.* Sham rich man picks teeth in public. He creates
the impression of having eaten. <u>Lazarillo</u>: Tratado III
102a.

K1954.6.1.* Poor men at court scatter bones of animals and
feathers of fowls around their lodgings in order to make
neighbors believe that they eat well. Invited to rich
men's homes, they carve for them and eat meat.
<u>Buscón</u>: Bk. II, Ch. VI 1125a.

K1954.6.2.* Poor man appears to have fine breeches. He wears
pasteboard hoops around his waist and under his cloak to
give the illusion that fine breeches are pushing out his
cape. He has no breeches. <u>Buscón</u>: Bk. III, Ch. I 1127b.

K1954.6.3.* Poor man sprinkles crumbs in his whiskers and on
his cloak in order to make people think that he has
dined well. <u>Buscón</u>: Bk. III, Ch. II 1130b.

K1954.6.4.* Trickster counts fifty coins repeatedly at night. People on other side of thin wall think that he is rich. Buscón: Bk. III, Ch. V 1137b.

K1954.6.5.* Sham rich man disguises himself as a majordomo and inquires about himself ("his master"). Would-be bride and her family are impressed. Buscón: Bk. III, Ch. V 1138a.

K1954.6.6.* Poor man rents horse and rides with two wealthy gentlemen. He creates the impression that he is rich by stopping lackeys and asking if their horses are for sale. Buscón: Bk. III, Ch. VI 1140a.

K1954.6.7.* Impoverished lover rides rented horse down street following a pedestrian. He gives the impression to his fiancée that he has a lackey. Buscón: Bk. III, Ch. VII 1144a.

K1954.7.* Sham rich woman. Penniless courtesan poses as rich widow and rents house opposite that of a rich man. She attracts the latter as her lover. Harpías: Estafa II 71-82.

K1954.7.1.* Sham rich woman tricks priest into advancing money on her "jewel" box. She makes priest think she is rich and will build a chapel. Harpías: Estafa III 107-137.

> K347.5.* Woman tricks priest into advancing money on her "jewel" box. K455.9. Worthless chests offered to obtain credit. K476.2.1.1.* Box of supposed jewels given to help build church.

K1954.7.2.* Sham rich woman exposed. Actor identifies her, by scar on cheek, as former actress. Teresa: Ch. XVII 1411b.

> H51. Recognition by scar.

K1955. Sham physician.

P424.7.* Two kinds of doctors. P424.8.* Physicians
criticized for excessive purgings and blood-letting.

K1955.2. Sham physician pretends to diagnose entirely from
urinalysis. Stupid doctor pours all urine specimines
together in order to diagnose the illness of a community.
Lozana: Mamotreto LIX 194.

J1734.2.* Urine analysis to diagnose illness of
community.

K1955.2.2.* Sham physician diagnoses from what he sees on
floor near patient. Observing cherry pits he says, "Oh,
how many cherries you have eaten!" Seeing straw and a
pot of donkey urine placed by pranksters: "Oh, how
many packsaddles you have eaten!" Manzanares: Ch. X 63.

K1955.8.2.* Sham physician becomes a doctor in thirty days.
He reads medical treatises and observes techniques of
blood-letting. He decides against practising medicine
because doctors are too ignorant or too greedy.
Torres: Trozo III 1951b.

P424.7.* Two kinds of doctors.

K1955.9.1. Sham physician hands out prescriptions haphazard.
He always says, "May God dispose it to good."
Guzmán: Pt. I, Bk. I, Ch. III 255b.

K1955.9.2.* Sham physician's prescriptions bring him great
success. Nobody dies from using the worthless prescriptions, and the doctor becomes wealthy and respected.
Torres: Trozo II 1939b.

K1955.10.* Sham surgeon nearly kills a man in attempted
blood-letting. Estebanillo: Bk. I, Ch. III 1746a.

K1955.11.* Sham physician could rid the world of sickness,

if only he had a mule for traveling. <u>Necio</u>: Ch. III
243.

 J953. Self-deception of the lowly.

K1956. Sham wise man. <u>Necio</u>: Ch. I 168.

 N685. Fool passes as wise man by remaining silent.

K1956.0.1.* Blind beggar poses as wise man. He predicts sex
 of unborn children, and gives medical and spiritual
 advice to gullible people. <u>Lazarillo</u>: Tratado I 86b.

K1956.1. Sham wise man gives a purgative and helps find a
 lost horse. <u>Lozana</u>: Mamotreto XLVI 154.

K1956.3.1.* Thief posing as astrologer declares who
 committed the theft: the officer's assistant.
 <u>Urdemalas</u>: p. 7b.

K1956.11.* Sham wise woman. Tells another woman who has lost
 a hen to climb on house and bring her some grass. Woman
 finds hen on roof and sham profetess gains fame.
 <u>Lozana</u>: Mamotreto XLVI 154.

K1956.12.* Sham wise woman. Tells man who has lost donkey
 to give himself an enema of cold water. When man goes
 into orchard to defecate, he finds donkey.
 <u>Lozana</u>: Mamotreto XLVI 154.

K1956.13.* Sham wise man's "modesty" prevents him from
 publishing many books. <u>Necio</u>: Ch. I 171.

  U111.2.* False scholar's "modesty" prevents him
  from publishing many books.

K1958. Sham teacher.

  K1822.2.1.* Soldier disguised as scholar.

  P340. Teacher and pupil.

K1958.1.* Sham teacher loses textbook and cannot teach class.
 Pupils talk and play. <u>Torres</u>: Trozo II 1935b.

P345.* Teacher loses textbook and cannot teach
class.

K1961.1.2.2.* Sham priest speaks poor Latin to the uneducated.
He uses the vernacular, if people understand Latin.
Lazarillo: Tratado I 105b.

K1961.1.5. Sham holy man.

    K1826.2.1.* Trickster disguised as pious hermit
    fleeces victims in card game.

K1961.1.5.2.* Sham holy man deceives with the truth.
Accused of fraud, he admits his fraudulence in such a
way that his fame increases. Hija: p. 913b.

K1961.1.5.3.* Sham holy man collects money for poor. He
and moll abscond with it. Hija: p. 913b.

K1961.1.5.4.* Sham holy man robs church. He is detected
and sent to prison. Guzmán: Pt. I, Bk. I, Ch. I 242a.

K1961.1.5.5.* Sham holy man pretends to be faith healer.
Collects much money for cures and for "subscriptions"
for Masses. Buscón: Bk. III, Ch. III 1133a.

K1961.1.5.6.* Sham holy man is ally of robber band. He
stores robbers' loot in a secret room of the monastery.
He is later robbed by woman guest. Garduña: Bk. III
1578b.

    K675. Sleeping potion given to man who is to pass
    the night with a girl.

K1961.1.5.7.* Sham ascetic obtains money to get a soul out
of purgatory. The "soul" was a girl in need of money to
pay off debts before eloping with the "hermit."
Urdemalas: p. 144a.

    K359.7.* False hermit obtains money to get a soul
    out of purgatory.

K1963.1.1.* Sham magician exposed by **observant** man. Latter discovers magnet in magician's glove. The magnet caused a metal figure to turn and point to a letter when asked a question. <u>Marcos</u>: Bk. III, Descanso IV 1041a.

K1963.2.1.* Sham magician promises to make short man grow taller. Dupe is made to fast and to perform certain rituals. He is finally frightened and discomfited by trickster and confederates. <u>Marcos</u>: Bk. I, Descanso XXIII 996b.

    J2285.2.* A short man can grow tall.

K1966.2. Alchemist secures payment for his "secret." He can make gold from his "philosopher's stone." <u>Garduña</u>: Bk. II 1569a.

    J2300. Gullible fools. J2325.2.* Gullible rich man made to believe urine from red-headed boy is an essential ingredient for making gold. K476.2.2.* Reward for "philosopher's stone" which makes gold.

K1969.5.* Sham horseman. Old lover falls from horse while trying to impress woman with his horsemanship. <u>Urdemalas</u>: p. 41a.

    K330.3.* Old would-be lover fleeced by woman and two male companions.

K1970. Sham miracles.

    J2285.2.* A short man can grow tall.

K1972.3.* Priest makes congregation believe that God has smitten a disbeliever. Confederate of indulgence-seller priest falls to the floor when priest prays that God will smite the protesting skeptic. Impressed people buy many indulgences. <u>Lazarillo</u>: Tratado V 106a.

K1972.4.* Indulgence seller makes congregation believe that God has seared disbelievers' lips. He presents a secretly-heated red-hot iron cross for people to kiss. When they burn their lips, he claims a miracle. Many people buy indulgences from priest. Lazarillo: Tratado V 109a.

K1975.4.* Sham miracle: tooth pulled without pain and without blood. Trickster pulls a fake borrowed tooth from accomplice's mouth. He sells worthless poultices to people suffering from toothache. **Estebanillo**: Bk. II, Ch. I 1794a.

K1980. Other impostures.

K1983. Trickster poses as helper and eats woman's stored provisions. Justina: Bk. II, Pt. III, Ch. II 836a.

K317.2.3.* Woman thief gains entrance into sick woman's pantry when doctor prescribes poultice of bacon grease.

K1983.1.* Thieves pose as rich man's **helpers** and assist him in burying money and jewels. They rob him while he is away from home. Garduña: Bk. II 1571a.

K1988.2.* Imposters: Women rent "relatives" to appear more imposing at court. Diablo: Tranco III 1648a.

K1988.3.* Imposters: Men and women come to baptismal font to add "don" or "doña" to their names. Titles will give name more prestige. Diablo: Tranco III 1648a.

K2000 - K2099. HYPOCRITES

K2000. Hypocrites.

J261. Loudest mourners not greatest sorrowers. J261.1.* Hypocritical fox goes to bed when his wife dies. K352.1.* Fake doctor steals purse of dying man. T231.6.* Faithless widow puts dead husband

in her bed at night in order to feign discovery
of his death the next morning.

K2010. <u>Hypocrite pretends friendship but attacks</u>.

K2016. Friendship pretended to gain access to girl (wife).
<u>Guzmán</u>: Pt. II, Bk. III, Ch. V 548b.

    K1388.2.* Trickster judge gives husband commission
away from home then seduces man's wife.

K2030. <u>Double dealers</u>.

K2031.2.* Gang shouts "Peace, peace," before attacking man.
Latter is saved when an officer approaches. <u>Guzmán</u>
(Luján): Pt. II, Bk. II, Ch. VII 634b.

K2038.* Fox incites dogs to chase cats, then tells cats that
he prayed to Jupiter to free them from dogs.
<u>Peregrinación</u>: p. 12.

K2039.* Trickster double-crosses four confederates. He
pulls one confederate's tooth to make nobles laugh. He
then denounces this accomplice and three other helpers.
<u>Estebanillo</u>: Bk. II, Ch. I 1794b.

K2050. <u>Pretended virtue</u>.

K2051.5.* Adulteress pretends to admonish lovers. She has
her room decorated with skulls and hangmen's ropes in
order that her lovers will take heed how they live.
<u>Buscón</u>: Bk. I, Ch. I 1093a.

K2051.6.* Adulteress pretends sensitivity toward certain food.
She will not eat snails because they have horns; fish,
because they have bones; rabbits, because they have tails.
<u>Estebanillo</u>: Bk. II, Ch. II 1801a.

    K1550.1.5.* Husband hides adulterous wife from
public in a rented house with no balcony.

K2052.4.4.* Hypocritical widow "faints" after burying husband. She entertains men before and after funeral. <u>Manzanares</u>: Ch. VI 32.

    T231. The faithless widow.

K2054.2.* Thief pretends honesty to mulct **victim.** Takes articles stolen by confederate to mayor (an accomplice) and has town crier announce that these articles have been found. Thieves escape with loot. <u>Codicia</u>: Ch. VIII 1180a.

    K341.15.2.* Thief and confederate rob merchant.

K2054.3.* Sailor given permission to go to chapel to fulfill vow made during storm. He never returns to ship. <u>Estebanillo</u>: Bk. I, Ch. V 1762a.

K2058.1.1.* Apparently pious men are thieves. They pose as devout men and loiter around churches, robbing money at night. <u>Codicia</u>: Ch. VII 1177b.

K2058.3.* Criminals pretend to be religious. They light candles and pray before improvised altar in gang chief's house. <u>Rinconete</u>: p. 183b.

K2058.4.* False ascetic carries skull when begging to admonish people that they are going to die. In an ensuing fight with a man, bystanders side with the hermit and beat up the man. <u>Urdemalas</u>: p. 136a.

K2060. <u>Detection of hypocrisy</u>.

    Q241.2. Lover refuses to take back unfaithful paramour. Q267.2.* Rival lovers abandon hypocritical mistress. Q267.3.* Man feigning death denounces hypocrisy of weeping woman.

K2090. <u>Other hypocritical acts</u>.

K2091.2.* Illness feigned to escape having guests for lunch.
Poor nobleman pretends illness on day he has agreed to
invite guests for lunch. Trapaza: Ch. XII 1491a.

> W152.9.1.* Stingy man cancels invitation to his
> guests. Feigns illness.

> K2100 - K2199. FALSE ACCUSATIONS

K2100. False accusation.

> J1820.0.1.* Officers arrest men engaged in foot
> race. K1956.3.1.* A thief posing as an astrologer
> declares who committed the theft: the officer's
> assistant. N347.1.1.* Innocent man arrested for
> murder when he intervenes with duelers.

K2104.1.* Cloak entrusted to man brings false accusation
of theft. Trickster thus avenges himself on man who
has previously tricked him. Marcos: Bk. I, Descanso IX
958b.

> K1641.2.* Trickster planning to sell entrusted
> cloak is arrested for theft.

K2105.* Falsely accused travelers arrested as robbers.
Highwaymen, thwarted in an attempted robbery, return to
town and accuse travelers of beating and robbing them.
Pindaro: Bk. II, Ch. VII 334b.

K2110. Slanders.

K2111. Potiphar's wife. A woman makes vain overtures to a
man and then accuses him of attempting to force her.
Alonso: Pt. I, Ch. V 1235a; and Periquillo: Discurso
III 1861b.

K2112.0.1.* Jewish woman slandered as adulteress saved from
death by Virgin. She becomes a Christian and gives her
life to the church. Alonso: Pt. II, Ch. XI 1323a.

J1184.1. Adulteress hurled from high rock escapes injury; she may not be punished again.

K2114.1.* False tokens of man's unfaithfulness. Maid steals man's belt and some jewels and accuses him of having deflowered her. Mistress of house tricks maid into confessing her treachery when she says that she has selected a rich huband for her. Periquillo: Discurso II 1860a.

> J1141.1.13.* Mistress tricks maid into confessing false accusation of manservant.

K2114.2.* Teacher-poet falsely accused of heresy. He is jailed because an ignorant judge does not understand his satirical poems. Torres: Trozo III 1949b.

K2116.2.3.* Man falsely accused of murder when he stops to hear dying man's confession. Police later free him. Garduña: Bk. II 1564a.

K2118.1.* Servant accused of stealing master's gold-trimmed hat band. Innocent servant is sent to galleys. Hat band is found later in a rat's nest, and servant is freed. Guzmán: Pt. II, Bk. III, Ch. IX 574b.

K2121.3.* Man slandered as having deflowered innocent girl. Rogues exact money from old man, stating that his nephew has seduced an innocent girl. They produce youth's stolen dagger as evidence. Hija: p. 897a.

> K443. Money acquired by blackmail. K2150. Innocent made to appear guilty.

K2122.* Man falsely accused of rape. Prostitute wants additional money and has man arrested for raping her. Man bribes officer and he "settles" the case. Guzmán: Pt. II, Bk. III, Ch. II 511a.

K1213. Terrorizing the paramour (importunate lover).

K2129.5.* Man is accused falsely of being a sorcerer, magician, and ravisher of virgins. Necio: Ch. VIII 329.

K2158.* Innocent man's satirical sonnets interpreted as sinister conjurations.

K2130. Trouble-makers.

K2132.1.* Trickster tells girl's father that his daughter sends notes to a rich neighbor's son. Father intervenes at night and attacks the real lover, a poor man. Girl is forced to marry poor lover. Urdemalas: 129a - 131a.

K2134.1.* Woman sews together the skirts of two women. Makes trouble between them. Justina: Bk. II, Pt. II, Ch. IV 808a.

K2150. Innocent made to appear guilty.

K443. Money acquired by blackmail. K1817.6.* Man disguised as prostitute. K2121.3.* Man slandered as having deflowered innocent girl.

K2150.1.* Robbed man imprisoned for bringing suit against rich man's thieving son. Thief's father states that the honor of his house has been discredited by the lawsuit. Guzmán: Pt. II, Bk. II, Ch. II 443b.

K2152.3.* Dummy set up in front of dupe's window at night. Dupe shoots the "man" and, on advice from a trickster, takes sanctuary in a monastery. Thieves ransack dupe's house, stealing money and jewels. Garduña: Bk.I 1546b.

K343.0.3.* Thief advises man to leave home.

K2155.1.2.* Corpse in chest carried by innocent man brings accusation of murder. Trapaza: Ch. VI 1455b.

K2155.3.* Corpse of rival in front of man's house brings

accusation of murder. Man is jailed for two years.
He later avenges himself on former mistress and man she
married. <u>Manzanares</u>: Ch. IX 59.

    N347. Innocent man accidentally suspected of crime.

    Q261.2.2.* Treacherous couple killed by explosion.

K2157.* Innocent hermit compelled to give woman gold chain.
Hermit is accused of forcing woman's daughter who had
slipped into his room. Chain is later stolen by
trickster and returned to hermit. <u>Manzanares</u>: Ch. VIII
49.

K2158.* Innocent man's satirical sonnets interpreted as
sinister conjurations. Jealous man gives false inter-
pretations to the police. <u>Necio</u>: Ch. VIII 331.

    K2129.5.* Man is accused falsely of being a
    sorcerer, magician, and ravisher of virgins.

    K2200 - K2299. VILLAINS AND TRAITORS

K2210. <u>Treacherous relatives</u>.

K2211.0.1. Treacherous elder brother(s). Motivated by
jealousy, Cain kills Abel. <u>Alonso</u>: Pt. II, Ch. IV
1290a.

    S73.1. Fratricide.

K2213.4.3.* Samson's secret betrayed by his wife. She cuts
his hair while he sleeps, and he is captured by enemies.
<u>Periquillo</u>: Discurso XVI 1912b.

    D1831. Magic strength resides in hair.

K2213.11.1.* Treacherous queen tricks king into allowing her
to reign for five days. On first day she orders king's
death. <u>Periquillo</u>: Discurso XVII 1917a.

K2214.2.2.* Daughter-in-law destroys portrait of mother-in-
law. Portrait seems to be spying. <u>Alonso</u>: Pt. I,

Ch. IV 1222a.

P260. Relations by law.

K2230. <u>Treacherous lovers</u>.

K2231.1.2.* Adulteress betrays false lover to another man
while latter sleeps. She keeps jerking sleeper's foot
while pronouncing lover's name. Sleeper awakens and
attacks the lover. <u>Guadaña</u>: Ch. XII 1717b.

K2231.2.* Treacherous mistress refuses to admit endangered
lover into her house. She is entertaining her other
lover. <u>Guadaña</u>: Bk. II, 1558b.

K2232.1. Treacherous lover betrays woman's love and deserts
her. She has robbed her aunt in order to flee with lover.
<u>Teresa</u>: Ch. I 1345a.

K2240. <u>Treacherous officers and tradesmen</u>.

K2241.1.* Innkeeper's wife serves a rotten-egg omelet to
soldiers. They throw it in her face. <u>Guzmán</u>: Pt. I,
Bk. I, Ch. IV 260a.

    K1600. Deceiver falls into own trap.

    K1694.* Woman's rotten-egg omelet thrown in her
    face.

K2241.2.* Innkeeper serves guests mule flesh for veal.
<u>Guzmán</u>: Pt. I, Bk. I, Ch. V 264b.

    K1840. Deception by substitution.

K2245.1.* Treacherous judge: has deflowered many maidens.
When a mother asks that her daughter be sent back home,
judge denies any knowledge of the girl. He give the
mother money and tells her to pray that Saint Anthony
will restore the girl's hymen. <u>Guzmán</u>: Pt. II, Bk. III,
Ch. V 548a.

    J1280. Repartee with ruler (judge, etc.).

K2249.5.* Governor sends spoiled meat to prisoners in jail.
Alonso: Pt. I, Ch. VI 1246a.

    R51. Mistreatment of prisoners.

K2250. Treacherous servants and workmen.

K2250.1.1.* Treacherous servant murders woman's small son in
vain hope of seducing the woman. The latter kills the
servant when he breaks into her room. Alonso: Pt. I,
Ch. VII 1251b.

    K1227.9.1.* Importunate lover left at dining table
while woman goes for more food.

K2250.2.* Treachersous servants give new boy a severe "hot-
foot" treatment. The sleeping boy thinks that he is
being carried away by the devil, and his screams
frighten his master. Guzmán (Luján): Pt. II, Bk. I,
Ch. IV 596a.

    J1781.4.* Sleeping boy dreams that "hot-foot"
treatment is the devil carrying him away.

K2250.3.* Treacherous manservant writes an indecent letter
to a maidservant, forging another servant's name. He
shows the letter to the mistress of the house, and she
discovers the forgery and dismisses the offender.
Periquillo: Discurso II 1859b.

K2251.2.* Treacherous galley slave. Kills ship's captain
for having punished him. Slave: "Lower the yard. I
know that I will be hanged, but I don't care. I have
avenged my heart." Guzmán (Luján): Pt. II, Bk. III,
Ch. XI 701a.

    P170 Slaves.

K2252.1.* Treacherous maidservant sends false love letter to
nobleman enamoured with her mistress. The servant

expects money or jewelry as reward. <u>Necio</u>: Ch. II
218; and Ch. III 231.

K2259.4.1.* Treacherous sailor throws himself and enemy
overboard. Enemy cannot swim, but saves himself by
grabbing sailor's leg. Both are rescued. <u>Marcos</u>: Bk. I,
Descanso XXI 989b.

K2259.5.* Treacherous dueler. After receiving a wound, he
calls two friends who attack his opponent, leaving him
for dead. <u>Teresa</u>: Ch. IX 1373b.

K2260. <u>Dark traitors</u>.

K2261.0.1.* Treacherous Moors. Attack a woman in a broken-
down carriage. When she wounds one, the others decapitate
her and take her small daughter as captive. <u>Teresa</u>:
Ch. IX 1376a.

    S133. Murder by beheading.

K2280. <u>Treacherous churchmen</u>.

K2285. Villain disguised as ascetic or nun.

    K443.1.1.* Woman exacts money from thief disguised
    as hermit.

        K2300 - K2399. OTHER DECEPTIONS

K2310. <u>Deception by equivocation</u>.

K2319.1.1.* Family had descended from the royal house of
Aragon. Man's boast is true: His ancestors were
servants in the palace and had escaped by descending in
a basket from the top of the palace wall. <u>Justina</u>:
Bk. I, Ch. II 730b.

    J1114.3.* Servant deceives master with polite phrase.

    K475.4.* Lineage descended from royal house.

K2320. <u>Deception by frightening</u>.

K2320.1.* Students frightened away by muleteer who wants to be alone with a woman. He accuses them of having stolen his money bag, and threatens to call the police.

Marcos: Bk. I, Descanso X 960a.

K2350. Military strategy.

K2357.2. Disguise as pilgrim to enter enemy's camp (castle). Offended enemy kills nobleman during siesta.

Harpías: Estafa I 26ff.

K1817.2.1.* Disguised as pilgrim, offended enemy kills nobleman.

L. REVERSAL OF FORTUNE

L100 - L199. UNPROMISING HERO (HEROINE)

L110. <u>Types of unpromising heroes (heroines)</u>.

L115.1.* Foolish son inherits half of father's estate. His
two normal brothers receive one-fourth each. The foolish
one willneed more money, states the father in his will.
<u>Necio</u>: Ch. V 288.

L123.2.* Poor chestnut vendor becomes wealthy as mistress of
merchant. She returns home, unrecognized, and poses as
a lady. <u>Trapaza</u>: Ch. XV 1509a.

L400 - L499. PRIDE BROUGHT LOW

L400. <u>Pride brought low</u>.

B469.9.2.* Helpful parrot humbles arrogant statesman.

L410. <u>Proud ruler (deity) humbled</u>.

L415.1.* God punishes Herod for his pride in rich clothing.
When Herod sets himself up as a god, heaven punishes him
by sending down spots on his clothing, and the spots
penetrate into his soul. <u>Justina</u>: Introduction, p. 716b.

L430. <u>Arrogance repaid</u>.

L431.4.* Lovers get revenge on woman trickster. They trick
woman's maid into stealing all of her mistress' jewels
and clothes under pretext that the woman will oppose
the maid's marriage. <u>Teresa</u>: Ch. XIX 1423a.

L450. <u>Proud animal less fortunate than humble</u>.

L451.5.* Beetle and the snail. Beetle feels superior to
snail because his wings will take him away from danger
of water. When he starts to fly away, the snail throws
water on him and he drowns. <u>Marcos</u>: Bk.III, Descanso X
1056a.

L460. <u>Pride brought low - miscellaneous</u>.

L473.1.* Wealthy host and guests humbled at banquet. Philosopher brings in corpse and tells revelers to observe the present he has brought and to eat. No one eats. <u>Alonso</u>: Pt. II, Ch. IV 1290a.

L473.2.* **Pride** of soldier brought low by servant's action. Servant places a sharp goad in clothes on soldier's backside. Pricks from goad are so painful that they force soldier to leave reception parlor. <u>Estebanillo</u>: Bk. II, Ch. I 1788a.

L482. Men too prosperous (happy): things are made more difficult. <u>Necio</u>: Ch. III 250.

    A1330. Beginnings of trouble for man. A1346.2.3. **Men** are too happy: pain and sickness created.

M. ORDAINING THE FUTURE

MO - M99. JUDGMENTS AND DECREES

M10. <u>Irrevocable judgments</u>.

M11. Irrevocable judgment causes judge (emperor) to suffer
first. Emperor has decreed that no one enter a meeting
armed. He forgets to remove his sword. Kills himself.
<u>Coloquio</u>: p. 213a.

M50. <u>Other judgments and decrees</u>.

M52.* All literary works should be written in Castilian.
Youthful president of Seville Academy gives many rules
of taste to writer-members. <u>Diablo</u>: Tranco X 1674b.

M53.* King decrees that begging on streets be prohibited.
Poor will be provided for in poorhouses supported by
the government. <u>Torres</u>: Trozo VI 2006b.

M54.* Royal decree that private slaughterhouses be prohibited.
University maintains its own slaughterhouse and protests
the decree. It is allowed to continue processing its
meat. <u>Torres</u>: Trozo VI 2015b.

M57.* Decree that woman must be killed for refusing love and
money. Council of men issue the decree to evesdropping
woman to test her constancy. Although terrified, the
woman remains constant. <u>Necio</u>: Ch. VI 301.

     H387.2.* Man tests hoped-for bride's constancy
     by threat of death.

M100 - M199. VOWS AND OATHS

M150. <u>Other vows and oaths</u>.

M172.3.* Sick alcoholic soldier vows never to touch another
drop of wine - until he gets out of the hospital. The
first part of the vow is in a loud voice; the second,
in a low tone. <u>Estebanillo</u>: Bk. II, Ch. VI 1838b.

M200 - M299. BARGAINS AND PROMISES

M200. **Bargains and promises**.

  K1610.1.* Blind deceiver outwitted by boy guide.

M202.3.* Abused judge promises friendly courtesan that he
would grant freedom to a gallant, if he should be in her
house. A man walks out of a closet and escapes.
Guadaña: Ch. IV 1692b.

  J1193.3.* The gallant goes free. P421. Judge.

M205.0.2.* Lover refuses to marry adulteress after her
husband dies. She has been unfaithful to one husband
and will be so to another. Teresa: Ch. XVII 1411a.

  J1532.2.* Unfaithful to one husband, unfaithful
to another.

M205.5.* Captain breaks promise to pay for trip taken on
horseback. The horse's owner appeals to the magistrate,
and captain pays when he sees officers coming to arrest
him. Estebanillo: Bk. II, Ch. V 1821b.

M206.2.* Host offers guest a free salad if it does not please
him. Guest leaves without paying, saying that the salad
lacked three ingredients: (1) correctness (in amount of
vinegar), (2) liberality (in amount of oil), and (3)
stinginess (in amount of salt). He tosses a coin into
the garden, saying that he and the host lose the same
amount. Estebanillo: Bk. II, Ch. IV 1816a.

M250. **Promises connected with death**.

M256.1. Sons break promise to have masses for father's soul.
"If he is in Hell it will do him no good; if he is in
Heaven he won't need it; and if he is in Purgatory he
can purge himself." Alonso: Pt. I, Ch. X 1269b.

  P236.8.* Undutiful sons do not execute father's will.

M256.1.1.* Executor breaks promise to have masses for testa-
tor's soul. "If he is in Heaven, he doesn't need any help;
if in Hell, it will be more torment for him; if in Purgatory, he will come out sooner or later." Alonso: Pt. II,
Ch. IV 1289b.

M260. Other promises.

M273.* Trickster "promises" Saint Francis to eat with friars
on feast days. Priest "absolves" the uninvited guest of
his vow, and turns him away from the convent. Alonso:
Pt. II, Ch. I 1275a.

> J1563.9.* Priest "absolves" parasitic guest.

M290. Bargains and promises - miscellaneous.

M291.1.* Ruffian cannot slash merchant's narrow face. He
slashes merchant's lackey instead and collects money.
Rinconete: p. 192b.

> J1040.3.* "Hate a man, hate his lackey."

M300 - M399. PROPHECIES

M300. Prophecies.

M302.7. Prophecy through dreams.

> M341.0.4.*. Woman's dream about big tree.

M302.7.1.* Courtesan dreams of pimp's fight. She dreams
that he tried to kill a man. Later, the pimp quarrels
with a man and is taken to prison. Lozana: Mamotreto
XXI 112.

M310. Favorable prophecies.

M312.7.1.* Owl calls: prophecy that abandoned child will
be a wise man. Periquillo: Discurso I 1855a.

M327.* Prophecy: girl's future husband will be the first
being she meets on Saint John's Day. She meets a donkey,

then a castrated sexton. <u>Justina</u>: Bk. III, Ch. VI 868a.

M340. <u>Unfavorable prophecies</u>.

M341. Death prophesied.

    M302.7. Prophecy through dreams.

M341.0.4.* Woman's dream about big tree. Everyone is trying
to break off leaves or branches; this indicates that
she will soon die. <u>Lozana</u>: Mamotreto LXVI 211.

    M302.7. Prophecy through dreams.

M341.1.2.1.1.* Prophecy: death of king within the year.
Publisher of almanac predicts correctly the death of
king. He is considered to be a wise astrologer.
<u>Torres</u>: Trozo III 1958b.

M345.1.2.* Prophecy: Youth's future wife will be unfaithful.
Blind man prophecies that his guide will be given horns
(will be a cuckold) some day. <u>Lazarillo</u>: Tratado I 89a.

    H425.2.1.* Horns will be placed over youth's
    door some day.

M360. <u>Other prophecies</u>.

M363.1.2.* Antichrist to bring much wealth to people who will
follow him. Avaricious man asks priest, "When will the
rich man be here?" <u>Alonso</u>: Pt. II, Ch. III 1283b.

    J1269.14.* When is the rich man coming?

M391.2.1.* Skull is burned, fulfilling the enigmatic prophecy
written on it: "Here I am, but I do not know what will
happen to me." <u>Periquillo</u>: Discurso II 1857b.

    T257.2.3.* Jealous wife burns skull which her
    husband has found and placed in oratory.

M411.1.0.1.* Hangman curses son for shunning his profession.
He will place his son with a shoemaker where he will have
to chew sumach. <u>Marcos</u>: Bk. III, Descanso XIV 1062b.

M414.6. Poet curses. <u>Buscón</u>: Bk. II, Ch. III 1116a.

      P427.7.9.0.1.* Poets banished by proclamation.

M414.11.1.* Woman curses lover for betraying their secret love.

    Sick lover tells his brother about secret love trysts.

    <u>Píndaro</u>: Bk. II, Ch. V 330a.

M470. <u>Curses on objects or animals</u>.

      A2433.3.1.2.* Fox puts curse of coldness on

    unborn kittens.

N. CHANCE AND FATE

N0 - N99. WAGERS AND GAMBLING

N0. Wagers and gambling.

N1. Gamblers.

> J1115.1. Clever gambler. J1115.1.1.* Youths win muleteer's money with marked cards. J1115.1.2.* Youth wagers his mule by quarters. K92.4.* Servant wins conserves by deception. N57. Wager: to teach donkey to read.

N1.3.1.* Betting contest between two birds. Crested lark and heron bet as to which one is better dressed. All the birds helped dress the lark; the heron's husband helped her. The heron won. Justina: Bk. IV, Ch. V 882a.

N5.1.* Dying gambler says "flush" instead of "Jesus." He is given a deck of cards instead of rosary. Diablo: Tranco II 1646b.

N5.2.* Card-playing soldier. He wins money from muleteer, who angrily throws cards in soldier's face. The soldier hits the muleteer with his hat and a lamp, but avoids a duel by escaping in the darkness. Estebanillo: Bk. II, Ch. VI 1843a.

N9.1.1.* Gambler loses much of his wife's dowry. Father-in-law's chief worry is that youth's future games to recoup will take all his money. Alonso: Pt. I, Prologue, p. 1199b.

> J346.1.* Better small gambling loss than trying to recoup and lose everything.

N9.2.* Woman refuses to give lover more money to lose in gambling. He mistreats her, and she runs away with another man. Trapaza: Ch. VIII 1461a.

N9.3.* Losing gambler betrays winner as heretic to Inquisition.

The winner is imprisoned and forced to pay a fine. Trapaza: Ch. IX 1476b.

> Q225.1.1.* Man falsely accused of heresy is punished by imprisonment and fine.

N50. Other wagers.

N57.* Wager: to teach donkey to read. Trickster must make school examiners think his donkey can read. He starves donkey, then puts barley between pages of book. Donkey "reads" by turning pages seeking food. Lozana: Mamotreto LXV 209.

> H1024.4. Task: teaching an ass to read.

N63. Wager: more doctors than men of other professions. Trickster wraps bandage around one arm and one foot and collects people's remedies for his "swellings." He gives the names of all these "doctors" to his master, who has each pay the trickster the agreed on fee for doctors. Lozana: Mamotreto LIV 178.

> N100 - N299. THE WAYS OF LUCK AND FATE
>
> N100 - N169. NATURE OF LUCK AND FATE

N100. Nature of luck and fate.

N101.5.* Thief fated to be hanged. Woman tells thief that he was fated by the stars to be hanged. By-stander slaps woman, telling her that she was destined for such fate. Alonso: Pt. I, Ch. IV 1220a.

> J1459.* One cannot escape his fate.

N110. Luck and fate personified.

> U110. Appearances deceive. Z125. Virtue personified. Z134.2.* Fortune personified as a matron with two daughters (Falsehood and Truth).

N111.2.6.* Fortune has huge worldly retinue. She rewards the undeserving. Diablo: Tranco VII 1661b.

N250. Persistent bad luck.

N251.8.* Misfortune pursues lover. He is in hiding because of a duel. He marries, but his bride dies from an accident on returning home. The bridegroom is wounded when he returns to bride's home, and he leaves the area. Periquillo: Discurso X 1888b.

N270. Crime inevitably comes to light.

N271.3.2.* Jackdaws are witnesses to man's murder. They later cause murderers to talk about their crime; men are overheard, arrested, and punished. Periquillo: Discurso XVI 1914a.

N271.8.1.* Murderer traced through letter of challenge discovered on victim of duel. Píndaro: Bk. I, Ch. I 278a.

N279.* Mule betrays thieves by braying when they inadvertently pass through its hometown. The thieves escape in the night. Píndaro: Bk. II, Ch. XXII 361b.

N300 - N399. UNLUCKY ACCIDENTS

N300. Unlucky accidents.

K1218.9.2.* Importunate lover falls off roof on way to woman's window. N382.1.* Fugitive steals mare in heat and is battered by pursuing stallions. N385.2.* Good singer becomes deaf and makes ridiculous errors.

N310. Accidental separations.

N311.1.* Christ separated from Mary and Joseph at temple. Alonso: Pt. I, Ch. III 1213a.

N320. Person unwittingly killed.

N326.* Two men unwittingly kill each other. Each kills a robber and dresses in his clothes. When the two disguised men meet, they kill each other. Urdemalas: pp. 124b-125a.

N330. Accidental killing or death.

N338. Death as result of mistaken identity: wrong person killed. Assassins kill servant instead of the master. Trapaza: Ch. XII 1492b.

N339.1.1.* Man drinks a jar of cold water and dies. He had never tasted water for forty-four years. Marcos: Bk. I, Ch. XI 963b.

N340. Hasty killing or condemnation (mistake).

N342.0.1.* Woman accuses fiancé of falsifying receipt of her jewel box. She gave it by mistake to another man at night. The lovers separate permanently. Píndaro: Bk. I, Ch. XIX 313a.

N347. Innocent man accidentally suspected of crime.
         K2155.3.* Corpse of rival in front of man's house brings accusation of murder. Q261.2.2.* Treacherous couple killed by explosion.

N347.1.1.* Innocent man arrested for murder when he intervenes with duelers. Píndaro: Bk. I, Ch. IX 292b.
         K2100. False accusation.

N350. Accidental loss of property.

N353.* Cat sets house on fire. Knocks over candle in escaping from dog and fire destroys house. Manzanares: Ch. II 7.

N380. Other unlucky accidents.

N382.1.* Fugitive steals mare in heat and is battered by pursuing stallions. Marcos: Bk. III, Descanso IV 1040b.
         J2650. Bungling fool. N300. Unlucky accidents.

N385.2.* Good singer becomes deaf and makes ridiculous errors. Marcos: Bk. III, Descanso XIV 1062a.

N386.3.* Lover's ladder falls while he is climbing to mistress' window. Excited woman accidentally knocks loose one of ladder's clamps. Píndaro: Bk. I, Ch. XII 299b.

N388.1.* Blind poets in confusion knock each other off platform. Devil gets revenge on poets who were mocking him with their verses. Diablo: Tranco VI 1659b.

    K1081.4.* Blind men duped by devil into fighting.

    Q288. Punishment for mockery.

N391.2.* Woman intercepts note from rival addressed to her lover. Woman goes to rendez-vous in rival's place. Trapaza: Ch. IX 1467a.

    K1223.3.1.* Woman substitutes for rival at rendez-vous with lover.

N391.3.* Woman planning to elope mistakes strange man at night for her lover and gives him a locked chest containing letters, pictures, jewels, and money. Píndaro: Bk. I, Ch. XIV 304a.

    K1317.7.1.* Woman at night gives passer-by box of jewels and money intended for her elopement.

N396.1.* Guard fleeing from dogs runs into a blind man and breaks eggs which the latter is carrying. Marcos: Bk. I, Descanso XXII 994a.

N400 - N699. LUCKY ACCIDENTS

N440 - N499. VALUABLE SECRETS LEARNED

N450. Secrets overheard.

N455.2.1.* Robbers' plans overheard by other thieves. Robbers will take stolen goods to hermit in a monastery. The evesdropping thieves scheme to rob them. Garduña: Bk. II 1574a.

N500 - N599. TREASURE TROVE

N510. <u>Where treasure is found</u>.

N511.1.8.1.* Gold coins buried in cask; silver, in six money
bags. Female thief tells confederates about the silver,
but she steals the gold for herself. Garduña: Bk. I
1548a.

> K302.3.* Female thief advises enamoured man to hide
> his treasure in the garden.

N524.2.* Money found in dead beggar's packsaddle. Rich
beggar wills packsaddle to duke who finds a treasure in
it. <u>Guzmán</u>: Pt. I, Bk. III, Ch. V 353a.

> N630. Accidental acquisition of treasure or money.

N530. <u>Discovery of treasure</u>.

N535.2.* Enigmatic inscription on stone indicates "union"
and "pearl." Youth raises stone and finds two lovers
united in death, and a large pearl and costly necklace
around the girl's neck. <u>Marcos</u>: Bk. I, Prologue, p. 925a.

N600 - N699. OTHER LUCKY ACCIDENTS

N630. <u>Accidental acquisition of treasure or money</u>.

> J1510.3.* Thieving innkeeper hands stolen money
> at night to guest instead of wife. N524.2.* Money
> found in dead beggar's packsaddle.

N630.1.* Passer-by receives money and jewels intended for
another. Woman planning to elope at night mistakes
passer-by for her lover. She hands him money and jewels.
<u>Trapaza</u>: Ch. XIV 1497b.

N636.* Nobleman finds treasure in beggar's packsaddle. Dying
beggar wills packsaddle to duke. <u>Guzmán</u>: Pt. I, Bk. III,
Ch. V 353a.

N640. <u>Accidental healing</u>.

N641.3.* Feverish patient accidentally cured. Doctor puts
her in straight-jacket and leaves her to die. She
sweats profusely and is cured. Guzmán (Luján): Pt. II,
Bk. III, Ch. VIII 681b.

N646.1.* Feverish man drinks filthy bath water and is cured.
Profuse vomiting empties his stomach and he gets well.
Marcos: Bk. I, Descanso XI 963a.

    D1500.1.18.1.3.* Man's bathwater as remedy.

N649.* Sick woman accidentally cured. Man presses so hard
on her stomach that she vomits and gets well.
Guadaña: Ch. VI 1703b.

N650. Life saved by accident.

N659.3.* "Drowned" man revived when thrown face-down on back
of mule. He is being transported for burial when his
lungs suddenly empty out water. Lazarillo (Luna):
Pt. II, Ch. VII 123b.

N659.4.* Sailor's beard saves his life. Beard becomes
entangled in rigging during storm, keeping sailor from
falling into sea. Marcos: Bk. II, Descanso VII 1013a.

N680. Lucky accidents - miscellaneous.

    U164* Cock's crowing reveals hidden chickens.

N680.3.* Lucky soldiers. Discover hidden chickens when
rooster crows. Alonso: Pt. I, Ch. II 1205b.

N681.1.1.* Fiancé arrives home just as mistress is to marry
a sham nobleman. Exposes fraudulent lover.
Trapaza: Ch. II 1435a.

    K1917.5. Man wins girl's love by pretending to
    wealth and nobility.

N685. Fool passes as wise man by remaining silent.
Necio: Ch. I 168.
    K1956. Sham wise man.

N696.3.* Rider and horse fall into privy pit during street
brawl. The man is so covered with filth that officers
cannot lay hands on him to arrest him. Buscón: Bk. I,
Ch. II 1095b.

N700 - N799. ACCIDENTAL ENCOUNTERS

N730. Accidental reunion of families.

N738.2.* Nephew unexpectedly meets uncle and saves him from
prison. Uncle is being taken to jail because he could
not deliver an inheritance to the nephew. Necio:
Ch. V 285.

N741.2.1.* Husband and wife meet in captivity after long
separation. Captor frees them. Marcos: Bk. III,
Descanso XXIV 1084b.

N770. Experiences leading to adventures.

N777.2.1.* Overturned tub leads to adventures. Lovers are
exposed when water accidentally spilled in room above
falls on woman and priest. They run outside and are
arrested for indecent exposure. Lazarillo (Luna):
Pt. II, Ch. V 122a.

K1271. Amorous intrigue observed and exposed.

N778.1.* Man hides meat in tomb at night to escape patrol
during lent. Dog steals meat and man thinks that tomb
is haunted when he hears tinkling of bell tied to dog's
tail. Marcos: Bk. I, Descanso V 942a.

N785.2.* Water-carrier's donkey bumps donkey of another carrier,
upsetting it and breaking jugs. Fight ensues and offending
carrier is taken to jail. Fregona: p. 158b.

N800 - N899. HELPERS

N810. Supernatural helpers.

H983.1.* Unfinished portrait of Virgin finished while artist slept.

N819.5.* Death, Deceit, and Truth help judge from other world. Man dreams that judge from other world sets up tribunal in city and is aided by Death, Deceit, and Truth in carrying out his decisions. <u>Manzanares</u>: Ch. XVIII 119-128.

J1170.1.1.* Wise judgments of judge from other world.

P. SOCIETY

P0 - P99. ROYALTY AND NOBILITY

P10. Kings.

P12.2.1.1.* Tyrant steals costly cape from statue of a temple
   god. He orders a servant to replace the rich cape with
   a plain one: "It protects in winter and is light for
   summer." Alonso: Pt. II, Ch. III 1283a.

P50. Noblemen (knights).

P56.* Ceremonious noblemen block door while they determine
   who will enter first. An ox kicked one nobleman,
   flattening him and thus freeing the entrance.
   Píndaro: Bk. II, Ch. XII 343b.

   B411.2. Helpful ox.

P90. Royalty and nobility - miscellaneous.

P96.* Poor nobleman must pay taxes. His claim to nobility
   does not exempt him. Magistrate says that it would be
   good for him to pay as others do. Guzmán: Pt. II,
   Bk. II, Ch. II 444b.

P97.* Nobleman insults fishmonger. Changes from flattery to
   insults when merchant tells him the price of fish.
   Marcos: Bk. III, Descanso VIII 1050b.

P100 - P199. OTHER SOCIAL ORDERS

P150. Rich men.

   Q272.1.2.* Devil carries off rich men with chain
   made of women's tongues. R11.2.1. Devil carries
   off wicked people.

P160. Beggars.

   K341.2.2.2.* Beggar shams illness in order to
   fleece guardian. N524.2.* Money found in dead
   beggar's packsaddle. Q383.1.* Beggar has hot

water poured on him. Q383.2.* Punishment for
persistent begging. Q458.0.4. Flogging as punishment for imposture. U130.2.* Newly-rich beggar-
girl becomes ill.

P170. <u>Slaves</u>.

K2251.2.* Treacherous galley slave.

P190. <u>Other social orders - miscellaneous</u>.

P192.0.1.* House of madmen. Crazy people do many foolish
things. A blind fool looks at lady's portrait; a
grammarian seeks a lost Greek gerund... <u>Diablo</u>:
Tranco III 1649a.

P192.2.1.* Wicked judge becomes wealthy and respected. His
honest deputy is poor and discredited. <u>Necio</u>: Ch. IV
264.

P200 - P299. THE FAMILY

P230. <u>Parents and children</u>.

P232.3.* Mother allows younger daughter to become nobleman's
mistress in exchange for household accommodations.
<u>Harpías</u>: Estafa I 20-23.

P233. Father and son.

M411.1.0.1.* Hangman curses son for shunning
his profession.

P236.8.* Undutiful sons do not execute father's will. Father
leaves three falcons to two sons: one falcon to each son
and the third to be sold to pay for masses for the father.
One falcon escaped - the one for their father's masses,
they reasoned. They kept the other two. <u>Alonso</u>: Pt. I
Ch. X 1269b.

M256.1. Sons break promise to have masses for
father's soul.

P236.9.* Undutiful son thinks it unnecessary to lament over father's death. If he is in Heaven, no ill can befall him; if in Hell, he has received what he deserves, and weeping will not help; and if he is in Purgatory, he has hopes of being liberated. Necio: Ch. V 287.

P250. Brothers and sisters.

P250.2.* Brother avenges himself on sisters who serve him bad wine. He throws dishes and upsets the table. Estebanillo: Bk. I, Ch. III 1749a.

Q292. Inhospitality punished.

P260. Relations by law.

K2214.2.2.* Daughter-in-law destroys portrait of mother-in-law.

P262.2.* Daughter-in-law cannot tolerate likeness of mother-in-law. Sugar or clay likeness of mother-in-law is objectionable to daughter-in-law. Alonso: Pt, I, Ch. IV 1221b.

P300 - P399. OTHER SOCIAL RELATIONSHIPS

P310. Friendship.

P319.3.1.* Spanish noble's intercession saves Moorish lover from execution. Lover is reunited with his abducted fiancée. Guzmán: Pt. I, Bk. I, Ch. VIII 295a.

R10.1.1. Maiden abducted by soldiers.

P340. Teacher and pupil.

K1822.2.1.* Soldier disguised as scholar.

P344.* Pupils humiliate master who attempts to punish them. They set upon him with knives. One pricks his finger and the other brings a surgeon to take his blood. The master is given a cooky and wine. Manzanares: Ch. XII 77.

P345.* Teacher loses textbook and cannot teach class.
Pupils talk and play. <u>Torres</u>: Trozo II 1935b.

    K1958.1.* Sham teacher loses textbook and cannot
    teach class.

P346.* Master punishes impudent student. He hits him on the
mouth with a heavy compass. This act inspires awe and
quietude among students. <u>Torres</u>: Trozo IV 1958b.

    Q326. Impudence punished.

P360. <u>Master and servant</u>.

    J1289.22.* Ruler rebukes critics. J1561.4.3.*
    Servant refuses to defend stingy master a second
    time.

P361.7.1.* Captain must obey general's order not to kill his
enemy. From his fortified position, captain can laugh
at enemy when he passes ambush. <u>Guzmán</u>: Pt. I, Bk. I,
Ch. IV 261b.

    H1552.3.* General orders captain to mock enemy
    but not to kill him when he passes ambush.

P365.3.* Faithless servants rob money from mistress and
flee undetected. <u>Castigo</u>: p. 1637b.

P367.* Ruler saves servant from drowning. Reprimanded by
his generals for his temerity in swimming the swollen
river, the ruler replies: "You do not know what it is
to love a servant well." <u>Guzmán</u> (Luján): Pt. II,
Bk. II, Ch. III 619b.

    J1289.22.* Ruler rebukes critics.

      P400 - P499. TRADES AND PROFESSIONS

P410. <u>Laborers</u>.

P411. Peasant.

    J1705.1.1.* Stupid peasants refuse to change

route of procession.

P420. <u>Learned professions</u>.

P421. Judge.

J1193.3.* The gallant goes free. M202.3.* Abused judge promises friendly courtesan that he would grant freedom to a gallant.

P421.0.1.* Smiling judge. Condemned persons do not appeal sentences because judge is always smiling. <u>Alonso</u>: Pt. I, Ch. V 1232a.

P421.2.* Judge fails to catch culprit, but confiscates jewels and other property for himself. <u>Guadaña</u>: Ch. IV 1692a.

P422.2.* Lawyers banished by royal decrees. Kingdom will have peace if lawyers learn new professions, or if they are banished. <u>Guzmán</u> (Luján): Pt. II, Bk. III, Ch. II 659b.

P424. **Physician.**

J166.3.* Bible teaches man to honor the doctor.

J1435.* Church no sanctuary from doctor.

W117.3.* Boastful doctor.

P424.3.2.* Physician receives no pay when patient dies. <u>Alonso</u>: Pt. I, Ch. VI 1240a.

P424.6.* Doctor has three faces: face of man when he is not needed; face of angel when he is needed; and face of devil when he keeps calling after patient has recovered. <u>Guzmán</u>: Pt. I, Bk. I, Ch. IV 259a; and <u>Alonso</u>: Pt. I, Ch. VI 1239b.

P424.7.* Two kinds of doctors. Some practise without understanding or knowing medicine; others are doctors merely to make money. Youth decides not to be a doctor.

<u>Torres</u>: Trozo III 1952a.

K1955.8.2.* Sham physician becomes a doctor in thirty days.

P424.8.* Physicians criticized for excessive purgings and blood-letting. Sick man says that his enemies would pity him if they could see him. <u>Torres</u>: Trozo V 1983b.

K1955. Sham physician.

P424.9.* Physicians' "cures" rejected: man gets well. By refusing to let doctors give him purgatives and blood-lettings, sick man gets well. <u>Necio</u>: Ch. III 247.

P425. Scribe.

J1263.1.5.* "It would be a miracle to see a scribe in heaven."

P425.2.* Scribes are the worst of sinners. Priest excoriates scribes for disloyalty and thievery. There is no absolution nor salvation for them. <u>Guzmán</u>: Pt. I, Bk. I, Ch. I 243b.

P426.1.2.* Priest harangues against the selling of public offices. Weighers for markets subsequently are given their offices free of charge. <u>Alonso</u>: Pt. II, Ch. X 1321a.

P427.7.2.2.* Poet and actor closely allied. Poet reads play to actor and crowd. All leave except the actor. <u>Coloquio</u>: p. 229b.

P427.7.9.0.1.* Poets banished by proclamation. Trickster reads false proclamation against poets in order to silence a poet companion. <u>Buscón</u>: Bk. II, Ch. III 1116a.

M414.6. Poet cursed.

P440. <u>Artisans</u>.

P441. Tailor.

J1115.4. Clever tailor. W116.2.2.* Tailor erects showy coat of arms over door.

P446. Barber.

J1484.1.* Skinning or shaving? J1484.2.* Howling dog must be getting a free haircut.

P446.3.* Apprentice barber burns off man's moustache. He uses an iron which is too hot. Estebanillo: Bk. I, Ch. I 1729a.

P446.4.* Apprentice barber cuts a man severely while shaving him. He staunches the blood flow with spider webs. Man's wife fails to recognize him when she comes to his cries. Estebanillo: Bk. I, Ch. III 1743a.

P446.5.* Apprentice barber cuts off half of a youth's ear while cutting his long hair. Master barber punishes apprentice. Estebanillo: Bk. I, Ch. III 1745a.

P460. Other trades and professions.

P461. Soldier.

J1442.1.2.* Cynic rebukes bold and reckless soldier.

P471.2.* Actors satirize doctors in a play. Actress drinks "urine" (white wine) while actor imitates confused doctors. Enraged friends of doctors beat actor to death. Teresa: Ch. XVI 1405a.

K1858.1. Substitute specimen in urinalysis.

P471.3.* Actress starts a fight when she does not get leading role. Police come to arrest the devil and student for a previous disturbance, but arrest actors instead when the devil becomes invisible. Diablo: Tranco V 1657b.

G303.6.2.1.1.* Devil appears invisible among actors.

P471.4.* Heathen actor is converted to Christianity while presenting a rôle satirizing Christian baptism. Alonso: Pt. I, Ch. IX 1261b.

> V330. Conversion from one religion to another.

P471.5.* Intoxicated actor impersonating Bacchus falls from seat, upsetting table where other bacchanal actors are drinking. Crowd stones actors, who escape on horse-drawn float. Estebanillo: Bk. II, Ch. II 1799b.

P471.6.* Comic actors in tableau represent sick-room scene. Whenever the doctor asks for a urine sample, beer is poured into a pot. The doctor examines the "specimen," then drinks it. Estebanillo: Bk. II, Ch. II 1802a.

P475.3.* Robbers loot store at night in presence of dead owner. They get lost and return next morning to the same store. Wife of dead owner tells them about the robbery. Pindaro: Bk. I, Ch. XXIII 321b.

P481.1.* Astrologer unable to predict or prevent his own death. Councillor warned him that he would come to a bad end if he did not quit star-gazing. Astrologer was killed a few days later. Guzmán (Luján): Pt. II, Bk. III, Ch. IV 666b.

P482.1.* Bad painter is advised to paint house first, then whitewash it. He has talked of the opposite procedure. Guzmán: Pt. II, Bk. II, Ch. III 449a.

> J953.2.2.* Bad painter is reprimanded.

P500 - P599. GOVERNMENT

P550. Military affairs.

> H1550. Tests of character. P361.7.1.* Captain must obey general's order not to kill his enemy.

P600 - P699. CUSTOMS

P600. <u>Customs</u>.

P618.* Handkissing as greeting custom. <u>Estebanillo</u>: Bk. II,
Ch. VI 1831a.

    J1840.* Woman misinterprets hand-kissing custom.

P665. Custom: boasting of sexual prowess. "Can swim the
river twice." Man copulates with sleeping courtesan, then
again when she awakens. <u>Lozana</u>: Mamotreto LIII 174.

    H915.2.* Courtesan has man copulate twice with her
to test his boast. W117.2.* Man "can swim the
river twice."

P672. Pulling a man's beard as an insult. <u>Estebanillo</u>:
Bk. I, Ch. III 1750a.

    K1631.1.* The bribed assistant detected by judge.

P677.2.* Military law takes precedence over civil law in
duels. Absent man refuses to accept challenge to duel
by letter. The challenger failed to state the name of
the absent man's servant who allegedly attacked him. A
council finally ruled that since military law deals with
honor and civil law with utility, the challenged man
was obligated to accept the challenge. <u>Guzmán</u> (Luján):
Pt. II, Bk. I, Ch. II 585b.

P682.1.1.* Greeting in God's name angers nobleman. Greeter
says, "May God help you" - a greeting to a common person.
Nobleman requires, "I kiss your lordship's hands."
<u>Lazarillo</u>: Tratado III 103b.

    J410. Association of equals and unequals.

P715.2.* Frenchman and Spaniard argue over merits of his own
country. A cynic sums up the evils of each country.
<u>Periquillo</u>: Discurso XVII 1915b.

Q. REWARDS AND PUNISHMENTS

Q10 - Q99. DEEDS REWARDED

Q40. **Kindness rewarded.**

Q40.1.* Scheming woman gives female confederate reward for
help in securing a rich fiancé. <u>Flora</u>: p. 494.

> Q111. Riches as reward.

Q53.3.2.* Maiden marries rejected lover who rescues her
from grave. <u>Urdemalas</u>: pp. 112b - 126b.

> H911.2.* Rivals assign themselves task of finding
> another woman similar to the one who seems to have
> died. T86.1.1.* Rivals kill each other over woman
> for whom they are searching.

Q80. **Rewards for other causes.**

Q91.3.1.* Judges reward erudite and obscure poem. They do
not understand the poem; therefore, they value it highly.
<u>Estebanillo</u>: Bk. II, Ch. VI 1834a.

> H509.4. Tests of poetic ability.

Q100 - Q199. NATURE OF REWARDS

Q100. <u>Nature of rewards.</u>

Q101.2.* Tax collector rewards four times monetary amount
to defrauded persons. <u>Alonso</u>: Pt. I, Ch. V 1227a.

Q110. <u>Material rewards.</u>

Q111. Riches as reward. Scheming woman gives female confederate 1,000 golden ducates for help in securing a rich
fiancé. <u>Flora</u>: p. 494.

> Q40.1.* Scheming woman gives female confederate
> reward for help in securing a rich fiancé.

Q111.2. Riches as reward (for hospitality). Stranger receives
shelter at young man's house. He becomes sick and dies
several days later, willing his entire fortune to his

young host. <u>Píndaro</u>: Bk. I, Ch. XXI 317b.

W27. Gratitude.

Q111.2.1.* Money as reward for rescue. Stranger opens iron
ring locked around debtor's throat, thus saving him from
slow starvation. Friends give rescuerer monetary reward.
<u>Píndaro</u>: Bk. II, Ch. XXIV 366a.

Q421.0.1.1.* Starvation as punishment for debt.

Q150. <u>Immunity from disaster as reward</u>.

Q151.1.1.* Life spared as reward for charitable act performed
years before. Robber's life is spared 23 years after he
had saved the life of a student. The latter, now a priest,
saves robber. <u>Marcos</u>: Bk. I, Descanso XIV 972b.

Q170. <u>Religious rewards</u>.

Q171.1.2.* Emperor is forgiven for raping girl. His generous
gifts to the poor ties hands of Virgin Mary. <u>Guzmán</u>:
Pt. I, Bk. III, Ch. VI 355b.

V250. The Virgin Mary.

Q200 - Q399. DEEDS PUNISHED

Q210. <u>Crimes punished</u>.

Q210.2.* Judge imprisons friends of escaped assassins. He
maintains his reputation as a severe judge.
<u>Guadaña</u>: Ch. III 1687b.

Q212.2.1.* Dead virgin punishes grave robber. She scratches
out his eyes when he tries to strip off her costly
burial clothes. <u>Alonso</u>: Pt. II, Ch. IV 1291a.

K426.1.* Apparently dead virgin revives when thief
tries to strip off her burial clothes.

Q451.7. Blinding as punishment.

Q212.5.* Son punished for stealing from father. He is caught,
flogged, and exiled. <u>Rinconete</u>: p. 178a.

Q220. Impiety punished.

Q221.1.2.* Bears kill children who mock Elijah. The latter curses the children for mocking his baldness. Alonso: Pt. I, Ch. X 1268b.

Q221.1.3.* Miriam becomes leprous for murmuring against Moses. Alonso: Pt. I, Ch. X 1268b.

Q221.3.1.* Priest threatens to denounce critical woman to Inquisition. He has overheard her criticizing some mal-practices of the church. Justina: Bk. II, Pt. III, Ch. I 826b.

Q223.4.2.* Revenant punishes dueler for letting him die without confessing. Corpse rises from casket and wounds his murderer. Píndaro: Bk. I, Ch. XVII 311b.

    E230. Return from dead to inflict punishment.
    K778.3.2.* Capture by luring to women's room, which closes around man.

Q223.6. Failure to observe holiness of Sabbath punished. Man's mule slips and falls down a steep slope. The man believes he has been punished for taking the trip on Sunday. Marcos: Bk. I, Descanso XVI 979b.

    C631.1. Tabu: journeying on Sabbath.

Q225.1.1.* Man falsely accused of heresy is punished by imprisonment and fine. Trapaza: Ch. IX 1476b.

    N9.3.* Losing gambler betrays winner as heretic to Inquisition.

Q240. Sexual sins punished.

Q241. Adultery punished.

    J1351.3.* Many women deserve the same punishment.
    K1551.1. Husband returns secretly and kills unwelcome suitor. Q411.0.3.* Husband beheads

adulteress. Q433.5.1.* Imprisonment for intercourse. S139.6. Murder by tearing out heart.

Q241.2. Lover refuses to take back unfaithful paramour. He
overhears mistress reading a note to another lover.
Garduña: Bk. II, 1562b.

> K2060. Detection of hypocrisy. Q267.2.* Rival
> lovers abandon hypocritical mistress.

Q241.2.1.* Woman (nun) refuses to take back lover who left
city without notifying her. Guzmán: Pt. II, Bk. I,
Ch. II 398a.

> T70. The scorned lover.

Q245. Punishment for refusal to marry after girl is pregnant.
Man is jailed; later breaks legs and an arm in attempted
jail break. He confesses and marries the girl shortly
before he dies. Trapaza: Ch. I 1428b.

Q252.2.* Prince punished for breaking betrothal. He has
promised a large sum of money to girl for her favors,
then refuses to marry her. Court forces him to pay her.
Guzmán: Pt. II, Bk. III, Ch. II 513a.

> K1353.2.* Prince promises to marry woman and give
> her a large sum of money for her favors. T455.
> Woman sells favors for particular purpose.

Q260. Deceptions punished.

Q261.2.2.* Treacherous couple killed by explosion. Man
avenges himself for imprisonment on false charge of
killing a rival. Manzanares: Ch. IX 59.

> K2155.3.* Corpse of rival in front of man's house
> brings accusation of murder. N347. Innocent man
> accidentally suspected of crime.

Q262. Imposter punished.

> Q458.0.4. Flogging as punishment for imposture.

Q267.2.* Rival lovers abandon hypocritical mistress. Each
discovers the lady's double dealing. The spurned woman
enters a convent. Garduña: Bk. II 1562b.

> K2060. Detection of hypocrisy. Q241.2. Lover
> refuses to take back unfaithful paramour.

Q267.3.* Man feigning death denounces hypocrisy of weeping
woman. She comes to his bedside only after learning of
"fortune" which he has willed her. The will is worthless.
Necio: Ch. IV 283.

> K2060. Detection of hypocrisy.

Q270. Misdeeds concerning property punished.

Q272.1.2.* Devil carries off rich men with chain made of
women's tongues. Guzmán: Pt. II, Bk. III, Ch. III
(in James Mabbe, The Rogue, London: Tudor Translations,
IV 151).

> P150. Rich men. R11.2.1. Devil carries off
> wicked people.

Q272.1.3.* Avaricious man punished in hell. Begs to have
Lazarus bring him water. Alonso: Pt. I, Ch. V 1233a.

Q280. Unkindness punished.

> W111.3.3.1.* Lazy wife hangs up hen instead of
> feeding sick husband. Doctor reprimands her.

Q285.2.1.* Doctor reprimands woman for neglect of sick husband.
Woman has a chicken hanging up, but she has not fed her
sick husband. Alonso: Pt. II, Ch. VI 1301b.

Q288. Punishment for mockery.

> K1081.4.* Blind men duped by devil into fighting.
> N388.1.* Blind poets in confusion knock each other
> off platform. Q221.1.2.* Bears kill children who
> mock Elijah.

Q292. Inhospitality punished. Estebanillo: Bk. I, Ch. III
1749a.

P250.2.* Brother avenges himself on sisters who
serve him bad wine.

Q300. Contentiousness punished.

W128.7.* Man and dissatisfied animals appear
before Jupiter seeking change of status.

Q313.1.* Angry soldier punished for insulting remarks. He
berates people of foreign country where he is visiting,
and is locked in an iron cage in the middle of town
square. Estebanillo: Bk. II, Ch. VII 1845a.

Q320. Evil personal habits punished.

Q393.0.1.* Man punishes self for swearing.

Q393.2.1.* Male gossiper reproved for evil ways.

Q325. Disobedience punished.

F1021.2.1. Flight so high that sun melts glue of
artificial wings.

Q325.1.* Icarus disobeys father and flies too high. Sun
melts his wings. Guzmán (Luján): Pt. II, Bk. III,
Ch. IV 664b.

Q325.2.* Son disobeys father's wishes and drowns. Father
refuses to allow son to engage in dangerous water sport.
Son persists, is granted permission, but drowns.
Marcos: Bk. I, Descanso XV 977a.

Q325.3.* Soldier punished for not accompanying prince on
deer hunt. He is forced to wear deer antlers with bells
attached, and to wear a deer skin. Estebanillo: Bk. II,
Ch. I 1790b.

Q325.4.* Soldier punished for failure to accompany master to
a baptism. He is forced to drink much wine, and is

terrorized with threats of castration. <u>Estebanillo</u>:
Bk. II, Ch. I 1792a.

Q326. Impudence punished.

    P346.* Master punishes impudent student.

Q330. <u>Overweening punished</u>.

Q331.0.1.* Two proud men knock each other down on narrow
bridge. Each is too proud to wait for the other to
pass. <u>Marcos</u>: Bk. III, Descanso VIII 1050a.

    W167. Stubbor**nness**.

Q338. Immoderate request punished.

    F930.2.1.* Waters of Tiber rise to drown imperti-
nent workmen. J514.7.* Greedy artist wants more
money for painting of horse. He gets nothing.
J957.1.* Presumptuous man asks university to postpone examination of candidates for faculty position
until he receives his degree. Q552.19.5. Miraculous drowning as punishment for haughtiness.
V311.4.* Mother asks Christ to grant her sons
special privileges in life to come. Request refused.

Q338.3.* Workmen punished for requesting emperor's son as
hostage for work payment. Tiber overflows, drowning
workmen and emperor's son. <u>Lozana</u>: Mamotreto LIII 173.

    Q552.19.5. Miraculous drowning as punishment for
haughtiness.

Q338.4.* Request for higher condition punished. Beetle
requests Jupiter to give him a more noble appearance,
and a louse supports his request. Both insects are
crushed under a man's foot. <u>Periquillo</u>: Discurso IX
1884a.

    A2232.3.1.* Beetle makes request for more noble
appearance.

Q340. Meddling punished.

  A2433.3.1.2.* Fox puts curse of coldness on
  unborn kittens.

Q340.1.* Cat receives fox's curse for ruining letter written
  to fish. Kittens will be born cold-natured. Justina:
  Bk. I, Ch. I 725b.

  M470. Curses on objects or animals.

Q380. Deeds punished - miscellaneous.

Q382.* Punishment for suspected thievery. Bully beats his
  moll when she gives him less money than he requested.
  He suspects thievery. Rinconete: p. 188b.

  J865.2.* Reconciliation will be sweet.

Q383.1.* Beggar has hot water poured on him. He is begging
  during siesta hour. Guzmán: Pt. I, Bk. III, Ch. III
  345b.

  P160. Beggars.

Q383.2.* Punishment for persistent begging. Irritated man
  asks beggar to extend cape to receive alms. He throws
  down excrement, befouling the beggar. Guadaña: Ch. I
  1684a.

  J1331.1.* Persistent beggar receives alms.

  P160. Beggars.

Q393.0.1.* Man punishes self for swearing. He pinches
  himself or kisses the earth every time he swears, but
  he cannot break the habit. Coloquio: p. 210a.

  Q320. Evil personal habits punished.

Q393.1.1.* Devil punishes foreigners for slandering king
  of Spain. He scatters gossipers with mighty blows.
  He and student get all the food. Diablo: Tranco V 1656a

Q393.2.1.* Male gossiper reproved for evil ways. He excused
himself: He had been misinterpreted. He had not meant
to offend anyone. Coloquio: p. 210a.

Q320. Evil personal habits punished.

Q393.2.2.* Ruler advises punishment for bearer of gossip.
The blows are not for the bearer; but since he brought
the gossip, he can take the blows to the gossiper.
Marcos: Bk. I, Descanso XXIV 999b.

Q395.1.* Captain's disrespect punished. He puts on his hat
in presence of king's favorite. The latter delays
captain's appointment, causing him anxiety and loss of
money. Guzmán: Pt. I, Bk. II, Ch. X 334b.

J410. Association of equals and unequals.

Q395.2.* Students are arrested for failing to raise hats
when officer passes by. They are freed and fed when a
respectful companion explains their plight.
Marcos: Bk. I, Descanso XII 965a.

J829.4.* Only one student raises hat when mayor
passes by.

Q400 - Q599. KINDS OF PUNISHMENT

Q410. Capital punishment.

Q411.0.3.* Husband beheads adulteress. Before a crowd of
onlookers, a husband beheads his faithless wife. A
male onlooker observes that many female witnesses deserve
the same punishment. Guzmán: Pt. II, Bk. II, Ch. IV,
454b.

J1350. Rude retorts. Q241. Adultery punished.

Q411.0.4.* Husband kills wife and paramour on ship. An
intercepted note informs husband that wife and lover
plan to escape by ship. Periquillo: Discurso XI 1893a.

K1844.1.2.* Husband has another man substitute
for him in bed. T258.1.1. Husband insists on
knowing wife's secret.

Q411.3.1.* Father dies of heart attack when about to kill
innocent daughter. He thinks that she has been disgraced
by lover. Urdemalas: p. 76b.

T97. Father opposed to daughter's marriage.

Q411.3.2.* Man executed for thievery. Girl reports that her
uncle died in a high place with a pain in his neck.
(He was hanged.) Flora: pp. 312 - 313.

Q411.7.1.* Brother killed for ravishing sister. Another
brother mixes his blood with mortar to build a house
for the sister. Justina: Bk. II, Pt. I, Ch. I 764b.

T415. Brother - sister incest.

Q411.7.2.* Brothers kill ravisher of sister. Ravisher's
heart is torn out and thrown to lions. Justina:
Bk. II, Pt. I, Ch. I 764b.

Q411.7.3.* Death as punishment for seducer who refuses to
marry girl. Father of seduced girl and relatives
murder the seducer. Píndaro: Bk. I, Ch. IV 283b.

Q411.11. Death as punishment for desecration of holy places
(images, etc.). Alonso: Pt. I, Ch. III 1211a - 1212b.

Q413.1. Hanging as punishment for theft. Buscón: Bk. I,
Ch. VII 1110b.

J2174.6.* Man about to be hanged shows much bravado.

Q413.4.1.* Paramour is hanged for killing husband of mistress.
Latter laments near gibbet. Her cries, together with
worms falling from the corpse, awaken man who has fallen
asleep underneath at night. Marcos: Bk. I, Ch. X 961a.

T232.2.1.* Adulteress remains by hanging corpse of lover who has killed her husband.

Q421.0.1.1.* Starvation as punishment for debt. Creditor clamps an iron ring around man's throat when he does not pay gambling debt. Victim is later rescued by a stranger, who receives a reward. <u>Pindaro</u>: Bk. II, Ch. XXIV 366a.

Q111.2.1.* Money as reward for rescue.

Q421.0.5.1.* Nuns are beheaded by Moors. Hoping to avoid being ravished by conquering Moors, nuns disfigure themselves. Their faces are so repugnant that the Moors behead them. <u>Guzmán</u> (Luján): Pt. II, Bk. II, Ch. VI 630a.

T326.3. Martyrdom to preserve virginity.

Q421.1.2.* King's head cut off and placed in container of human blood. Conqueror: "Fill yourself with blood; you were so thirsty for it." <u>Guzmán</u> (Luján): Pt. II, Bk. III, Ch. V 669b.

Q430. <u>Abridgment of freedom as punishment</u>.

Q433.0.1.* Punishment: imprisonment in the galleys. Brothers are falsely betrayed by innkeeper to Inquisition. <u>Lazarillo</u> (Luna): Pt. II, Ch. XII 134b.

Q433.5.1.* Imprisonment for intercourse. Master imprisons manservant for intimacy with maidservant. Servant cannot pay heavy fine, and remains in jail until he marries the girl. He becomes a pilgrim and the girl a prostitute. <u>Guzmán</u>: Pt. II, Bk. III, Ch. II 513b.

Q241. Adultery punished.

Q434. Fettering.

J2183.0.1.* Hunter decides to pacify fighting servants before rescuing fettered women.

Q580.1.* Women who have abandoned sick male
companion are later fettered to trees and abandoned.

Q450. Cruel punishments.

Q451.7. Blinding as punishment.

Q212.2.1.* Dead virgin punishes grave robber.

Q458.0.4. Flogging as punishment for imposture. Beggar
pretends to have a broken leg. Official has imposter
flogged. Guzmán: Pt. I, Bk. III, Ch. V 354a.

K254.3.* Trickster receives double portion of food
on pretense of taking some to other unfortunates.

K729.* Beggar lured to officer's house by
promise of a shirt.

Q458.0.4.1.* Men flog prostitutes who often have tricked
them. Manzanares: Ch. VI 35.

Q469.1.1.* Adulterer caused to fall down stairs from which
steps have been removed. Marcos: Bk. III, Descanso
VII 1046b.

S139.6. Murder by tearing out heart.

Q470. Humiliating punishments.

Q471.3.* New student is spit upon by older students. His
clothes are ruined. Buscón: Bk. I, Ch. V 1104a.

Q475.3.* Glue in breeches as punishment for impersonating
prostitute. Breeches have to be ripped apart to free
man's pubic hairs. Guzmán: Pt. I, Bk. III, Ch. VIII 366a.

Q497.2.* Tricksters cut off half of bully's formidable
moustache while he sleeps. Bully becomes meek on discovering loss. Marcos: Bk. III, Descanso XII 1059a.

Q499.4.2.* Satirizing as punishment for master's dismissing
of servant. Latter's poem satirizes master's short
stature. Master is enraged and plans vengeance, but

servant leaves town. <u>Trapaza</u>: Ch. V 1446a.

Q500. <u>Tedious punishments</u>.

Q501.5. Punishment of Ixion. Lashed to a wheel which revolves
continually, Ixion is punished for having fallen in love
with Hera (Juno). <u>Guzmán</u> (Luján): Pt. II, Bk. III,
Ch. V 668a.

    A132.6.2.1.* Goddess in form of cloud. Ixion
unites with cloud in form of goddess Juno.

Q552.3.5.1.* Goatherd garroted for cutting off town's water
supply in order to receive money for restoring it.
<u>Marcos</u>: Bk. I, Descanso XIV 971b.

Q552.14. Storm as punishment. Priest tells ship's captain
that the storm is punishment for captain's illicit
relations with a woman passenger. Captain disembarks
the woman and her male companion. <u>Urdemalas</u>: p. 27a.

Q552.19.5. Miraculous drowning as punishment for haughtiness.

    Q338. Immoderate request punished. Q338.3.* Work-
men punished for requesting emperor's son as hostage
for work payment.

Q580. <u>Punishment fitted to crime</u>.

    Q434. Fettering.

Q580.1.* Women who have abandoned sick male companion are
later fettered to trees and abandoned. <u>Hija</u>:p.906b.

Q581.1.1.* Mutilator of girl's hand suffers death by having
both hands cut off. <u>Guzmán</u>: Pt. I, Bk. III, Ch. X 375b.

    S161.0.2.* Rejected suitor cuts off hand of maiden.

Q590. <u>Miscellaneous punishments</u>.

Q591.0.1.* Heathen actor (Genesius) is converted to Christianity while acting rôle of Christian. He confesses and
is killed. <u>Alonso</u>: Pt. I, Ch. **IX** 1261b.

V330. Conversion from one religion to another.

Q591.1. Punishment: death pretended becomes real. <u>Alonso</u>:
Pt. I, Ch. V 1227a.

K1860. Deception by feigned death (sleep).

Q591.1.2.* Punishment: pretended beating becomes real.
Trickster has arranged with another man to stage a fake
beating to appease a third party. Trickster beats and
slashes man later for betraying him to police.
<u>Guadaña</u>: Ch. X 1711a.

Q595.0.1.* Foxes set fire to inn to punish treacherous
innkeeper. The latter proposes to foxes that they
rob drunken monkey actors. The foxes refuse.
<u>Peregrinación</u>: p. 52.

R. CAPTIVES AND FUGITIVES
RO - R99. CAPTIVITY

R10. <u>Abduction</u>.

R10.1.1. Maiden abducted by soldiers. Moorish maiden is
abducted by Spanish soldiers and sent as servant to
Spanish queen. Her Moorish lover find her and after a
series of adventures is reunited with her. <u>Guzmán</u>:
Pt. I, Bk. I, Ch. VIII 273b - 295b.

>P319.3.1.* Spanish noble's intercession saves
Moorish lover from execution.

R11.2.1. Devil carries off wicked people.

>P150. Rich men. Q272.1.2.* Devil carries off
rich men with chain made of women's tongues.

R11.3. Abduction by giant.

>G121.1.2.* Giants sieze men.

R12.2.2.* Children abducted by robbers. Latter mutilate
them and sell them to professional beggars.
<u>Codicia</u>: Ch. VII 1177b.

>S160. Mutilations. S161.1.2.* Robbers break
stolen children's arms and legs.

R18. Abduction by rejected suitor. Lover overhears beloved
and her mother denouncing him. He determines to get
revenge on the haughty women. <u>Necio</u>: Ch. V 291.

>T75.2.1. Rejected suitor's revenge.

R40. <u>Places of captivity</u>.

R43. Captivity on island.

>G121.1.2.* Giants sieze men.

R50. <u>Conditions of captivity</u>.

R51. Mistreatment of prisoners.

>K2249.5.* Governor sends spoiled meat to prisoners

in jail. S161.2.* Prisoner's arm cut off and
used as club.

R100 - R199. RESCUES

R110. Rescue of captive.

R121.11.* Men escape from giants' cave by means of bone
ladder. Marcos: Bk. III, Descanso XXI 1077a.

R150. Rescuers.

R153.1.2.* Mother and servants rescue baby. Drunken nurse-
maid was lying on it. Guadaña: Ch. II 1687a.

R161.3.1.* Poet falls in love with "nymph." (Macías
falls in love with woman whom he saves from drowning.)
Alonso: Pt. II, Ch. VI 1300a.

R165.3.1.* Abducted woman freed unharmed by abductor. Her
constancy impressed him, and he had a friend escort her
home at night. Necio: Ch. VII 319.

R200 - R299. ESCAPES AND PURSUITS

R210. Escapes.

R211.4.1.* Pirates abandon ship, leaving Christian captive
in charge. He is captured and freed by Christian forces.
Marcos: Bk. II, Descanso XIV 1032a.

R211.10.* Captive promises jailer to make him rich by
turning iron into gold. Trickster escapes by blowing
sleeping powder into jailer's face. Marcos: Bk. III,
Descanso I 1036a.

R211.11.* Male thief escapes from prison dressed as a woman.
Garduña: Bk. III 1595a.

K307.5.* Thieves betray hiding place of other
thieves.

R213.2.* Moorish brother and sister escape from Africa to
Spain. They have been converted to Christianity and

want to live in captive father's homeland. <u>Marcos</u>:
Bk. III, Descanso XVI 1063b.

V330. Conversion from one religion to another.

R213.3.* Trapped man escapes from woman's apartment by
dropping through hole in floor. <u>Píndaro</u>: Bk. II,
Ch. V 331b.

K1213.5.* Adulteress contrives with swordsmen to
attack her unarmed lover.

R215.4.* Man escapes execution when king's letter of pardon
arrives at last minute. <u>Píndaro</u>: Bk. I, Ch. II 279b.

R216.2.* Escape from ship while captors revel. Christian
captives freed from Moors when latter indulge in
drinking orgy to celebrate victory. <u>Marcos</u>: Bk. III,
Descanso XVII 1070b.

R219.3.* Escape from jail sentence. Master and servant
flee to another country to escape jail sentence.
Master has wounded another man with his sword, and the
servant is an accomplice. <u>Torres</u>: Trozo IV 1961a.

R220. <u>Flights</u>.

R227.2.1.* Christian wife flees from infidel husband. She
escapes in boat from Africa to Spain, aided by Christian
servant. <u>Marcos</u>: Bk. II, Descanso XIII 1030a.

R300 - R399. REFUGES AND RECAPTURE

R310. <u>Refuges</u>.

R325.4.* Fleeing men receive sanctuary in convent. They are
fired upon at first, but were admitted to convent when
identified. <u>Píndaro</u>: Bk. II, Ch. XIII 345a.

S. UNNATURAL CRUELTY

S0 - S99. CRUEL RELATIVES

S10. Cruel parents.

S11.1.1.* Beggar father mutilates son. Latter's deformity elicits alms from sympathetic people and father becomes wealthy. Guzmán: Pt. I, Bk. II, Ch. V 352b.

N524.2.* Money found in dead beggar's packsaddle.

S30. Cruel step - and foster relatives.

S37.1.* Stepsons turn foster father out of house when father's wife dies. They dispossess him of all property. Alonso: Pt. II, Ch. VI 1304a.

S50. Cruel relatives-in-law.

S52.1.* Cruel father-in-law. Sets son's fiancée adrift in boat. She is rescued by boatman, sells a ring which she had hidden in her mouth, and returns. Lozana: Mamotreto IV 22.

S141. Exposure in boat.

S60. Cruel spouse.

Q241. Adultery punished. S139.6. Murder by tearing out heart.

S62.2.1.* Jealous woman attempts to have rival drowned in order to marry latter's lover (husband). Octavia has Portia thrown into Tiber, but she is rescued. Through Caesar's intervention, Portia and Claudius, her secret husband, are re-united. Trapaza: Ch. VI 1447.

S70. Other cruel relatives.

S73.1. Fratricide.

K2211.0.1. Treacherous elder brother(s).

S100 - S199. REVOLTING MURDERS OR MUTILATIONS

S110. <u>Murders</u>.

      K1551.1. Husband returns secretly and kills unwlecome suitor.

S133. Murder by beheading. Woman is beheaded by Moors after she wounds one of them. They take her daughter captive. <u>Teresa</u>: Ch. IX 1376a.

      K2261.0.1.* Treacherous Moors.

S139.2.2.2.1.* Dead man mutilated by hungry dog. <u>Justina</u>: Bk. I, Ch. III 745b.

S139.2.2.3.2.* Corpses' clothing removed and sold by grave robbers. <u>Diablo</u>: Tranco III 1650a.

S139.6. Murder by tearing out heart. Husband places heart of paramour between fettered wife and murdered suitor. <u>Marcos</u>: Bk. III, Descanso VII 1046b.

      Q241. Adultery punished. Q469.1.1.* **Adulterer** caused to fall down stairs from which steps have been removed.

S141. Exposure in boat.

      S52.1.* Cruel father-in-law. S322.1.0.1.* Father casts daughter forth.

S160. <u>Mutilations</u>.

S161.0.2.* Rejected suitor cuts off hand of maiden. Latter's fiancé avenges her death by cutting off both hands of murderer and by hanging him near dead girl's house. <u>Guzmán</u>: Pt. I, Bk. III, Ch. X 375b.

      Q581.1.1.* Mutilator of girl's hand suffers death by having both hands cut off.

S161.1.2.* Robbers break stolen children's arms and legs. They sell them later to professional beggars. <u>Codicia</u>: Ch. VII 1177b.

      R12.2.2.* Children abducted by robbers.

S161.2.* Prisoner's arm cut off and used as a club. Master
of galley ship cuts off Christian's arm and uses it as
a club to make other slaves row faster. <u>Alonso</u>: Pt. II,
Ch. XIII 1335b.

R51. Mistreatment of prisoners.

S300 - S399. ABANDONED OR MURDERED CHILDREN

S310. <u>Reasons for abandonment of children</u>.

S312.4.1.* Woman abandons baby boy to keep her father from
learning of her illicit relations with her lover. She
lowers basket with baby in it to a stranger as he passes
her house at night. <u>Píndaro</u>: Bk. II, Ch. XIV 346b.

S321.2.* Destitute parents abandon baby boy at convent door.
Baby is found by childless couple who rear him, naming
him Pedro, as note accompanying the baby asked finders
to do. <u>Periquillo</u>: Discurso I 1854b.

S322.1.0.1.* Father casts daughter forth. She resembles too
closely her mother who has run away with another man.
<u>Periquillo</u>: Discurso XII 1898a.

S141. Exposure in boat.

S322.1.3.1.* Father murders daughter. She resembles too
closely her mother who has run away with another man.
Later, the father asks to be buried in a certain place
where the daughter's skeleton is found. <u>Periquillo</u>:
Discurso XII 1897b.

S350. <u>Fate of abandoned child</u>.

S351.2.2.* Abandoned baby boy reared by goatherd.
<u>Periquillo</u>: Discurso XII 1897a.

S353.3.* Abandoned baby boy of king's daughter reared by
water nymphs. Later he falls in love with a nymph and
is banished by nymph's father. <u>Garduña</u>: Bk. III 1583a.

T. SEX

TO - T99. LOVE

T10. <u>Falling in love</u>.

T11.2. Love through sight of picture.

>H1381.3.1.2.1. Quest for unknown woman whose picture has aroused man's love. J2323.1.* Numskull is tricked into marrying ugly woman. K1915.4.* Ugly woman substituted for beautiful one whose picture dupe had seen.

T11.2.0.2.* Love through sight of picture. Man falls in love with woman in picture which he has stolen. He determines to find the original of the **portrait**. <u>Trapaza</u>: Ch. XIV 1497b.

T30. <u>Lovers' meeting</u>.

>K1271.2.2.* Lovers observed in intrigue in the garden.

T41.2. Communication of lovers through hole in floor. Woman drops letter to man's room, inviting him to come to her apartment. He is to go to a church, be blindfolded, and carried to the **apartment** in a sedan chair. <u>Píndaro</u>: Bk. II, Ch. III 325b; and Bk. II, Ch. IV 329a.

>T55. Girl as wooer.

T41.3.1.* Cough is to be signal for lover's meeting with nun. He replies to persistent coughing only to discover that there was an old lady in church with a bad cold. <u>Buscón</u>: Bk. III, Ch. IX 1150b.

T50. <u>Wooing</u>.

T51.3. Match arranged by means of pictures of both parties. <u>Garduña</u>: Bk. IV 1602b.

T51.4.* Woman emissary intercedes for her female friend.
Emissary retracts a lie concerning the identity of her
female friend, and helps secure a rich fiancé for her.
Flora: p. 493.

T53.0.2.* Master tries to be matchmaker with servants. Maidservant embraces the manservant, but the latter escapes
and abandons the service of his master. Periquillo:
Discurso IX 1884b.

T55. Girl as wooer.

T41.2. Communication of lovers through hole in floor.

T70. The scorned lover.

K1214.1.2.* Importunate lover is tricked into
paying for woman's trip. Q241.2.1.* Woman (nun)
refuses to take back lover who left city without
notifying her.

T71.2.1. Woman scorned in love complains of man's coldness.
She tries to seduce him, but he resists her advances.
Pindaro: Bk. II, Ch. VIII 336a.

T75.0.3.* Woman deserts lover. She tricks him into paying
for her trip to city in order to seek justice against
an alleged seducer. She never returns. Lazarillo
(Luna): Pt. II, Ch. I 116b.

T75.2.1. Rejected suitor's revenge. Disguised as coachman,
suitor abducts woman. Necio: Ch. V. 291.

R18. Abduction by rejected suitor.

T75.3.1.* Unrequited love expressed by charade. Unsuccessful
lover has himself carried about on hairless skins with
a sign which reads, "Remember a forgotten man who because
of you is plucked (skinned)." Justina: Introduction, p. 711b.

T86.1.1.* Rivals kill each other over woman for whom they are searching. **According** to their previous agreement, the first one to see the woman is to woo her, but both rivals see her at the same time. <u>Urdemalas</u>: pp. 112b - 126b.

    H911.2.* Rivals assign themselves task of finding another woman similar to the one who seems to have died. Q53.3.2.* Maiden marries rejected lover who rescues her from grave.

T90. <u>Love - miscellaneous motifs</u>.

T92. Rivals in love.

    K1350.0.1.* Rival lover compromises widow's honor by adjusting clothes in front of her house in early morning.

T92.1.3.* Widow marries, then kills, rival lover who has compromised her honor. Her preferred lover enters a monastery, and she enters a convent. <u>Guzmán</u>: Pt. II, Bk. II, Ch. VIII 481b.

    T173.2.1.* Hostile bride kills husband who has compromised her honor before marriage.

T92.3.1.* Seduced woman recovers her honor. At night, man meets woman whom he has seduced, while fiancée of the seducer meets her true lover. Police raid the house , and the two pairs of lovers are betrothed. Thus, the seduced woman recovers her honor. <u>Garduña</u>: Bk. IV 1612a.

T92.10. Rival in love killed. <u>Garduña</u>: Bk. I 1542b.

    K929.8.1.* Lover slain while eloping with the other man's fiancée.

T93.6.* Disappointed lover reveals that master's (priest's) mistress has another lover. Master has servants attack rival lover, wounding him severely, Master leaves town. <u>Necio</u>: Ch. III 255.

T96. Lovers reunited after many adventures. They finally
locate their long-lost son. Píndaro: Bk. II, Ch. XIV
348a.

    H94.12.* Son identified by ring and mother's letter.

T97. Father opposed to daughter's marriage. Urdemalas: 76b.

    Q411.3.1.* Father dies of heart attack when about
to kill innocent daughter.

T100 - T199. MARRIAGE

T160. Consummation of marriage.

T165.8.* Consummation of marriage postponed two days.
Daughter-in-law persuade new husband of aged woman not
to consummate marriage until third night. Wife complains
that husband talks only about his debts; but after consummation of marriage, she is not sure whose debts he
talked about. Lozana: Mamotreto LX 197.

T173.2.1.* Hostile bride kills husband who has compromised
her honor before marriage. Guzmán: Pt. II, Bk. II,
Ch. VIII 481b.

    K1350.0.1.* Rival lover compromises widow's honor
by adjusting clothes in front of her house in
early morning. T92.1.3.* Widow marries, then
kills rival lover who has compromised her honor.

T200 - T299. MARRIED LIFE

T230. Faithlessness in marriage.

T230.2.1.* Faithless wife causes husband to faint. He
returns home after an absence of a year and overhears two
women say that his wife is with child by the priest.
Husband faints and almost drowns in a tub of water.
Lazarillo (Luna): Pt. II, Ch. VI 122b.

T231. The faithless widow.

K2052.4.4.* Hypocritical widow "faints" after
burying husband.

T231.6.* Faithless widow puts dead husband in her bed at
night in order to feign discovery of his death the next
morning. Husband had died while writing a note exposing
wife's infidelities and his plan to kill her. Wife
burned the note and wildly lamented husband's death.
Garduña: Bk. I 1536b.

J261. Loudest mourners not greatest sorrowers.

T232.2.1.* Adulteress remains by hanging corpse of lover who
has killed her husband. Marcos: Bk. I, Ch. X 961a.

Q413.4.1.* Paramour is hanged for killing
husband of mistress.

T250. Characteristics of wives and husbands.

T251.1.5.1.* Man throws wife into sea. Ordered to throw the
heaviest articles overboard in a storm, a man throws his
wife into the sea. She was the heaviest (most burdensome)
thing he had. (Pun is on the expression "de más peso.")
Guzmán: Pt. II, Bk. III, Ch. III 527a.

T251.2.2.1.* Husband reforms shrewish wife by veiled threats
on first day of marriage. No disfigured face, no scars
on the head, no broken arm from her previous marriage;
therefore, she must have been a saint with her late
husband. Alonso: Pt. II, Ch. V 1298b.

T251.4. Socrates and Zanthippe: "After thunder rain."
He thus remarks as she empties slops on his head.
Alonso: Pt. II, Ch. VI 1299a.

J1250. Clever verbal retorts - general.

T251.6.1.* Browbeaten husband, to doctors who were discussing
the phenomenon of milk in some men's breasts: "Speak
softly lest women learn this and make us rear our own
and other people's children." Guzmán (Luján): Pt. II,
Bk. III, Ch. VIII 681a.

T255.1. The obstinate wife: cutting with knife or scissors.
At the end of the argument the man throws his wife into
water. As she sinks she makes with her finger the motion
of shearing with the scissors. Alonso: Pt. I, Ch. IV
1221b.

T255.2.1.* Obstinate wife drowned when thirsty mule rushes
with her into swollen stream. Husband had withheld water
from mule for three days. Guzmán: Pt. II, Bk. III,
Ch. IX 573a.

> K1567. Husband tricks wife into riding a mule which
> has been denied water.

T256.0.2.* Husband and wife quarrel by day, but sleep together
at night. Time will eventually change conditions: The
wife will become quiet, or the husband will tire of
beating her. Alonso: Pt. I, Ch. IV 1219a.

> J862.* Consolation found in sexual relations.

T256.2.1.* Quarrelsome wife pacified by "magic" water held
in her mouth. She is thus unable to answer back when
her husband becomes angry, and domestic peace is restored.
Alonso: Pt. I, Ch. IV 1220b.

T257.2.3.* Jealous wife burns skull which her husband has
found and placed in oratory. She thinks it may be the
skull of a former mistress. Periquillo: Discurso II,
1857b.

> M391.2.1.* Skull is burned, fulfilling the
> enigmatic prophecy written on it...

T257.2.4.* Jealous wife forces husband to send away foundling
boy. She will not let husband adopt boy because she thinks
he may be the son of her husband's mistress.
Periquillo: Discurso IV 1866b.

T258.1.1. Husband insists on knowing wife's secret. He forces
her to give him the note which he saw her receive in
church. He later kills wife and her lover. Periquillo:
Discurso XI 1893a.

> K1844.1.2.* Husband has another man substitute for
> him in bed. Q411.0.4.* Husband kills wife and
> paramour on ship.

T280. Other aspects of married life.

T299.3.* Recipe for becoming a widower without violence or
poison. Tell wife that a person of her age should not
eat breakfast. She will become angry with husband and
refuse to eat dinner. Talk of the beauty of other women.
The wife will soon die. Manzanares: Ch. XVII 115-117.

T300 - T399. CHASTITY AND CELIBACY

T320. Escape from undesired lover.

> K1227. Lover put off by deceptive respite.
> K1227.11.* Girl escapes from undesired lover by
> telling him entertaining stories all night.

T320.3.2.* Woman saves herself from would-be ravisher by
threatening to call her servants. The bluff works,
and the man runs away. Justina: Bk. II, Pt. III,
Ch. I 829a.

> K1700. Deception through bluffing.

T320.3.4.* Woman escapes from undesired lover by telling him
that her noble sweetheart will "take care of him." The
lover runs away. Justina: Bk. III, Ch. V 866a.

T322.3.1.* Seductress drugs rich gambler and robs him.

   Harpías: Estafa IV 174ff.

T323.3.* Woman escapes from captors when they fight over her.
   Each man wants to be first. Teresa: Ch. VIII 1370a.

T326.3. Martyrdom to preserve virginity.

   Q421.0.5.1.* Nuns are beheaded by Moors.

T326.3.1.* Nuns mutilate their faces to repel Moors. The
   latter behead them. Guzmán (Luján): Pt. II, Bk. II,
   Ch. VI 630a.

T326.3.2.* Martyrdom to preserve chastity. Saint Ursula
   is killed by the Huns for preserving her chastity.

   Guzmán (Luján): Pt. II, Bk. II, Ch. VI 630a.

T360. Chastity and celibacy - miscellaneous.

T361.* Betrothed woman proposes to faithful rejected lover
   that they live chastely together until they learn if
   her absent fiancé is still alive. Urdemalas: p. 118b.

   T400 - T499. ILLICIT SEXUAL RELATIONS

T410. Incest.

T415. Brother-sister incest.

   Q411.7.1.* Brother killed for ravishing sister.

T450. Prostitution and concubinage.

T452.2.* Mother acts as procuress for her "virgin" daughter.
   The latter had been deflowered by a sexton instead of
   a shovel's handle. Lozana: Mamotreto XVI 63.

T452.3.* Prostitute will never enter bordello again if she
   can leave with "honor." She is satiated after 40 years.

   Lozana: Mamotreto LIII 170.

T453. Getting advice from a woman in bed.

   J1115.8. Clever prostitute.

T455. Woman sells favors for particular purpose.

    K1353.2.* Prince promises to marry woman and give her a large sum of money for her favors.

    Q252.2.* Prince punished for breaking betrothal.

T455.1.2.* Woman sells favors to obtain a ring. She needs something on her finger to remind her to go to man's house. He gives her a costly ring. Lozana: Mamotreto XXXVII 128.

T455.1.3.* Courtesan "loses" a ring when she enters man's house. He gives her another one. Lozana: Mamotreto XXXVII 131.

T455.1.4.* Woman "loses" a ring when she fakes a fall in front of man's house. Would-be lover gives her money to buy a new one. Guzmán (Luján): Pt. II, Bk. I, Ch. VI 602b.

    K347.2.* Trickster gets lover to replace "lost" ring (jewel).

T455.2.2.* Woman sells favors to support her husband and household. Husband and wife enjoy the luxuries which her lovers provide. Guzmán: Pt. II, Bk. III, Ch. V 544b.

T470. Illicit sexual relations - miscellaneous motifs.

T475.2.1. Intercourse with sleeping girl.

    W117.2.* Man can swim the river twice.

T481. Adultery.

    K1500. Deceptions connected with adultery.

    T500 - T599. CONCEPTION AND BIRTH

T550. Monstrous births.

T554.2. Woman bears dog. Witch causes woman to give birth to two dogs. Coloquio: p. 221b.

T600 - T699. CARE OF CHILDREN

T610. <u>Nurture and growth of children</u>.

T611.3.1.* Royal infant nursed by thieving woman. He grows up to be a thieving emperor. Latter has own house searched first if anything is missing in his kingdom. <u>Justina</u>: Bk. I, Ch. II 734b.

T611.3.2.* Nurse covers breasts with blood while child is suckled. Child grows up to be a blood-thirsty tyrant. <u>Alonso</u>: Pt. II, Ch. II 1276b.

T611.3.3.* Abandoned child nursed by dark frowning woman. He imbibes her characteristics. <u>Necio</u>: Ch. II 198.

U. THE NATURE OF LIFE

U0 - U99. LIFE'S INEQUALITIES

U10. Justice and injustice.

U11.1. Ass punished for stealing mouthful of grass (grain);
lion, bear, and wolf forgiven. Alonso: Pt. I, Ch. V
1230a.

U15.2.* Preacher denounces women's vanities. They should
anoint their hair and wash their faces on fast day;
however, they do things in reverse. They anoint their
faces and wash their hair. Justina: Bk. I, Ch. III 750b.
W116. Vanity.

U15.3.* Man resolves to remain a fool for the remainder of
his life. His greatest successes have come from his
foolishness; his misfortunes, from his rationality.
Necio: Ch. VIII 337.

U60. Wealth and poverty.

U62.* Poor philosopher rebukes rich ruler. The latter has
much money but few friends, while the philosopher lacks
only money. Guzmán: Pt. II, Bk. II, Ch. I 432a.
J1251. Baffling malice with ready answers.

U100- U299. THE NATURE OF LIFE -
MISCELLANEOUS MOTIFS

U110. Appearances deceive.
J264.1.* Apparent affluence may be deceiving.
J2286.* Foolish interpretation of physical
appearances. N110. Luck and fate personified.

U111.2.* False scholar's "modesty" prevents him from
publishing many books. Necio: Ch. I 171.
K1956.13.* Sham wise man's "modesty" prevents him
from publishing many books.

U120. <u>Nature will show itself</u>.

U121.2. Hind, like his mother, flees before the hounds. Useless for her to urge him to stand up against them.
<u>Alonso</u>: Pt. II, Ch. X 1320a.

U121.6.1.* Butcher cannot revere statue of Venus made from chop-block. "Since I knew you as a chop-block, I cannot have respect for you." <u>Justina</u>: Bk. IV, Ch. IV 881a.

    J1454.1.* The butcher and the statue.

U129.1. Thieving nature of the fox will show itself.
<u>Peregrinación</u>: p. 11.

    J1391.5.1.* Foxes pillage henhouse after condemning cats for stealing meat.

U130. <u>The power of habit</u>.

U130.2.* Newly-rich beggar girl becomes ill. Recovers health when she starts begging again from servants and before portraits in her house. <u>Guzmán</u>: Pt. II, Bk. II, Ch. I 438a.

    P160. Beggars.

U160. <u>Misfortune with oneself to blame the hardest</u>.

U163.* Courtesan becomes pregnant by priest whom she had cured of venereal disease. <u>Lozana</u>: Mamotreto XXIV 87.

U164.* Cock's crowing reveals hidden chickens. Soldiers kill all of them. <u>Alonso</u>: Pt. I, Ch. II 1205b.

    N680. Lucky accidents.

U240. <u>Power of mind over body</u>.

U241.1.* Man grows lean from fear of inquisitor. Fat and happy man becomes thin and emaciated when inquisitor moves next door. <u>Guzmán</u>: Pt. II, Bk. III, Ch. VIII 567b.

U242.2.* The donkey's last will. Dying donkey, surrounded
by greedy, disputing relatives, wills to them parts of
his body with sarcastic implications. <u>Guzmán</u>: Pt. II,
Bk. II, Ch. V 467a.

V. RELIGION

V0 - V99. RELIGIOUS SERVICES

V20. <u>Confession of sins</u>.

V23.3.* Moorish slave starts talking Spanish to master in
order to confess before he dies. Master discovers that
the man is a long-lost friend. <u>Pindaro</u>: Bk. II,
Ch. XXVI 369a.

> K1816.13.1.* Disguised slave turns out to be
> master's long-lost friend.

V40. <u>Mass</u>.

V49.3.* Woman skips Mass when crowd prevents her from seeing
altar. To appease the Virgin, she bows 100 times: 34
times toward altar and 64 before statues in side chapels.
<u>Justina</u>: Bk. II, Pt. II, Ch. IV 818b.

V50. <u>Prayer</u>.

V51.6.* Heathen more devout in prayer than Christian. Artist's
picture presents attentive, fervent heathen; Christian
is inattentive and wordly. Perhaps the labels under
each man's picture should be changed. <u>Alonso</u>: Pt. I,
Ch. III 1212b.

V52.16.* Prayers of poor cause water in Roman wells to turn
bad. They want pilgrims to buy water from Tiber from
them. <u>Lozana</u>: Mamotreto LIV 176.

V100 - V199. RELIGIOUS EDIFICES AND OBJECTS

V110. <u>Religious buildings</u>.

> C51.1.1.1.* Tabu: birds not to perch on holy
> temple.

V200 - V299. SACRED PERSONS

V220. <u>Saints</u>.

V221.0.4.* Miraculous healing power of saints. John and
Barnabas heal the sick "in the name of Jesus Christ."
Alonso: Pt. I, Ch. III 1213b.

V221.9.1.* Saint Peter cures Saint Agatha. Her breasts had
been cut off. Alonso: Pt. I, Ch. VI 1245a.

V223.1.1.* Saint advises married couples. Alonso: Pt. I,
Ch. IV 1220a.

V223.1.2.* Saint advises man to drink wine instead of water
for stomach ailment and other sickness. Alonso:
Pt. I, Ch. VI 1246b.

V250. The Virgin Mary.

    Q171.1.2.* Emperor is forgiven for raping girl.

    V300 - V399. RELIGIOUS BELIEFS

V310. Particular dogmas.

V311.4.* Mother asks Christ to grant her sons special
privileges in the life to come. Request refused.
Alonso: Pt. II, Ch. XIII 1338a.

    Q338. Immoderate request punished (rebuked).

V320. Heretics.

    J1262.10.* Spaniard calls Reformationists heretics.

V330. Conversion from one religion to another.

    K1831.0.1. Disguise by changing name.

    Q591.0.1.* Heathen actor (Genesius) is converted
to Christianity while acting rôle of Christian.

    R213.2.* Moorish brother and sister escape from
Africa to Spain.

V337.* Conversion to Islam. Captured Spaniard marries
Turk's daughter, converts to Islam, and becomes rich.
On deathbed he reconverts to Christianity.

Píndaro: Bk. II, Ch. XXVIII 374b.

V400 - V449. RELIGIOUS VIRTUES

V440. Other religious virtues.

V441.2.* Saint forgives man who has assailed him. Guzmán:
Pt. I, Bk. I, Ch. IV 262a.

> J1269.9.1.* "If I were not a Christian I would get
> revenge on you." J1269.9.2.* "It is not right for
> us to avenge the wrong done us by others..."

V441.2.1.* Saint Stephen pardons those who stone him to
death. Guzmán: Pt. I, Bk. I, Ch. IV 262a.

V441.3.* Constantine the Great forgives enemies who have
stoned his picture. He feels no wounds or injury.
Guzmán: Pt. I, Bk. I, Ch. IV 262b.

> J1288.* He feels no wounds or injury.

V450 - V499. RELIGIOUS ORDERS

V460. Clerical virtues and vices.

V465.1.1. Incontinent monk (priest). Keeps manservant's
wife as his mistress. Lazarillo: Tratado VII 110b.

> J2342.1.2.* Husband refuses to believe that his
> wife is unfaithful, although he shares her with
> archpriest.

V500 - V599. RELIGIOUS MOTIFS - MISCELLANEOUS

V510. Religious visions.

V513.1.1.* Monk sees vision of lawyer's soul carried away by
demons. The communion wafer pops out of lawyer's mouth.
Monk reveals dream to parishioners instead of eulogizing
lawyer. Píndaro: Bk. I, Ch. XIII 301b.

> D1731.2. Marvels seen in dreams.

W. TRAITS OF CHARACTER

WO - W99. FAVORABLE TRAITS OF CHARACTER

W10. Kindness. . . . .

W11.5.0.1.* Exiled philosopher pardons his enemy and praises him. His wise and patient conduct contrasts with the injustice of his punishment. Guzmán (Luján): Pt. II, Bk. I, Ch. IV 593b.

W11.5.2.1.* Christ pardons Judas who has come to betray him. Alonso: Pt. I, Ch. V 1233b.

W11.7.2.* Friends' generosity enables impoverished lover to entertain his lady and friends. Buscón: Bk. III, Ch. VII 1141b.

W11.10.1.* Officer protects thieves. Constable comes to gang chief's house to recover wallet stolen from a relative. Chief orders thieves to return wallet because constable is a friend of the gang. Rinconete: p. 186a.

W11.17.* Generous son shares dead father's ill-gotten wealth with former customers. Son becomes impoverished, but later receives a legacy from a stranger who died in his house. Pindaro: Bk. I, Ch. XXI 317a.

W20. Other favorable traits of character.

W27. Gratitude.

Q111.2. Riches as reward (for hospitality).

W32.2.* Old man fights twenty ruffians. He detects card sharks trying to cheat a youth, and the tricksters fight him. Others come to old man's aid and he takes sanctuary in a church. Pindaro: Bk. I, Ch. XV 306a.

W34.3.1.* Captain tells cowardly soldier to die defending the faith, or give the king a victory. Soldier: "If

his majesty is waiting for me to give it to him, he
has already negotiated his account. Estebanillo:
Bk. I, Ch. VI 1777a.

W37. Conscientiousness.

> W197.* Lack of conscience.

> W100 - W199. UNFAVORABLE TRAITS OF CHARACTER

W110. Unfavorable traits of character - personal.

W111.3.3.1.* Lazy wife hangs up hen instead of feeding sick
husband. Doctor reprimands her. Alonso: Pt. II,
Ch. VI 1301b.

> Q285.2.1.* Doctor reprimands woman for neglect
> of sick husband.

W116. Vanity.

> U15.2. Preacher denounces women's vanities.

W116.2.1.* Man wants to learn to write his name for business
purposes. He does not want to confess his ignorance
if a business deal presents itself. Guzmán: Pt. I,
Bk. II, Ch. IV 305b.

W116.2.2.* Tailor erects showy coat of arms over door. He
is allowed to keep it because it is a memorial to his
pilgrimages to Santiago. In reality, he keeps it
because he is rich. Justina: Bk. I, Ch. II 730a.

> P441. Tailor.

W116.4.1.* Mother and daughters in mourning give excuses for
looking into mirror. They really want to see if mourning
is becoming to them. Justina: Bk. I, Ch. III 746b.

W116.9.* Woman rebuked for vanity in dressing. She wears
long cloaks which sweeps the streets. Man: "Is that
dress which you are wearing yours, or did you borrow or
rent it?" Alonso: Pt. II, Ch. XIII 1334b.

W117.2.* Man "can swim the river twice." Copulates twice
with courtesan: once while she sleeps, and again when
she awakens. <u>Lozana</u>: Mamotreto LIII 174.

    H915.2.* Courtesan has man copulate twice with her
to test his boast. P665. Boasting of sexual
prowess. T475.2.1. Intercourse with sleeping girl.

W117.3.* Boastful doctor: can teach medicine in six months.
Rival doctor says that six days are sufficient for the
braggart to teach all he knows. <u>Alonso</u>: Pt. I,
Ch. VI 1241a.

    J1115.2.3.* Clever physician rebukes careless
boasting rival.

W121. Cowardice.

    J1161.12.* The arch-chicken of chickens.

W121.2.7.* Lapdog bites larger dog while mistress is near.
<u>Coloquio</u>: p. 232a.

    J951.6.* Lapdog bites larger dog.

W121.3.1.* Cowardly soldier hides under dead horse. He
tells another coward that his horse was shot from under
him. Second coward recognizes the deceit, and both men
share the horse. <u>Estebanillo</u>: Bk. I, Ch. VI 1776b.

W121.3.2.* Cowardly soldier hides under hay during battle.
Tells officer that he has been wounded twice in the
thigh, and that he is keeping the wound from getting
cold by covering with hay. <u>Estebanillo</u>: Bk. I,
Ch. VI 1777a.

W121.3.3.* Cowardly soldier "kills" enemy soldiers after
battle is over. One prone soldier yells when the coward
sticks his sword in him, and the coward runs away,
ruining his hopes to gain a reputation for bravery.

Estebanillo: Bk. I, Ch. VI 1778a.

W121.3.4.* Cowardly soldier's honor not tarnished by beating.
He need not fight his assailant because the latter strikes
him in a friend's home where he is taking sanctuary.
Estebanillo: Bk. II, Ch. I 1781a.

H504.3.* Contest in pot washing.

W121.3.5.* Cowardly soldier insults enemy. He is surrounded
by enemy soldiers which he mistakes for friends. Enemy
soldiers flog him and take him prisoner. Estebanillo:
Bk. II, Ch. I 1784a.

J2136. Numskull brings about his own capture.

W121.3.6.* Cowardly soldier hears victory cannons fired at
a distance and falls off his horse , thinking he is
wounded. When a surgeon finds no wound, he bribes the
doctor not to reveal his findings. Estebanillo: Bk. II,
Ch. II 1795b.

J1820. Inappropriate action from misunderstanding.

W121.8.2.* Peasant becomes ill with fear when asked to appear
before Inquisitor. The latter wants some pears. Peasant
digs up tree, fruit and all, and send it to the
Inquisitor so that he will not receive another summons.
Lazarillo (Luna): Pt. II, Introduction, p. 115b.

J829. Dealing with the great.

W125.2.1.* Gluttonous woman servant eats all the sausages
while cooking them. She chokes and dies from apoplexy
and from blows given her. Justina: Bk. I, Ch. III 747b.

W128.7.* Man and dissatisfied animals appear before Jupiter
seeking change of status. They want to be free. Man is
given free will, but he must struggle perpetually among
fools because he formerly sought wealth. Other animals

must stay subject to man, because a higher deity so
willed it. <u>Periquillo</u>: Discurso VIII 1881a.

   Q300. Contentiousness punished.

W141. Talkativeness.

   J1564.3. Incessant talker silenced by man who
   out-talks him.

W150. <u>Unfavorable traits of character - social.</u>

W151.8.1.* Three thieves quarrel over woman captured with
   mule team. One thief is shot to death, and the other
   two kill each other with swords. Owners of team come,
   free the woman, and recover their mules. <u>Periquillo</u>:
   Discurso XIII 1903a.

W151.9.1.* Greedy man sues imprisoned thief to force him to
   tell from whom he has bought stolen cloak. Man hopes to
   recover other stolen goods, but loses his money in lawsuit and is forced to sell his cloak. <u>Guzmán</u>: Pt. II,
   Bk. II, Ch. III 446b.

   J514.5.1.* Greedy man, dissatisfied with recovering
   stolen cloak, sues thief; loses cloak in payment
   for lawsuit.

W151.11.* Greedy druggist wants to be sold as medicine when
   he dies. His will states that he is to be put into a
   bottle and sold as medicine. <u>Guadaña</u>: Ch. I 1681a.

W151.12.* Greedy soldiers killed in effort to seize food.
   They try to take away a cooked chicken from outlaws at
   an inn. The outlaws escape on soldiers' horses.
   <u>Periquillo</u>: Discurso XIII 1902a.

W152.9.1.* Stingy man cancels invitation to his guests. He
   feigns illness. <u>Trapaza</u>: Ch. XII 1491a.

   K2091.2.* Illness feigned to escape having guests
   for lunch.

W152.12.5.* Stingy master refuses to repay servant for losses incurred while defending him. Servant refuses to aid master a second time. Guzmán: Pt. II, Bk. II, Ch. V 314b.

    J1561.4.3.* Servant refuses to defend stingy master a second time.

W152.18.* Stingy schoolmaster.

    F950.1.1.* House of miserly schoolmaster cures diseases. J1341.7.1.* Stingy schoolmaster breaks tooth on "pea" soup. J1341.14.* No need for toilets. J2021.2.* Starving student cannot find his mouth.

W152.18.1.* Stingy schoolmaster uses bacon over and over in stew. He places it in a perforated container and suspends it in stew to give flavor. Buscón: Bk. I, Ch. III 1099a.

W152.18.2.* Father removes son from stingy schoolmaster's school. Son reports to father that another student has starved to death. Father fails to recognize his emaciated son when he comes for him. Buscón: Bk. I, Ch. III 1100a.

W153.10.1.* Dead miser owes many debts to his body. Friend indicates that miser has received no benefits from his wealth. Alonso: Pt. I, Ch. I 1201a.

    J1380. Retorts concerning debts.

    J2199.4. Short-sighted economy.

W153.11.1.1.* Dying miser reproves son for simulating grief. Father knows that son is wanting to get his money. Alonso: Pt. I, Ch. I 1204a.

W153.11.1.2.* Dying miser advises son. Lend money only on silver, gold, or copper security. Select young men for farm workers. Alonso: Pt. II, Ch. XII 1327a.

W153.16.* Miser insists on eating four old withered radishes. Scolds wife for having lost them and forces her to eat one. Guzmán: Pt. II, Bk. I, Ch. I 392a.

W154.2. Monster ungrateful for rescue. Kills rescuer to get money. Periquillo: Discurso III 1863b.

B361. Animals grateful for rescue from pit.

W154.3.1.1.* Lion rescued from pit by following fettered lamb's advice, but is too proud to rescue lamb. Ungrateful man kills lamb before help arrives. Periquillo: Discurso III 1864a.

B335.6.1.* Fettered lamb warns lion of trap set by man.

W154.8. Grateful animals; ungrateful man.

B361. Animals grateful for rescue from pit.

W154.9.2.* Man rescued from hanging kills rescuer. Compassionate man cuts rope, freeing man from death by hanging. Freed man takes rescuer's sword and kills him. Periquillo: Discurso IV 1866a.

W165.3.* Nobleman exiles himself because of false pride. He leaves his hometown because another nobleman never removes his hat first when they meet. Lazarillo: Tratado III 103a.

J410. Association of equals and unequals.

W165.4.* Peddler sells his merchandise by singing rather than by shouting. His profession is that of a singer, which is higher than that of peddler. Estebanillo: Bk. II, Ch. I 1780b.

W165.5.* Job is beneath his dignity. After years, a water-seller saves enough money to buy fancy clothes. He abandons his job; it is beneath his dignity.

<u>Lazarillo</u>: Tratado VI 110a.

W167. Stubbornness.

Q331.0.1.* Two proud men knock each other down on narrow bridge. J1705.1.1.* Stupid peasants refuse to change route of procession.

W193.2.* Bodyguards extort money from fearful soldier under pretense that his life is in great danger.

<u>Estebanillo</u>: Bk. II, Ch. V 1827a.

W197.* Lack of conscience.

W37. Conscientiousness.

W197.1.* Consciences are lost from purses. School children lose consciences from unstitched purses. Schoolmaster saves found consciences, but does not know to whom they belong. He may return wrong conscience to a person; hence, the bad connotation connected with the word "conscience." <u>Guzmán</u>: Pt. I, Bk. III, Ch. V 351b.

X. HUMOR

X100 - X199. HUMOR OF DISABILITY

X130. <u>Other physical disabilities</u>.

X145.2.* A horse neighs better than the singer can sing. King has no appreciation for music. <u>Guzmán</u> (Luján): Pt. II, Bk. II, Ch. VII 333a.

> J1365.* A horse's neighing sounds sweeter.

X600 - X699. HUMOR CONCERNING RACES OR NATIONS

X650. <u>Jokes concerning other races or nations</u>.

X653.* Artist paints a naked man to represent Spaniard. He carries a bolt of clothing material on his shoulder, but he is so changeable in tastes that no one knows how he will dress. <u>Alonso</u>: Pt. II, Ch. VI 1300b.

> J730. Forethought in provision for clothing.

X900 - X1899. HUMOR OF LIES AND EXAGGERATION

X900. <u>Humor of lies and exaggerations</u>.

X907.2.* Second liar is reprimanded by first. "Be content with having more property than I without wanting to lie more than I do." (The lying was over having killed a deer with so many points.) <u>Guzmán</u>: Pt. II, Bk. I, Ch. II 396a.

X910 - X1099. LIE: THE REMARKABLE MAN

X960 - X1019. LIE: REMARKABLE PERSON'S SKILLS

X980. <u>Lie: occupational or professional skill</u>.

X1005. Lie: remarkable cook. <u>Necio</u>: Ch. IV 267.

> J2353.1.1.* Foolish boast about cook's remarkable ability gets man into trouble.

X1600 - X1699. LIES ABOUT WEATHER AND CLIMATE

X1620. <u>Lies about cold weather</u>.

X1623.4.* Lie: head frozen back on decapitated dueler's
    body. It thaws out later in tavern while victim and his
    murderer are drinking. <u>Estebanillo</u>: Bk. I, Ch. III
    1748a.

X1700 - X1799. LIES: LOGICAL ABSURDITIES

X1720. <u>Absurd disregard of anatomy</u>.

X1737.1.2.* Man stays under water a long time after ship sinks.
    Kills 500 tuna fish with sword, finds chest of jewels and
    coins, ties treasure to his leg, and begins to swim
    upward. Fishermen catch him in net. <u>Lazarillo</u> (Luna):
    Pt. II, Ch. II 118b.

Z. MISCELLANEOUS GROUPS OF MOTIFS

Z100 - Z199. SYMBOLISM

Z100. <u>Symbolism</u>.

> D1711.6.2.1.* Aesculapius as god of healing.
>
> H619.6.* Symbolic interpretation of jai-alai game.
>
> H619.7.* Symbolic interpretation of glove shop.

Z110. <u>Personifications</u>.

Z111.3.2.* Death allegorically pictured as three-bodied person. From the front, a skeleton; from one side, a maiden; from another side, a youth. <u>Alonso</u>: Pt. II, Ch. VIII 1312b.

Z114.1.* Old Age despised in heaven. Jupiter makes two brooms from thunderbolts and has the place swept where Old Age has stood. <u>Justina</u>: Bk. I, Ch. I 727b.

Z121.1. Truth leaves city because there is no place left for her. People prefer lies to truth. <u>Guzmán</u>: Pt. I, Bk. III, Ch. VII 359b; and <u>Periquillo</u>: Discurso VI 1873a.

Z121.1.1.* Truth is dumb. She remains speechless in order not to pay for debt of others. <u>Guzmán</u>: Pt. I, Bk. III, Ch. VII 360b.

> K455.4.0.2.* Falsehood alleges that she has paid debt for food.

Z121.3.* Two Truths personified: (1) "You are Old"; (2) "You are Ugly." Woman falsely accuses these two of being perverts, and they are burned publicly. <u>Justina</u>: Bk. I, Ch. I 727b.

Z121.4.* Truth dressed in rags; people despise her. At night Malice exchanges Truth's rich clothes for those of Falsehood's rags. Blind Fortune, mother of Truth and

Falsehood, dresses her daughters in wrong clothes.
Periquillo: Discurso XIV 1907a.

Z125. Virtue personified.

N110. Luck and Fate personified.

Z126. Energy (strength) personified . Venus overcomes
Strength (a woman) and puts her to work in her garden.
Strength, therefore, becomes the slave of love and women.
Justina: Bk. IV, Ch. I 871a.

Z127.1.1.* Sin personified as praying man before fountain
of Christ. His fingers thrust into holes in Christ's
hands and body represent his sins which prevent the
outpouring of divine grace. Alonso: Pt. II, Ch. XIII
1338b.

Z131.0.1.* Falsehood personified as a lame old woman. She
is old because she has existed an infinite number of
years; she is lame so that everyone can overtake her.
Periquillo: Discurso VII 1880a.

Z131.1.* Falsehood tries to get free meal through false
credit. Truth aids innkeeper and Falsehood must pay.
Guzmán: Pt. I, Bk. III, Ch. VII 360a.

K200. Deception in payment of debt.

Z134.2.* Fortune personified as matron with two daughters
(Falsehood and Truth). Periquillo: Discurso XIV, 1907a.

N110. Luck and Fate personified.

Z134.3.* Rich man personified. He controls a body guard of
fools and business and professional men. Devil takes all
to hell with a chain made of women's tongues. Guzmán:
Pt. II, Bk. III, Ch. III (in James Mabbe, The Rogue,
London: Tudor Translations, IV 151).

P150. Rich men. R11.2.1. Devil carries off

wicked people.

Z139.6. Modesty personified.

    J91.1.* Wind, water, and modesty.

INDEX OF AUTHORS AND TITLES

(The pagination under a given novel refers to where the
motifs of that novel are located in the text. Many of
these motifs have cross references, which are also listed.)

Cortés de Tolosa, Juan. Lazarillo de Manzanares, 26, 40, 42,
     48, 51, 54, 59, 65, 67, 72, 87, 89, 90, 101, 102, 103,
     106, 112, 114, 115, 129, 142, 150, 152, 168, 174, 178,
     193, 198, 201, 211, 219, 234.

Delicado, Francisco. La lozana andaluza, 2, 3, 12, 17, 19,
     22, 23, 30, 33, 34, 35, 36, 40, 56, 67, 69, 72, 76, 85,
     90, 91, 96, 146, 147, 148, 149, 153, 159, 162, 165, 168,
     169, 187, 188, 191, 207, 214, 225, 231, 235, 236, 239,
     241, 246.

Enríquez Gómez, Antonio. Vida de don Gregorio Guadaña, 7, 32,
     44, 45, 60, 61, 70, 88, 89, 100, 116, 125, 132, 133, 135,
     146, 153, 165, 179, 186, 196, 203, 209, 215, 221, 223,248.

Espinel, Vicente. La vida de Marcos de Obregón, 5, 6, 7, 8,
     10, 11, 12, 16, 17, 18, 21, 22, 24, 25, 26, 27, 32, 38,
     39, 40, 44, 45, 47, 48, 49, 52, 54, 55, 56, 57, 59, 62,
     63, 64, 67, 68, 77, 78, 80, 82, 83, 84, 86, 87, 89, 90,
     92, 93, 95, 98, 99, 100, 102, 107, 124, 125, 129, 130,
     133, 134, 135, 136, 137, 138, 139, 144, 150, 152, 153,
     155, 156, 161, 171, 175, 181, 182, 183, 188, 193, 194,
     195, 196, 197, 199, 209, 210, 213, 214, 216, 217, 219,
     220, 223, 224, 226, 232.

García, Carlos. La desordenada codicia de los bienes ajenos,
     3, 108, 112, 113, 119, 127, 128, 130, 132, 136, 137,
     174, 222, 226.

González, Estebanillo. Vida y hechos de Estebanillo González,
     17, 24, 31, 50, 58, 59, 65, 69, 70, 72, 74, 75, 82, 87,
     92, 96, 103, 105, 106, 112, 113, 115, 116, 117, 122, 125,
     127, 128, 133, 134, 138, 140, 151, 154, 155, 157, 159,
     168, 172, 173, 174, 184, 185, 186, 190, 201, 205, 206,
     207, 208, 213, 214, 245, 246, 247, 250, 251, 253.